DOHA AND QATAR

TRAVEL GUIDE

TONY WALSH

Arabesque.Travel

The spellings in this book are British English.

The publisher thanks Alan Fitz-Patrick & Ibrahim Al Busafi for their assistance in creating the book.

CONTENTS

1

BASIC FACTS

Geography: The State of Qatar is a peninsula situated halfway down the east coast of the Arabian Peninsula (the western coast of The Gulf (this term is used in throughout the book in preference to the Arabian Gulf that is used in the Arab World or Persian Gulf that is used elsewhere), bordered to the south by Saudi Arabia. The coastline is about 550 km long and bounds the country to the west, north and east. Low hills in the north-west and dunes in the south-east are the most distinct geography. There are several small islands including Halul, Shirawah and Al Ashat. The total land area of Qatar is approximately 11,627 square kilometres (sq km).

Capital: Doha is the capital, economic and population centre of Qatar.

Economy: Qatar is one of the world's wealthiest nations in terms of GDP per capita. Oil and natural gas is the basis of this wealth, a situation that is projected to continue for the next century.

Population: Mid-year population in July 2021 is estimated by the Qatar government (psa.gov.qa) at 2,380,011 appx giving a population density rate of 204 persons per sq km; most of which are located on Qatar's east coast.

Climate: Qatar has a hot, humid desert climate with long summers and from November to February short warm winters.

Language: Arabic is the official language; however, English, Hindi/Urdu & Bengali are widely spoken. Although English, in some form, may be spoken it might not be a form you will understand easily, do actively listen when people speak. Equally, your English might not be the form of English readily understood by a person you speak to, so speak clearly and slowly

Religion: Islam is the official religion of the country.

Qatar National Day: Qatar's National Day is the 18th of December & is an official holiday.

Flag: The flag is white and 'Qatar maroon'; having a serrated vertical border of nine white serrations between the two colours. The colour maroon represents the imperial purple of ancient civilizations, which used dye obtained from shellfish that were exploited in Qatar. The nine serrations represent the nine Gulf sheikhdoms under a British treaty in 1916.

Work Hours: Government: From 07:00-14:00. Friday and Saturday are weekend holidays. Companies: Office hours typically from 08:00-midday / 16:00-20:00 (or 08:00 – 17:00). Friday & Saturday is the weekend. Retail and services have longer hours and in major shopping malls these may be 10:00-22:00, with supermarkets also operating an hour, or so, either side of this.

Local Time: Three hours + Greenwich Mean Time

Currency: The official currency is the Qatari Riyal (QAR – sometimes QR), which is divided into 100 Dirhams. The exchange parity is fixed at US$ = 3.65 QARs.

The front of all notes have the value in Arabic numerals and letters with the flag of Qatar; stylised flower; and a door - the obverse has

1 riyal Traditional dhow & the Pearl Monument

5 riyalsDesert scene with Arab horses, Camel, Oryx and a Tent

10 riyals Lusail Stadium, Torch Tower, Sidra Medicine and Education City

50 riyals Qatar Central Bank building and Ministry of Finance building

100 riyals Imam Muhammad ibn Abd Al Wahhab Mosque

200 riyals Qatar National Museum, Museum of Islamic Art & Palace of Sheikh Abdullah bin Jassim Al Thani

500 riyals LNG ship & Ras Laffan LNG Refinery (at US$ 137 this is a very high value note)

Coins, use is increasingly reducing as they are of such little value, with 100 dirhams in 1 Qatari Riyal. Coins are 1 dirham, 5 dirhams, 10 dirhams, 25 dirhams, 50 dirhams, all having their value and on the obverse the date on top with the emblem of Qatar consisting of two crossed bent swords, and between them a sailing ship (dhow) sailing on waves beside an island with two Date Palms. There are several hundred QAR dirhams in 1 US$ (unlike the dirham - AED - of the UAE).

For the 2022 World Cup there will be a commemorative FIFA World Cup Qatar 2022 coin and banknote. The coins will be made in silver, gold-plated, and also pure gold in limited numbers (about 3,000) which will be available for the local market only. The banknote will be a single note currency that includes a QRcode, through which a QRcode reader will enable individuals to access information about Qatar in Arabic and English.

Credit and debit cards are widely accepted; to ensure they work do advise the supplier (bank) in your own country that you will be travelling into Qatar. ATMs are easy to find in major shopping areas. Apple Pay and Google Pay use is possible in many places. However in smaller shops its cash only, make certain you have some Qatari Rials, though in tourist places US$ are often accepted. Ensure your dollars are issued after 2007 as earlier notes are not accepted, and its ideal to have some small denomination notes for ease of payment or even tipping. If Qatari Riyals are not available in your own country Hamad International Airport does have exchange counters in arrivals & departures (so you do not have unexchangable notes when you return home – or donate to charity).

2

GEOGRAPHY

On the eastern coast of the Arabian peninsula, Qatar, a peninsula itself, is one of the world's smallest countries at 11,627 square (sq) kilometres (km) extending about 190km south to north and a maximum 90km east-west. This size includes offshore islands; such as Halul, some 97km to the north-east of Doha, Al Ashat 60km south of Doha and Fasht Ad Dibal north-west of Al Ruwais in northern Qatar. Though Qatar is smaller than the USA state of Connecticut or the British counties of Perth or Yorkshire, the size belies the extraordinary wealth of the country.

Qatar shares a single land border of 87km with Saudi Arabia and has sea borders with Bahrain to the west, the United Arab Emirates to the east and Iran to the north, in addition to the sea borders with Saudi Arabia to the south-west and south-east. In 2001 the border with Saudi Arabia was ratified, and the sea border with Bahrain was also agreed the same year. That ratification resulted in the Hawar Islands, a few hundred metres off Qatar's west coast, being confirmed as Bahraini territory. Areas disputed with Bahrain and awarded to Qatar at the same time were Al Zubarah in Qatar's north-west mainland, the scattered islets of Fasht Ad Dibal north-west of Al Zubarah and Jinan Island north-west of Dukhan on the west coast. The seas near the Hawar Islands (Bahrain) and Khor Al Udaid (also called the 'Inland Sea'), part of which is in Saudi Arabia's territory, are areas where small distances of water separate different states. With the political situation between Qatar and its neighbours being especially fractious, it is essential to ensure you do not enter the water, or land, within the jurisdiction of another state.

Qatar is part of the Arabian Shelf, the eastern sedimentary areas of the Arabian Plate that is moving north and being subducted under the Iranian/Eurasian plates. The geology of Qatar includes surface areas of gravels and sandstone of the Hofuf Formation formed by rivers over the last 1.5million years. The Hofuf Formation lies over the Dam Formation of the Miocene Period (23-5million years ago approximately) which has clays and limestones and is largely found in the south-west of the country. Below the Dam formation is the Dammam Formation, much of which is a chalky limestone and dolomite. The Dammam Formation extends over most of Qatar and was created during the Middle Eocene (48-38million years ago). The Dammam Formation is a karst limestone environment that contains sinkholes and caves. Typical sinkhole examples can be found off the Salwa Road to the north-west and south-east of the Rawdat Rashid Interchange (GPS 25.172, 51.327). The sinkholes and caves are thought to have developed from about 560,000 years ago. They often collect water run-off and are called *dahl* locally. Below the Dammam Formation is the Rus Formation a chalky limestone and marl/clay formed during the Early Lower Eocene (48-38 million years ago).

The key structural elements within the Qatar rock formations are anticlines; these are rock strata that have been forced into a convex arch. It is here that the wealth of Qatar, its oil and gas, is trapped in the upper part of the arch where suitable 'capping' rock is found. The major anticlines are the

Qatar Arch that extends from the south of the country into Iran; in this arch's north-east is the vast North Gas Field. Others include the Dukhan Anticline that flows from the south to the north-west a few kilometres inland from the coast up to the area of Dukhan. This uplift has exposed the fossiliferous Dam Formation and has trapped the Dukhan oilfield to its west.

Yardang at Zekreet

Almost devoid of notable contours, Qatar's highest point is in the south-west at Qurayn Abu al Bawl (24.717, 51.047) also noted as Al Galail, next to a security installation so do take care regarding photography and activities here and at all government buildings. The location overlooks the Saudi Arabian border 19 km away, taking advantage of the 103 metres elevation; access is west from route 59 at 24.713, 51.069. The land gradually drops in general elevation from there towards the north, though there is a series of low hills in the north and the general flatness makes any rock outcrop noteworthy. Shallow dry valleys that are locally called *wadi* are found throughout the country.

North of Khor Al Udaid (a *khor* is a natural inlet from the sea) on the south-east coast are dunes and *sabkha* (mud, sand, gypsum salt flats). The sands are aeolian (wind-blown) in origin while the *sabkha* that often looks a solid surface might be a quicksand-like trap waiting for unwary drivers. Khor Al Udaid is a sea inlet that forms part of Qatar's south-eastern border with Saudi Arabia. Many of the areas here are named 'pure' (نقيان) with a noun to identify the location. Perhaps the paleness of the sand gave rise to the description.

To Doha's west and north-west are areas of karst limestone with numerous depressions symptomatic of erosion and sinkholes. North of Doha the coast is sand, created following changes in the level of The Gulf which, when lower over 10,000 years ago, allowed sand from the extensive exposed seabed to be blown inland.

3

CLIMATE

Qatar's climate is a desert climate with scorching, humid summers, and warm winters. During July, Qatar's hottest month, the temperature peaks at over 48Celsius (C) in Doha and warmer inland, and drops to a night-time minimum of 29C, with humidity up to 90%. In the coolest month, January, the very highest temperature might be 31C and minimum 12C with humidity up to 100% if a night fog forms but typically during the day it's around 40%. Rain is unlikely at any time of year with the highest probability during December-March. Winds are usually very light coming from the south in the summer and from the north in winter when weather systems drop south from Asia. Springtime can have dust-storms, which may originate over Iran, and these can last up to a few days.

Note that the average (Celsius) is what it says and does not represent the absolute maximum.

Month	Jan	Feb	Mar	Apr	May	Jun	Jul	Aug	Sep	Oct	Nov	Dec
Avg Max (C)	23	25	30	35	41	43	44	43	40	37	31	26

4

NATURE

With Qatar's extreme desert climate, plants and animals have constant stress to survive. Add in an increasingly developed human environment and for many this pressure increases, though some have taken advantage of new man-made environments.

FLORA

Qatar's fauna ultimately depends on its 300+ species of flora. The dominant trees are;-

Ghaf, Prosopis cineraria, this large tree with its feathery leaves grows in sandy soils (though not usually in dunes) and in Qatar from the central region through to the north. The *ghaf's* leaves can trap fog and the resultant water dripping to the ground becomes the tree's own irrigation system.

The Christ's thorn tree, *Ziziphus spina-christi,* grows in rocky *wadi* environments; the flowers are a source of prized honey, and its small fruit is eaten by animals and, in the recent past and occasionally today, by humans. Its densely branched habit and 20 metres height make it an ideal shade tree, so it was planted in villages. A similar tree *Ziziphus mauritiana,* has been introduced, probably from Malaysia.

Acacia tortilis

Three species of Acacia are found, '*Salam*', *Acacia ehrenbergiana,* is found in open sandy soils. Its appearance varies but is usually a very ragged bushy shape of less than three metres in height. '*Garat*', *Acacia nilotica,* has a similar appearance to Salam, though slightly smaller and less bushy. '*Simr*', *Acacia tortilis / Vachellia tortilis,* is spread throughout Qatar and, as with other Acacias, prefers well-drained sandy soil. This tree is the classic umbrella Acacia found in Africa, and unlike the other Acacia of Qatar, its flower is creamy coloured rather than yellow. All Acacia have roots that can penetrate deep into the soil and rock, perhaps up to 30metres depth, in search of water. The trees respond to drought by dropping their leaves, which will regrow rapidly after rains.

On the north coasts and at Al Wakrah, south of Doha, Mangrove *Avicennia marina* grows on muddy areas in the intertidal zone. In Qatar, around Al Thakhira, they grow up to around five metres in height. Mangrove's aerial roots allow absorption of oxygen, water and nutrients in a muddy stagnant lagoon type environment, while the leaves excrete salts from seawater.

LAND MAMMALS

Qatar's land mammals in historical times may have included the Asiatic lion and Asiatic cheetah along with their prey that would have included antelope and gazelle. Today the numbers of land mammals and their variety has reduced. Smaller mammals are the most common.

Dwarf gerbil, *Gerbillus nanus;* Wagner's gerbil, *Gerbillus dasyurus;* Cheesman's gerbil, *Gerbillus cheesmani;* are widely dispersed small rodents. Cheesman's gerbil is probably the most readily seen towards dusk in sandy areas. Look for a light russet colour rodent about 11 centimetres (cm) in body length with a slightly longer tail, and rear legs that are somewhat longer than the forelegs. These are opportunistic feeders, preferring seeds & grain though eating insects if other food is scarce. They probably breed throughout the year, and each litter may have up to eight young and are vital food for owls and foxes. Jirds are related to gerbils, though they are larger at up to 16cm with a more rat-like appearance. The Libyan jird, *Meriones libycu's* and Sundevall's jird, *Meriones crassus,* are omnivorous and occupy sandy or rocky desert in Qatar. With its long kangaroo type rear legs, the Egyptian jerboa, *Jaculus jaculus,* occupy a similar niche to the gerbil. The more familiar house mouse, *Mus musculus,* and house rat, *Rattus rattus,* join these small rodents in Qatar.

The desert hedgehog, *Paraechinus aethiopicus,* at up to 25 cm is a relatively small hedgehog. As with most other hedgehogs, this is a nocturnal animal that eats insects and small animals. With a litter of perhaps six young, this hedgehog breeds once a year. Cape hare *Lepus capensis* is comparable to the European brown hare in appearance and is up to 68cm in length. As with most other desert animals, it is active from dusk to dawn; sheltering under vegetation during the day. This animal breeds throughout the year with perhaps up to six litters annually and four leverets in each. The hare's adult size and the lack of larger predators in Qatar, mean that it is most vulnerable only when young.

The largest predators in Qatar include three canids and possibly the honey badger, *Mellivora capensis,* which might live in the south of the country. The honey badger is omnivorous, about 75cm long excluding the tail and may have a couple of cubs annually.

Golden jackal, *Canis aureus,* is an adaptive predator with a body length up to 85cm long and a tail of about 25cm with a weight of 14kilograms (kg). This jackal possibly breeds with feral dogs in Qatar, though pure animals have a coat of a rusty brown colour, with black back. Like most jackals, this is omnivorous, feeding on small rodents, lizards and carrion which it supplements with fruit and vegetation, for a well-rounded diet. They breed once a year and give birth to up to six pups. The red fox *Vulpes vulpes arabica* is found throughout Qatar and is a subspecies of the red fox, though with a less intense red colour. Ruppell's fox *Vulpes rueppelli sabaea* is a pale coloured desert-living fox ,up to 74cm long including its tail, weighing in at less than 1.9kg. They breed once a year with up to six pups. As with the jackal these foxes are omnivorous, eating small animals, large insects and plant products.

Bats include desert long-eared bat, *Otonycteris hemprichii,* and Geoffrey's trident leaf-nosed bat, *Asellia tridens,* which are both insectivorous.

Reintroduced species include the Arabian oryx, *Oryx leucoryx,* which has become the logo of Qatar Airways. The oryx can be up to 175cm long, 100cm at shoulder height and weigh up to 100kg with both sexes having twin horns of up to 65cm. Their natural habitat is a desert environment, both stony and sandy, where they might roam in large family groups of about ten animals. The white colour of the coat helps reflect the heat, while in colder weather the hair raises to expose the darker skin, allowing it to absorb heat.

The Arabian oryx can breed throughout the year with a single calf born eight months after mating. With a mid brown coat, the calf is well camouflaged in desert conditions. Extinct in the wild throughout the world by 1972, due to hunting, a breeding population had been established in several zoos around the world, most importantly at Phoenix and San Diego Zoos, and animals were reintroduced into their original countries from the mid-1970s. In Qatar this reintroduction was focused initially on Al Wabra Wildlife Preservation, a private zoo; later other locations bred the animal. The Arabian oryx is a herbivore which in winter can obtain its water from fresh vegetation that includes grasses and leaves.

Gazella subgutturosa marica

The other major mammal reintroduced to Qatar is the Arabian sand gazelle, *Gazella subgutturosa marica,* locally called *reem*. Due to hunting, the animal was extinct in Qatar by the end of the 1950s and was reintroduced in the mid-

1990s, notably in Al Reem Reserve. The males can grow to a length of 120cm and weigh 30kg. Both sexes have horns, though the male's are substantially larger. In a safe environment population growth can be rapid, as this gazelle can breed after it is about 18months and in about 30% of live births twins are born after a gestation period of just over five months.

Qatar would hardly seem an Arab country without the **Camel**, *Camelus dromedaries*, the dromedary (the use of Camel, except where noted below refers to *Camelus dromedaries*). The world Camel comes from the Arabic جمل (Jamal, a male Camel) and the word dromedary, the single-humped variety, from the Greek *dromus*, meaning race/race course or running, all very apt in the world of Camel racing today. All living dromedaries are domesticated animals, the wild type having disappeared perhaps 2,500 years ago. This domestication started, at least, by 1,000BC, probably in south-east Arabia during the period of a substantial reduction in the wild Camel population.

Male Camels can be two meters in height at the shoulder and weigh 600kg, females are perhaps 10% smaller in height and 30% less in weight. The single hump is a fat bearing organ and as fat can release water, if used due to lack of food, it allows better survival in drought. The diet for the Camel is plants, both by grazing on the ground and browsing bushes and trees, though nowadays a large proportion is supplied as hay or other animal feed. As with a cow, the Camel is a ruminant; therefore much of the day is normally spent either eating or ruminating! To cope with the desert climate, the body temperature can fluctuate by more than 10C and can deal with a 30% water loss; either of these changes would kill most mammals. Camels, fortunately, can replenish water at around 20 litres a minute, useful if finding water in a desert climate.

From around four years, the Camel can breed, with

typically a single baby born after a gestation period of some 15 months, which may then live for some 50 years. In captivity, the dromedary has bred with the llama, and in the wild in areas such as Iran where their ranges overlap, dromedaries can breed with the two-humped Bactrian Camel. In Turkey, the breeding of Bactrian and dromedary is specifically done at Izmir Province where the result is large single-humped animals, whose males compete in Camel 'wrestling' events. Camels have been used historically for transport, milk, meat, clothing and more; it therefor is probably more useful than cattle.

Camels and Robot Jockeys

Today in Qatar, Camels are bred for the prestige they bring, especially for racing. Camels are used for short races from about aged 18 months – 24months, the prime age is around six years, and these older Camels can race at around 40kmph. Though children were used as jockeys for their lightweight, from 2007 the 'rider' has been a simple robot, with a rotating whip to encourage the animal's speed. Prizes can be hundreds of thousands of Qatari Riyals and luxury cars. However, the most sought after rewards are the prestige of owning a winning animal though the sales value of the winner, which can reach US$ 1,500,000, must be an added benefit. These high prices are obtained for animals which, like thoroughbred racehorses, have a known and admired lineage. Other Camels might take part in Camel beauty contests, or milking contests. Again the value of a successful animal might run to more than US$1,000,000, with the most expensive Camel ever being sold for US$ 2,720,000, in the UAE (though rumours say one has been sold for US$9,500,000). As they say, beauty is in the eye of the beholder.

BIRDS

Currently, there have been 325 birds recorded in Qatar, excluding introductions such as the red-necked Ostrich that is effectively a zoo-based bird in Qatar. Of these about 119 species are relatively common, 83 are scarce but expected to be seen at some stage in the year, 38 are seen regularly but are uncommon, some 39 have only been seen one or two times, and there are around 46 vagrant species. The overall number of species seen in Qatar is gradually increasing, principally as a result of new environments being created by man. These critical environments include vegetated areas such as farms, parks and golf clubs and, less attractively, rubbish dumps which birds such as Eagles, especially Steppe Eagles, feed from.

Indian mynah, *Acridotheres tristis*

Three invasive species are probably amongst the most easily birds seen around Doha. The Indian mynah, *Acridotheres tristis,* is an aggressive resident, breeding throughout Doha and surrounds. It out-competes, and can kill young of similar sized birds and lives very freely alongside people. The Indian house crow, *Corvus splendens,* nests in trees and is found towards the coast in areas of human habitation. The house crow scavenges refuse and, like the mynah, can live alongside people. From Africa or India the rose-ringed parakeet, *Psittacula krameri,* is a common resident breeder and like the mynah probably results from escaped cage birds. This is the parakeet seen in London and other cities worldwide that were not part of its original range. Another parakeet, the larger Alexandrine, *Psittacula eupatria,* is also found in Doha. These birds feed on nuts, fruit and seeds and therefore can damage cultivation in Qatar.

Socotra cormorant *Phalacrocorax nigrogularis*

Off the coast of Doha at Al Aaliya Island (a restricted location north of The Pearl) some 500 pairs of Socotra cormorant *Phalacrocorax nigrogularis* nest. This endangered species breeds in winter in various months, but always as a synchronised event in any given colony. The great cormorant, *Phalacrocorax carbo,* also occurs, though in lower numbers.

Readily seen coast birds include greater flamingo *Phoenicopterus roseus* from around November to April. They might also be found inland at Irkhaya Farm (25.013, 51.163) along with the black-crowned night Heron, *Nycticorax nycticorax*, grey heron, *Ardea cinerea*, purple heron, Ardea *purpurea*. Smaller shorebirds are mostly winter visitors and include Grey Plover, *Pluvialis Squatarola*, Common Ringed Plover, *Charadrius Hiaticula*; Little Ringed Plover, *Charadrius Dubius*; Kentish Plover, *Charadrius Alexandrines*; Lesser Sand Plover, *Charadrius Atrifrons*; Greater Sand Plover, *Charadrius Leschenaultia*; Common Snipe, *Gallinago*; European Black-Tailed Godwit, *Limosa*; Bar-Tailed Godwit, *Limosa Lapponica*; Eurasian Whimbrel, *Numenius Phaeopus*; Eurasian Curlew, *Numenius Arquata*; Common Redshank, *Tringa Tetanus*; Marsh Sandpiper, *Tringa Stagnatilis*; Common Greenshank, *Tringa Nebularia*; Green Sandpiper, *Tringa Ochropus*; Wood Sandpiper, *Tringa Glareola*; Terek Sandpiper, *Xenus Cinereus*; Common Sandpiper, *Actitis*

Hypoleucos; Ruddy Turnstone, *Arenaria Interpres*; Sanderling, *Calidris Alba*; Little Stint, *Calidris Minuta*; Dunlin, *Calidris Alpine*.

Gulls and terns, which are mostly migratory species, include Slender-Billed Gull, *Chroicocephalus Genei*; Common Black-Headed Gull, *Chroicocephalus Ridibundus*; Great Black-Headed Gull, *Larus Ichthyaetus*; Steppe Gull, *Larus Barabensis*; Gull-Billed Tern, *Gelochelidon Nilotica*; Caspian Tern, *Hydroprogne Caspia*; Lesser Crested Tern, *Thalasseus Bengalensis*; White-Winged Tern, *Chlidonias Leucopterus*; Saunders's Tern, *Sternula saundersi* (seen throughout the year); whiskered tern, *Chlidonias hybrid* (seen throughout the year).

European roller, *Coracias garrulous*

Inland from Doha, some attractive migrants that should be seen include the flashing blue of the European roller, *Coracias garrulous*; the deeper blue of the Indian roller, *Coracias benghalensis*, both these rollers are similar in size to a jackdaw or feral pigeon, blue-cheeked bee-eater *Merops persicus*;

European bee-eater *Merops apiaster*, Eurasian hoopoe, *Upupa epops,* which though most migrate through Qatar some stay rather than moving on.

Expect to see common kestrel, *Falco tinnunculus,* and Western osprey, *Pandion haliaetus,* which is resident along much of the coast and breeds in Qatar. Arriving in winter are Western Marsh Harrier, *Circus aeruginosus,* and Pallid Harrier, *Circus macrourus.*

Smaller migratory species include the much sought after hypocolius, *Hypocolius ampelinus,* found in scrub, Rufous-Tailed Scrub Robin, *Erythropygia Galactotes*; Spotted Flycatcher, *Muscicapa Striata*; Ed-Spotted Bluethroat, *Luscinia Svecica*; Black Redstart, *Phoenicurus Ochruros*; Common Redstart, *Phoenicurus*; Rufous-Tailed Rock Thrush, *Monticola Saxatilis*; Whinchat, *Saxicola Rubetra*; European Stonechat, *Saxicola Rubicola*; Northern Wheatear *Oenanthe*; Isabelline Wheatear, *Oenanthe Isabellina*; Desert Wheatear, *Oenanthe Deserti*; Pied Wheatear, *Oenanthe Pleschanka.*

Less common birds include crab-plover, *Dromas ardeola,* a distinctive wader with black & white plumage and a heavy bill, at Simaisma, though the resort may impact their numbers. North African red-necked ostrich, *Struthio Camelus,* has been introduced to the Al Reem reserve.

REPTILES

Geckos are the most numerous lizard, in species and overall numbers; Arabian desert gecko, *Bunopus tuberculatus,* rough-tailed gecko, *Cyrtopodion scabrum*; Heyden's gecko, *Hemidactylus robustus,* are all found.

The yellow-belly house gecko, *Hemidactylus flaviviridis,* as its name suggests is the species commonly seen inside buildings where they feed on insects. This may well be the most commonly seen lizard in Qatar.

Other lizards include Persian Leaf-Toed Gecko, *Hemidactylus Persicus*; Arabian Short-Fingered, Gecko *Stenodactylus Arabicus*; Slevin's Short-Fingered Gecko,

Stenodactylus Slevini; Gulf Short-Fingered Gecko, *Pseudoceramodactylus Khobarensis*; Persian Rock Gecko, *Pristurus Rupestris*; Arabian Desert Lizard, *Acanthodactylus Opheodurus*; Blanford's Short-Nosed Desert Lizard, *Mesalina Brevirostris*; Hadhramaut Sand Lizard, *Mesalina Adramitana*; Yellow-Spotted Agama, *Trapelus Flavimaculatus*; Arabian Toad-Headed Agama, *Phrynocephalus Arabicus*; Eastern Skink, *Scincus Mitranus*.

Arabian Toad-Headed Agama, *Phrynocephalus Arabicus*

The strangest lizard of Qatar is Zarudny's worm lizard, *Diplometopon zarudnyi*, a limbless subterranean lizard. The largest lizards are Desert Monitor *Varanus griseus* which can reach over 90cm from the nose to the tip of the tail. They are active hunters and eat other reptiles including the Egyptian spiny-tailed lizard *Uromastyx aegyptia* which is slightly smaller at up to 80cm.

Snakes include Sindh Saw-Scaled Viper, *Echis Carinatus Sochureki*, a venomous ambush hunter of perhaps up to 50cm in length; possibly the Desert Black Snake, *Walterinnesia Aegyptia*, this can exceed a meter in length and is a venomous hunter of small animals; Hooded Malpolon / False Cobra, *Malpolon Moilensis*, a venomous rodent eater that grows to over 1.5m; Flowerpot Snake, *Rhamphotyphlops Braminus*, a worm-like snake of only a few cm in length, found in soil; Crowned Dwarf Snake, *Eirenis Coronella*, a small non-venomous snake of only about 30cm length; Crowned Leaf-Nosed Snake, *Lytorhynchus Diadema*, again this is non-venomous but slightly larger at up to 50cm; Clifford's Diadem

Snake, *Spalerosophis Diadema Cliffordi,* a six foot long hunter of rodents that is very mildly venomous.

There is a **toad** species, the African common toad *Sclerophrys regularis* that may have been introduced from Egypt. Though Qatar is a hyper-arid country, these toads are expanding their distribution making use of artificial irrigation systems.

Moths and butterflies of Qatar are thought to number less than 35 species including the Blue Pansy *Junonia Orithya*; Clouded Yellow *Colias Croceus*; Painted Lady *Vanessa Cardui*, whose family is also familiar in Europe.

SEA MAMMALS

Despite being almost landlocked and shallow, The Gulf has many sea mammals including Orca / Killer Whale *Orcinus Orca*, Byrdes Whale *Balaenoptera Edeni*, Indo-Pacific Bottlenose Dolphin *Tursiops Aduncus*, Indo-Pacific Humpbacked Dolphin *Sousa Chinensis*, Spinner Dolphin *Stenella Longirostris*, often seen leaping out of the sea and rotating its body and Dugong, *Dugong Dugong*. The Dugong can grow to around three metres and weigh some 500kg. They feed in shallow waters on seagrass, which means The Gulf is an ideal habitat. A single calf is born after a year's pregnancy and is dependent for almost two years after which it might live for a further 65 years.

SEA REPTILES

Turtles

The Arabian Sea is home to several sea reptiles including the Hawksbill Turtle *Eretmochelys imbricate* and Green Turtle *Chelonia mydas* both of which are found in Qatar's seas. Perversely Green Turtles are the most common in Qatar's waters where they feed on seagrass but do not appear to nest in Qatar, while Hawksbill do nest, but the adults move elsewhere to feed in coral reefs. The Hawksbill has a hawk beak-like shaped mouth, while the Green Turtle's is more rounded. The Green Turtle gets its name from the green tinge to its fat.

The most detailed knowledge of any turtle is for the Green Turtle; however, it is likely that in most respects the Hawksbill has a similar lifestyle.

Only female turtles return to the land and then only to lay eggs; males never return to land after hatching. The female Hawksbill may reach maturity around 20 years and Green Turtle from 25 onwards. A mature adult Green Turtle may measure 120cm shell length and weigh 170kg while a Hawksbill may measure 85cm and weigh 65kg. The eggs are laid in a sandy beach, with a relatively shallow slope; in Qatar, Fuwayrit beach is a prime location. This beach is closed, as a result, at peak nesting season 1st April to 31 July.

Mating for turtles takes place at sea near the beach, following which the female will lay eggs perhaps up to 140, with the Green Turtle repeating this four times over a few weeks. They then leave, migrating to feeding grounds that may be hundreds of kilometres away. Each turtle returns to breed after 2-3 years, undoubtedly returning to their hatching beach to breed when they mature. As with many other reptiles, the temperature of the environment that surrounds the egg determines the sex of the hatchling, with more females developing with a temperature over 30C and more males under 30C. The impact that global heating will have on the sex ratio is clear, and presumably will have an impact on total numbers over the long term unless they relocate to different, cooler areas, to nest.

Green Turtle *Chelonia mydas*

The nesting process is designed to camouflage the location of the eggs, but even so, foxes may locate and dig up a nest and eat the eggs. Around 60 days after the eggs are laid they hatch, and the hatchlings will co-ordinate their eruption from the nest so they emerge en-mass and scramble together towards the sea. On their way to the sea the hatchlings are predated by Ghost Crabs, *Ocypode rotundata*, gulls, foxes and in the sea by fish. The result of this predation and other death-causes is that perhaps 990 out of every 1,000 eggs laid may never give rise to an adult. The young turtle may spend the next five years in open waters feeding on krill and other small marine life before moving to shallow waters. The Green Turtle feeds on seagrass and algae while Hawksbill are omnivorous, though preferring sea sponges, which though toxic to many sea animals do not affect the Hawksbill turtle.

Other sea reptiles include various sea snakes, which are found generally in shallow waters and are best given a wide berth. They include the Annulated Sea Snake *Hydrophis cyanocinctus*, the Gulf Sea Snake *Hydrophis lapemoides*, Reef

Sea Snake *Hydrophis ornatus* in shallow water including sandy bottomed areas, Yellow Sea Snake *Hydrophis spiralis*, Yellow Bellied Sea Snake *Pelamis platurus* which may reach over two metres and does inhabit shallow water.

NATURE RESERVES

There are 12 land reserves in Qatar, two of which also include marine areas. The reserves, in most cases, seem little different in development from areas outside the reserve's boundary. Most are freely accessible.

Ash Shahaniyah covers 12 sq km in central Qatar. It was a sanctuary for the endangered Arabian Oryx from Muaither farm. Today there is also a pen for ostriches.

The 54 sq km Al Masshabiya reserve is in south-west Qatar, near the Abu Samara border. The reserve has sandy plains with some hills and valleys, and seasonally grass, herbs and wild trees grow on sand dunes in the reserve. The reserve resettled Arabian Oryx, gazelle and other endangered animals in Qatar.

The Al Eraiq reserve is adjacent to Al Masshabiya and is intended to protect its vegetation from overgrazing.

In north-east Qatar, 64 km from Doha, Al Thakhira was designated as a natural land and sea reserve and includes the small island of Um Far opposite the housing at Al Thakhira and natural mangroves. The reserve has rich marine biodiversity and *Avicenna marina* mangrove.

The Al Reem reserve lies on the western coast and covers around 16 percent of Qatar's total land area and has distinctive calcareous formations alongside the western coast. The reserve is recognized under UNESCO's Man and the Biosphere Program.

The Al Wasil nature reserve measures around 36 sq km. It was chosen in line with the biodiversity strategy objectives and to limit the rapid urbanization on Qatar's eastern coast.

Khor Al Udaid Also known as the 'Inland Sea' was designated as a land and sea nature reserve in 2007 and stretches over around 1833 sq km. It has large, white sand dunes and presents a unique mix of geological terrains and environmental factors, creating potential natural habitats for various flora and fauna species. Despite it being a reserve, 4x4 vehicles use it as a recreation area and tourist camps line the shore.

The 53 sq km Al Rafa reserve is located near Al Rayyan and Al Wajba areas, to the west of Doha.

The Sunai reserve lies north-west of Doha. It was designated as a protected area due to its biodiversity and to limit urbanization.

Um Al Amad Reserve is located 25 km north-east from Doha.

Um Qarn Reserve is located 30 km north from Doha.

Irkaya Farm is located off the Abu Samra Road about 50 km west of Doha in the south central plain of Qatar. Though a nature reserve, the area is a man-made environment of sewage settling ponds and agricultural pivot fields and it is these that attract the wildlife.

5

AGRICULTURE

Searing heat, intense sun and lack of rain mean that agriculture in Qatar depends on man-made assistance, including permanent irrigation. Farming, as a result, has in the past been subsistant, with limited scope for crops and a vast range area needed for animal grazing. Perhaps the key reason that man has been able to survive on the Qatar peninsula has been access to the sea and a symbiotic relationship with the Camel.

There are no permanent rivers in Qatar so most water, until recently, was as a direct result of local rains with the run-off fed into localised water catchment features. Qatar's soils are relatively shallow, with high salt levels and low nutrients as a result of the high evaporation and high temperatures. These issues do make any form of crop cultivation difficult.

Today most water for agricultural use in Qatar is pumped up from two aquifers, the Aruma aquifer in south-west Qatar (that is recharged from the west and Saudi Arabia) and the more important Rus aquifer north-west of Doha.

Agriculture is probably possible over less than 300sq km of Qatar, while the actual use is around 83sq km. The quintessential tree of Arabia the Date Palm *Phoenix dactylifera* is grown over about 24sq km in Qatar. Date Palms have been cultivated in The Gulf region since the Bronze Age. In Qatar the lack of large quantities of water needed for successful growth must have made their cultivation a peripheral activity.

Date Palm *Phoenix dactylifera*

The date tree, in modern agriculture, is almost entirely dependent on man for fruit production. The tree is single sex, and therefore female flowering trees need a separate male tree for pollination. As male trees do not produce fruit and thus 'waste' space, an artificial ratio is created of around one male tree to 100 female trees, resulting in each female tree requiring artificial pollination. Propagation is typically by using the natural offshoots (suckers) at the base of a tree. These are carefully cut off, their base soaked in water and planted in a hole, that has been fertilised. Artificial irrigation is needed, in Qatar today this is typically by drip-feed irrigation. After about 8 years the tree can produce fruit. Date Palms can grow to a height of around 20 metres, and live up to approximately

90 years, depending on the variety. All aspects of the tree and date fruit cultivation are labour intensive, however the fruit which ripens in mid-summer, has a high value so there is a reward. Ripe dates have a high sugar content and this means that the fruit, after either drying or compressing into a mass, is not easily damaged by bacteria or fungus. The date fruit can therefore be stored and used after perhaps two years. With all this work, Qatar now has some 500,000 trees producing about 21,000 tons of fruit.

Root vegetables grown in Qatar include beet, carrots, onions and potatoes, while greenhouse crops include cucumbers, peppers, strawberries and tomatoes. Wheat imports are over 250,000tons and other fruit and vegetables are almost all imported.

Livestock animals in Qatar include more than 128,000 head of sheep, 78,000 goats, over 22,000 cattle that are principally used as dairy cows. These animals are mainly imported or the descendants of recently imported animals. Most of the cows are at the Baladna Farm (the name means 'our country' farm), north of Doha at Al Khor. Poultry and egg production can provide over 600,000kg of meat a year and 250,000,000 eggs. Following the economic blockade of Qatar, the country hopes to further improve its food security. In addition there are well over 1,000 horses, a newly favoured animal, seen in equestrian centres and also in Souq Waqif. There are also around 24,000 Camels, which are a mix of local origin and imported animals.

All these animals are reliant on feed being provided, and so the grass fodder is grown on large pivot fields in the south and north of the country. Baladna Farm is investing in farm land in Romania to grow fodder, which will then be imported to the Qatar farm. This fodder may be fed fresh if grown on the Qatar cattle farm, or as hay. The company is also setting up a dairy operation in Malaysia.

Excavations at Purple Island (also called Jazirat Bin

Ghanim and Al Khor Island after the town it is located near) have revealed ample evidence of fish and mollusc exploitation, tools included fishhooks dating to 5610BC. This name reference to purple comes from its use in the exploitation of purple dye from a shellfish *Thais savigny,* a murex sea snail. Vast quantities of the shellfish produce a dye that is a variety of 'Tyrian purple' the imperial purple of Rome and elsewhere. Shell middens excavated here attest to a lengthy timeline of occupation of this site by possibly nomadic herders/fishers along with structures that appear to have had a cycle of use, abandonment and then reuse, over hundreds of years, perhaps as a base for seasonal activities such as Pearling. At Ras Abrouq, on the coast of west Qatar, occupation from as early as around 5,000BC is shown with potsherds and fish remains. Clearly the coast and sea was exploited by early occupants of Qatar.

Diving for Pearls has been suggested from excavations at more than a dozen sites on the coast of Eastern Arabia that date from between the 6th-4th millennium BC. This Pearl diving was a seasonal practice, which in historical times was concentrated between April-September with the Pearls exported, probably to Mesopotamia. This practice enabled the local population to rise above a simple subsistence economy.

6

HISTORY

Qatar's history is interwoven with the surrounding regions and in many cases it has to be inferred from the larger picture of the region.

On the slopes of Wadi Fatimah in central Saudi Arabia, an archaeological site at Saffaqah has archaeological remains from the Acheulean Period (1,760,000 – 130,000 years ago). Saffaqah lies in the headwaters of the major extinct river Wadi Sahba, which flowed east to towards what is now The Gulf (Arabian / Persian) in the area of Khor Al Udaid in Qatar. This natural route allowed humans to travel very easily during an 'Out of Africa' event along a fertile river valley into the region of Qatar. The earliest dated human evidence found in Qatar have been 'Abbevillian' stone cores (a period around 600,000-500,000 years ago) corresponding to the Lower Acheulean Period, identified by Dr Julie Scott-Jackson and team of the University of Oxford. These were found in south-west Qatar (near the Saudi Arabian border) at sites collectively named 'Kapel'.

The Gulf's water size has varied with the increase and decrease of ice cover in northern and southern latitudes over the last 300,000 years. Over the last 19-15,000 years, sea level changes a result of the Holocene glacial retreat, will have covered evidence of occupation by humans in the valley of a pre-historic river formed by the waters of the modern Tigris/Euphrates system, which previously flowed though Iraq to the Strait of Hormuz. Sea water levels have risen by some 120m over the last 15,000 years, covering what must have been ideal living space used by both animal and human populations in The Gulf. At times the rise in sea levels created swamps to the south of Qatar, effectively making Qatar an island. As recently as perhaps 7 or 8,000 years ago, the historic river was surrounded by a fertile valley flood plain with lakes and the now fossil river valley flowing from Wadi Sahba entered into this river's valley, to the east of modern Qatar.

On the west coast at Al Daasa, 6km south-east of Dukhan, pottery from the Mesopotamian civilisation of Ubaid 6500-3800 BC has been excavated scattered in a seasonal fishing settlement. Also from this period, 18 cairn burials have been found on low hills just north-west of Al Khor, north of Doha, with a pit burial covered with slabs of limestone. More recent evidence of human occupation has also been found on nearby Purple Island (Al Khor Island), in the lagoon at Al Khor. Here remains of tools, shell and fish have been carbon dated to a period between 5610 and 5080. Ceramics from the Dilmun civilisation 2000-1750BC (Bronze Age) occupation have also been found, with evidence of circular huts, post-holes, stone-lined pits and fire hearths. Kassite pottery (from Mesopotamia) 1530-1160BC were widely distributed over this island and it is this period to which the name 'Purple Island' refers. The Kassites traded in this dye, 'Tyrian purple' which was colour-fast. Evidence on this island has also been found from the Sassanid (AD224-651) Persian occupation in the form of pottery and also pottery from AD1700-1900. This small island, of less than 17 hectares, was remarkably considered an excellent location to work on, for some 4,000 years.

At another long established site, Ras Abrouq north of

Zekreet, Ubaid period potsherds have been found. Also at Ras Abrouq are some 100 Seleucid (312-63BC) period burial cairns.

The number of these sites suggest that Qatar was a flourishing location for pre-historic man.

The first definitive reference to Qatar in historical records is by Pliny the Elder (AD23-79) in his Natural History when he referred to a tribe the 'Catharrei'.

Persian domination

Qatar became subsumed by the rising power of the new ruling dynasty in Persia, the Sassanids. In AD224 Ardashir I, the Sasanian king, defeated Artabanus V, the Parthian king, and founded the Persian Sassanid Empire becoming *Shahanshah* (King of Kings). He conducted military excursions around Yamama (south of modern Riyadh) in 240, where he is reputed to have killed the ruler, and in Mazun (modern northern Oman) which became a province of the Persian Empire under the Arab Julanda governors. A successor, *Shahanshah* Shapur II (309-79) occupied Yamama following raids from Arabs into the Persian coast, setting up a buffer kingdom that eventually was ruled by the neighbouring Arab Lakhmid rulers, who may well have been the source of those raiding ships. Shapur II also set up frontier posts along the eastern coast of Arabia through Qatar to northern Oman and crossed west into the Hijaz and up to Syria. In 363 after the Battle of Ctesiphon, between Rome and Persia, in the Persian territory of Mesopotamia, the Roman Emperor Julian was killed, marking a highpoint in Persian suzerainty of The Gulf region. Following a period where little subsequent Persian activity in the region is known, further expansion into Arabia was made during the time of *Shahanshah* Kusrow I in 532. This expansion by Persia included the Red Sea areas of Hijaz and Yemen, bringing Qatar from the western edge of the Persian Empire towards its geographical centre. However by 588 Arabs were again raiding into Iran and the new

Shahanshah Khosrow II occupied north-east Arabia and deposed the Lakhmid dynasty in 600. The buffer client Lakhmid kingdom having been removed, the next wave of Arab invasions into Persia would therefore have unopposed access into the Persian Empire.

Christianity

Christianity was established in Qatar before the middle of the 4th century AD. This establishment of Christianity might have been a result of the relocation of monks after the persecutions carried out by *Shahanshah* Shapur II in Persia, which was probably a reaction to the Roman Emperor Constantine the Great's support of Christianity after the Edict of Milan in 313. A publication the 'Vitae Ionae' which is the story of a monk who lived during the time of Catholicos Barbashemin (343-346), mentions a monastery of Rabban Thomas in 'Beth Qatraye', modern Qatar. Beth Qatraye was one of several Christian establishments belonging to the Eastern Church in The Gulf area including on Sir Bani Yas Island (near Abu Dhabi), Bahrain, Darin Island (on the coast near Dammam Saudi Arabia) and Rew-Ardashir in Fars, north-west Persia that oversaw the others. Rew-Ardashir itself was under the administration of the bishop (later titled Catholicos) of Seleucia-Ctesiphon, the Persian capital in modern Iraq. Beth Qatraye was also the name of the ecclesiastical province that covered the current regions of Kuwait, Eastern Saudi Arabia, Bahrain and Qatar. The neighbouring ecclesiastical province of Beth Mazunaye (the Persian province of Mazun, modern Oman) was noted as attending the Markabta Synod represented by their Bishop Yohannon. In 576 a Bishop mentions a monastery from Beth Qatraye participated at the Synod of *Mar* Ezekiel who was the patriarch of the Eastern Church from 570-581 (*Mar* is an honorific used for Saints and, in this case, Bishops). *Mar* Ezekiel personally visited the region and reported on the Pearl fishing to *Shahanshah* Khosrow I (also known as Chosroes and

Anushiruwan the Just). Beth Qatraye hermit monks requested that Patriarch Ishoyahb I (582-95) of Seleucia-Ctesiphon correspond directly to them, effectively creating their independent role in Qatar. In 613 a man, Ishaq an-Naynuwi, was born in Beth Qatraye and was later created Bishop of Ninevah in modern Iraq and after his death in about 700, he became St Isaac of Ninevah. In 676, well after the establishment of Islam, the Catholicos of Seleucia-Ctesiphon held a synod at Darin Island (off the west coast of the Arabian Peninsula opposite Bahrain, and a Metropolitan of Beth Qatraye attended. Beth Qatraye continued as a Christian establishment, becoming tax collectors for the Muslim rulers until the end of the 7th Century. It was still recorded in the 9th Century and perhaps disappearing around the time of the rise of the Qaramita state that was based in Bahrain from 899.

The Rise of Islam

In 628, Prophet Mohammed sent an envoy, Abu Al Alaa Al Hadrami, to Munzir ibn Sawa Al Tamimi, the Sassanid governor of Qatar and the surrounding area. Similar requests were sent to all rulers of lands abutting the Hijaz. The letter asked for his allegiance to the Islamic faith, which Munzir ibn Sawa Al Tamimi and some of his subjects did. After more correspondence, Mohammed advised that those who did not become Muslims should pay *Jizya* (taxation on non-Muslims). After the death of the Prophet Mohammed in 632, a widespread revolt occurred throughout the Islamic world. Abu Al Alaa Al Hadrami was sent again to eastern Arabia by the new Caliph, Abu Bakr, to defeat the rebels there, in which he succeeded. The next military action by the Caliph in the region was against Persia, which without a buffer state had an open border against the Islamic empire. In 633 the conquest of Persia began, the capital Ctesiphon (south of modern Baghdad) was occupied in 637. This was done during the period the Byzantine areas of Palestine and Syria were conquered by the Caliph. After several pauses in military activity in Mesopotamia, by 651 the Persian Empire was occupied and the last Sassanid ruler, (Yazdegerd III 632-651) was killed during his lengthy retreat after the siege of Ctesiphon (by an inhabitant of Merv in central Asia). Qatar was firmly within a new Arab Muslim empire.

After the rise of the Islamic Abbasid Caliphate from 750, the capital of the Islamic world became Baghdad in 762, relocated from Damascus & briefly Harran. This relocation of power to the region north of Qatar created a flow of wealth through The Gulf, into what was probably the most populous city in the world, who splendour was recounted in the One Thousand and One Nights. Little, however, is known about the history of Qatar during this period.

What may be the Abbasid governor of Qatar's palace from around 805–885 and its supporting settlement was at Murwab in north-west Qatar, an early suggestion of the importance that this area of Qatar would have.

From 874 a new Islamic group, the Qarmatians, developed a form of Shia Islam whose core area was eventually in Bahrain. In 899, they took advantage of a rebellion in Basra Iraq against Abbasid rule and seized power in Bahrain, Qatar and Eastern Arabia, at times stretching as far south-east as the coast of Oman. They became the most powerful force in eastern and central Arabia, exacting tribute and customs until a defeat in 976 by the Abbasid Caliphs. Around 1067 the Qarmatians were overpowered, and a successor state was ruled by the Uyunid dynasty who again ruled in eastern and much of central Arabia; they owed allegiance to the Abbasids.

The occupation and destruction of Abbasid Bagdad by the Mongol prince, Hulagu Khan, in 1258 ushered in a period of rule of Syria, Iraq and Persia by the various Ilkhanate successors of Hulagu Khan. Qatar was on the periphery of the Ilkhanate, whose capital was in Tabriz Iran. Although it is known that from 1253 the Bahrain based Usfurids ruled over eastern Arabia, Qatar was often vassal to the growing power of the Kingdom of Hormuz, based on Hormuz island at the entrance to The Gulf, itself a nominal vassal to various Persian princes.

Portuguese & Ottoman rivalry

The Portuguese arrival in The Gulf region in 1507 and its defeat of the rulers of the Kingdom of Hormuz shook up the power balance in the region. This island based kingdom had dominated the southern entrance to The Gulf, its subsequent occupation by Portugal, in 1515, enabled Portugal to establish other forts in The Gulf including three on Bahrain. From 1514, the Ottoman Turks campaigned against Persia's Safavid rulers, and in 1538 Basra (in southern modern Iraq) became an Ottoman town, giving them a port into The Gulf, where they could campaign against both Portugal and Persia. A peace treaty between the Ottoman Turks and the Safavids in 1555, allowed the Ottomans to focus on the Portuguese and other petty states in Arabia. The Portuguese and Ottomans clashed frequently between 1550 and 1560 with Portugal occupying the coastal town of Qatif on the eastern Arabian mainland, opposite their fort in Bahrain, and the Ottomans occupying Al Ahsa, a town in Arabia 70km west of Qatif. In 1602 Persia, expanding its territory under its Safavid dynasty ruler Shah Abbas the Great, occupied Bahrain. Subsequently Bahrain was ruled from Behbahan, a Persian town near the northern end of The Gulf. In 1622 Persia defeated Portugal, with the support of an English fleet from the growing power of the East India Company, and occupied the island of Hormuz.

Though Qatar was in the centre of an area of intense competition for territory by the Ottomans, Portuguese, Safavids and later the English East India Company, it does not seem to have been occupied by any of them, though presumably ships from Qatar's ports were forced to pay protection and customs duty to those various powers.

By 1670, Qatar came under the Bani Khalid tribe's rule, who had conquered Al Ahsa from the Ottomans. Elsewhere

Oman took advantage of Persia's increasing weakness following its disastrous defeat in Afghanistan in 1711 and occupied Bahrain in 1717. However, by 1736 Persia, under its new ruler Nader Shah Afshar, of the new Afshar dynasty, had reoccupied the island, once again bringing the eastern areas of Arabia under Persian domination.

The Start of Qatar's Modern History

It is following these episodes, that Qatar has a more defined history, and events from this period also resonate in the region's modern politics. In 1732 members of the Al Bin Ali family from Kuwait who were part of a tribal federation, the Utub, are thought to have settled in what would become Al Zubarah. Later the Al Khalifa family, also part of the Utub, moved between 1762-1768 from Kuwait to Al Zubarah under the leadership of Shaikh Muhammad bin Khalifa. This is the period, which is ascribed to the foundation of the town.

Al Zubarah grew partly because of the instability elsewhere and also because Sheikh Mohammad bin Khalifa, who had become the town's ruler, did not impose customs tax, possibly as he was already wealthy through his own ships and trade. The town developed trading links through The Gulf and attracted traders from Basra to settle in the town after they fled Iraq during the Ottoman–Persian wars between 1775/79. Families also moved from Al Ahsa after the seizing of that region by the Al Saud family in 1795.

In 1782, a skirmish, one of a series, took place on the island of Bahrain between a group from Al Zubarah and Bahraini merchants. The resulting deaths on both sides escalated the incident, and an invasion of Bahrain from Al Zubarah took place, which succeeded in destroying Manama, the main town on Bahrain. Part of their spoils was the ship used by Bahrain's Governor to collect customs. In retaliation, plans were made in Bahrain to invade Al Zubarah with 2,000 soldiers being sent from Persia, who still claimed rule over the island. In May 1783 the governor of Bahrain and Busher in Persia, Sheikh

Nasr Al-Madhkur, whose family originally came from Oman, sent ships to attack Al Zubarah. They landed away from the town and were defeated by a combined force from the town and surrounding region. Compounding this defeat was an attack on Bahrain itself, on the same day, by Utub tribe members from Kuwait who set fire to Manama. By July 1783, Bahrain was captured with a force from Al Zubarah by Shaikh Ahmad bin Muhammad Al Khalifa, and following that large numbers of people relocated from Al Zubarah to the more easily defended island of Bahrain.

From 1787 Al Zubarah came under increasing attacks by Amir Abdulaziz ibn Muhammad Al Saud, the ruler of the First Saudi State, from Al Diriyah (near modern Riyadh). Following the Al Saud capture of Al Ahsa (in eastern modern Saudi Arabia) large numbers of refugees fled from there and arrived in Al Zubarah in 1795. Al Saud forces who forced Al Zubarah to submit and pay tax as protection, tracked these refugees.

From the death in 1795 of Shaikh Ahmad bin Muhammad Al-Khalifa in Bahrain, two of his sons jointly ruled Bahrain and Al Zubarah. One ,Sheikh Abdullah bin Ahmed Al Khalifa, ruled until 1842. In 1797, the Al Khalifa family moved to Bahrain initiating the start of a decline in the fortunes of Al Zubarah. The governor of Al Zubarah, Rahmah ibn Jabir Al Jalhami, was tested between 1799 and 1802 by a series of attacks in the area by Omani forces, which ended after the Al Khalifa obtained support from the Al Saud family.

Al Zubarah was the target of a combined attack in 1809 by Al Qassimi forces (from Ras Al Khaimah in the modern UAE) and Al Saud forces. They were, probably in allegiance as a reaction to increased sea power projected against them by Britain and Oman. The town was occupied by the Al Qassimi/Al Saud forces, giving Britain and Oman, both of which had existing conflicts with the Al Qassimi and Al Saud, a new conflict centre to consider. In 1811, a combined

British/Omani force attacked Al Zubarah, and expelled the Al Qassimi/Al Saud forces, leaving the town in ruins, the finale of a period of decline for the town.

The political result of these conflicts was that from 1811 the Al Khalifa family were again the dominant power in Qatar. In the following years, Britain supported them through various agreements concerning Bahrain, notably the General Treaty (which also involved Abu Dhabi and Ras Al Khaimah) in 1820 and later a Perpetual Truce of Peace and Friendship signed much later in 1861.

Britain increased its impact on Qatar in 1821, when an East India Company vessel bombarded the town of Al Bidda, now part of Doha, as retaliation for what was said to be piracy committed by its inhabitants. This action forced between 300 and 400 people to flee, temporally, from Al Bidda.

Al Bidda was involved in a turning point in Qatar's modern history. A contender for power in Bahrain, Sheikh Abdullah bin Ahmed bin Khalifa, in alliance with Shaikh Isa Bin Tarif Al Bin Ali of Al Bidda, who was a leading power in the region and incidentally Sheikh Abdullah's previous military opponent, acted against Sheikh Mohammed bin Khalifa ruler of Bahrain and Al Zubarah. A battle occurred at Fuwayrit (often called the Battle of Umm Suwayya) on 17 November 1847, in which Shaikh Isa Bin Tarif, was killed and Sheikh Abdullah bin Ahmed escaped to Persia. Following the battle at Fuwayrit Sheikh Mohammed bin Khalifa attacked and destroyed Shaikh Isa's base of Al Bidda and relocated its population to Bahrain.

These events created a power vacuum in Qatar, and the Al Thani family, under the leadership of Sheikh Mohammed bin Thani relocated, possibly, in 1849 or 50 from Fuwayrit to the growing settlement of Doha, near Al Bidda.

The Perpetual Truce of Peace and Friendship, that was signed in 1861 with Shaikh Muhammad bin Khalifa Al Khalifa, collapsed in Qatar in 1867 following a series of small incidents that culminated in the imprisonment of Sheikh Jassim bin Mohammed Al Thani, the future ruler of Qatar, by Sheikh Mohammed bin Khalifa Al Khalifa. Led by the Al Thani family, who were now prominent at that time in Doha, there was a battle against Bahraini forces in Qatar, which the Qatari side won. Sheikh Jassim was released in exchange for Bahraini prisoners. Later in the year, 24 boats from Bahrain and 70 ships from Abu Dhabi, with a combined total of 2,700 men, attacked Qatar and destroyed the towns of Al Bidda and Al Wakrah. Despite this, Qatari forces were powerful enough to attack Bahrain, destroy 60 boats and kill 1,000 men. This conflict resulted in Britain forcing a change of ruler within Bahrain and the confiscation of all his ships. A substantial fine of $100,000 was levied on Bahrain.

The Leadership of the Al Thani Family

The British Political Resident (Administrator/Minister/Ambassador depending on your viewpoint of Britain's role in the region) in The Gulf, Colonel Lewis Pelly signed a treaty with Sheikh Mohammed bin Thani in 1868. This treaty represents the acknowledgement of Qatar as a separate political entity, rather than a political part of Bahrain, and the Al Thani family as its leaders.

Midhat Pasha, the Ottoman Governor of Bagdad, reoccupied eastern Arabia in 1871, following a conflict within the Al Saud family and also occupied Qatar. Despite the alarm of Britain the Ottomans then incorporated Qatar into the *sanjak* (administration area) of Najd (Eastern Arabia) in 1872 as a *kaza* (small administrative area). Sheikh Mohammed bin Thani was appointed as the *Qaim-makam* (sub-governor), once again supporting his dominant role in Qatar. In 1878 the future *Qaim-makam*, Sheikh Jassim bin Mohammed bin Thani (Al Thani), attacked and defeated the residents of Al Zubarah, who were allies of Shaikh Isa bin Ali Al Khalifa in Bahrain, and captured the nearby Al Murair Fort. In the following years, Bahrain once again attempted to regain control of Al Zubarah, probably assuming Britain would support them against the newly confirmed Ottoman *Qaim-makam* Sheikh Jassim bin Mohammed Al Thani; however Britain did little against Sheikh Jassim.

The role of the Ottomans, however, came under pressure because of historical local rivalry. In 1882 Abu Dhabi occupied Khor Al Udaid in south-east Qatar, which was at its territorial western limits and the Ottomans would not support the new *Qaim-makam* Sheikh Jassim bin Mohammed Al Thani in regaining it. Sheikh Jassim bin Mohammed Al Thani retaliated against the occupation of Khor Al Udaid by raiding 300km south-east of Khor Al Udaid into the Liwa Oasis in the south-west of the modern UAE; this oasis was the original home of the Abu Dhabi Sheikhs.

A conflict between the Ottomans and Sheikh Jassim bin Mohammed Al Thani followed a simmering dispute when the newly appointed Ottoman Governor of Basra, Mehmed Hafiz Pasha, arrived in Qatar from Al Ahsa, with 340 armed men. Sheikh Jassim bin Mohammed Al Thani relocated to Al Wajbah, 13km west of Doha, with men from several tribes. After unsuccessful negotiations, the Ottomans captured and then imprisoned several men on a ship, the Merrikh. The Battle of Wajbah in 1893 with over 4,000 men under Sheikh Jassim bin Mohammed Al Thani followed this imprisonment. There was a substantial loss on both sides; however the Qataris defeated the Ottomans, and the result was that Mehmed Hafiz Pasha withdrew to Al Ahsa and the Ottoman Sultan then deposed him as governor. This defeat consolidated Sheikh Jassim bin Mohammed Al Thani's position and reduced the ability of the Ottomans to govern.

The Ottomans officially renounced sovereignty over Qatar in 1913 though they remained in Doha until 1915. On 3rd Nov 1916, Britain signed a Protectorate treaty with Sheikh Abdullah bin Jassim Al Thani, where Qatar gave up independence in foreign affairs in exchange for Britain's support against external threats; similar agreements had previously been made throughout The Gulf. Despite this, Britain continued to have little interest in Qatar's internal affairs until initial negotiations for oil exploration took place in 1922.

Oil and natural gas have been a key part of Qatar's economy for almost 100 years. The Anglo-Persian Oil Company surveyed in 1926 but no oil was found. After an oil strike in Bahrain in 1933, a Qatari concession was signed on 17 May 1935 with Anglo-Persian representatives for a period of 75 years in return for 400,000 rupees on signature and 150,000 rupees per annum with royalties, with Britain agreeing to provide enhanced security. In October 1938, the first oil well was sunk in Dukhan, on Qatar's west coast, and oil was found in 1939, however due to World War II exports did not begin until 1949.

Over this period, the dispute with Bahrain over Al Zubarah continued, and in 1936 it expanded to include the Hawar Islands, just off the Qatari central west coast. A Bahraini police fort was built on the islands and Bahrain imposed a ban on trade and travel into Qatar. Qatar followed this by building Al Zubarah Fort, which was completed in 1938.

Following Britain's announced withdrawal from 'East of Suez' in 1968, The Gulf sheikhdoms future political situation needed to be addressed by them. For many months, it appeared that Qatar would become part of a union that would include Bahrain and what are now the constituent states of the United Arab Emirates, which includes Abu Dhabi, Qatar's immediate neighbour to its east. Ultimately on 3rd September 1971 Sheikh Khalifa bin Hamad Al Thani, the then Heir Apparent and Prime Minister but soon to be ruler, declared Qatar a separate, independent sovereign state.

In 1971, Qatar also discovered the North Dome Gas Field in The Gulf; this field straddles the maritime border between

Iran and Qatar as the South Pars/North Dome Gas Field. Production started in 1981 and it eventually turned out to be the largest gas field in the world.

On 27 June 1995, Sheikh Hamad bin Khalifa Al Thani, (known since his abdication as The Father Amir) the father of the current ruler Sheikh Tamim, assumed power and during his reign, the State of Qatar witnessed massive economic, social and cultural development.

The Al Zubarah dispute with Bahrain was settled in March 2001 by a decision by the International Court of Justice whereby Fasht ad Dibal sandbank, Janan Island and Al Zubarah were confirmed as territory of Qatar, while the Hawar Islands and Qitat Jaradah Island were part of Bahrain's territory.

In 2002, Qatar hosted the United States Central Command, which in 2009 relocated to its current base at Al Udeid Air Base, west of Doha. Other USA bases in Qatar have been transferred out of the country. (Al Udeid Air Base is a high security location to be avoided, unless you have business there.)

Sheikh Hamad Bin Khalifa Al Thani abdicated in June 2013 when his son Sheikh Tamim bin Hamad Al Thani, the current Amir of Qatar, became ruler.

From 5 June 2017, Saudi Arabia, the UAE, Bahrain and Egypt instated a political and economic blockade against Qatar. This followed years of disputes that notably included withdrawal of the ambassadors of Bahrain, Saudi Arabia and the UAE from Qatar in 5 March 2014. The blockade and resultant focus on self-sufficiency by Qatar has resulted in an increase in the national identity of Qatar. This blockade was officially resolved on 5 January 2021.

In July 2021 Amir Sheikh Tamim bin Hamad, confirmed that the country's first legislative polls would be held in October 2021. The elections would be for 30 members of a 45-seat Shura Council. The remaining 15 members will continue to be appointed by the Amir. The people who can vote are Qatari men and women aged over 18, with a grandfather who was born in Qatar. The candidates themselves must be Qatari and over 30. The specificity of those Qataris who can vote is not unusual throughout The Gulf, where identity based on tribal origins and previous, historic, allegiances still have importance. Current inclusion or exclusion and government patronage can result from ancestral actions.

7

PEARL DIVING

One of the oldest professions in the Gulf region is Pearl diving.

Archaeological evidence dating back to the Late Stone Age in 6000–5000 BC suggest trade and spiritual beliefs within in The Gulf included the natural Pearl.

The Epic of Gilgamesh a poem from 700 BC Mesopotamia tells that Gilgamesh searched for the 'flower of immortality', a well-known early allusion to Pearling, by diving using weights attached to his feet. Pliny the Younger, who died in AD 113, wrote about Cleopatra's sumptuous dinners, which included her consuming Pearls dissolved in vinegar. He also wrote that women in Rome 'glory in having these (Pearls) suspended from their fingers, or two or three of them dangling from their ears'. The Armada portrait of Britain's Queen Elizabeth I shows the victorious queen in a dress embroidered with dozens of large Pearls, an 8 strand necklace of Pearls as well as earrings and other Pearl embellishments; clearly Pearls were a majestic ornament for a powerful north-west European monarch in the 16th century.

The Gulf's Pearl industry boomed with increasing stability in the region in the early modern era and its incorporation into international markets. Divers from Oman's

Batinah Coast and the Yemeni island of Socotra, almost 3,000 kilometres away by sea, came to The Gulf to dive for this valuable resource. By around the middle of the 19th century, there can have been few families on the coasts of Eastern Arabia or Western Persia who did not have men working in the Pearl business.

Historical records illustrate the extent of Pearl diving and the money made. The value of the market in Pearls is estimated to have grown by over 600% between 1790 to 1905. Pearls from The Gulf created an income of about US$1.75 million a year from 1830 rising to US$4 million by the early 20th century.

In the 1829 book Travels in Assyria, Media and Persia, James Silk Buckingham wrote that Pearls from Bahrain brought in approximately £200,000. In the same period, James Wellsted in his 1838 book Travels in Arabia wrote that there were over 4,000 boats engaged in Pearling between Bahrain and Oman.

Pearls from The Gulf were traded to India, the Ottoman Empire, Persia and on to China, Europe and North America, where the aristocratic and emerging middle classes used Pearls as luxury items for jewellery and clothing. Sheikh Mohammed bin Thani of Qatar told William Palgrave in 1877 that: 'We are all from the highest to the lowest, slaves of one master, Pearl.'

The British Political Resident, John Lorimer, wrote that the industry was worth £625,933 in 1873/74 and £1,076,793 30 years later in 1904/05 in his Gazetteer of the Persian Gulf. Lorimer also included that there were 350 Pearl boats in Doha.

Two species of Molluscs were sought for their Pearls. The Akoya Pearl oysters *Pinctada imbricata fucata*, which grows to a shell length of 60–80 mm and create as a by-product 'Lengeh shells' named after the Iranian port, used for products such as buttons. The second and a bigger species *Pinctada margaritifera*, commonly known as the Black-Lip Pearl oyster, which grows to 200 mm in length.

Pearl grounds in the western shore of The Gulf run from Kuwait to Musandam in Oman. They also ran along nearly the whole coast of the Persian side of The Gulf, from near Bushehr (opposite Kuwait) to Lengeh (opposite Musandam) in the south.

Diving for Pearls was a seasonal activity from June to September with two diving periods: the big dive, a 60-day journey, and the small dive, a 40-day trip. Both seasons fell from June and September. Each season dozens of Pearling boats left Doha for coastal banks rich with oysters.

The captain, called the *nakuda*, was in command of the whole operation including the Pearl divers, *ghawas al lulu*. On the diver's fingers and toes were leather protection, *khabbal*, to protect against sharp rocks, shells and dangerous sea creatures. A wooden nose peg, *fitaam*, stopped seawater drowning the man under deep-water pressure, oil-soaked cotton plugs blocked the ears. They used a knife to cut the shellfish off the rock and a basket, *dadjin*, to put their catch in.

A diver used two ropes to descend which his assistant, the *saib*, held from the ship. The diver would remain underwater for 60 to 90 seconds, going as deep as 20 metres. Each vessel could have up to 40 divers, with each person diving perhaps 40 times a day. A crew could gather 8,000 Pearl oysters a day. In colder waters in The Gulf, some divers greased their body against the cold water, much as ocean swimmers do today.

These divers lived on credit given to them by their captain, who owned and operated the boats and kept the crew. Pearl merchants, *tawawish*, in turn advanced loans to boat captains in advance of the diving season. The Pearling industry, therefore, functioned on borrowed capital. The captain would collect all the Pearls, and after selling them to the Pearl merchant, he would pay the divers in cash, though despite them risking their lives they received the smallest proportion of the sale. The system depended on success each season, with financial ruin for everyone down the chain a possibility.

By 1924, however, the region's Pearling industry was already falling into rapid decline. A primary factor affecting that decline was the development of the cultured (artificially encouraged growth of the Pearl) Pearl industry in Japan from 1916, by the entrepreneur Mikimoto Kokichi.

From then the Pearl fishing fleets dwindled, and the men travelled elsewhere to look for work, perhaps to Baku, Iraq and Persia where oil was replacing Pearling as the engine of the region's economy.

8

EXPLORERS OF QATAR

Lieutenant J.H. Grubb of the Indian Navy (Bombay Marine) in 1822, described Bidda as a 'most miserable place: not a blade of grass nor any kind of vegetation near it; the water good, procured, they said, at some distance. The anchorage in the inner harbour very good, four fathoms, being about one-eighth of a mile from the shore, surrounded by a reef nearly dry, which forms a complete basin, the entrance to which is very narrow, but deep, and free from danger. Not so in approaching it, as the water is very shoal about seven miles out, there being two and a half fathoms, sand, and a good deal of sea in a north-wester.'

In the 20th Century, the description of Qatar by foreign visitors create a vivid impression of the country.

In January 1904 Hermann Burchardt, the German explorer and photographer, arrived in Doha after travelling by sea from Kuwait into Al Uqair and overland via Al Ahsa. He went to the Ottoman Fort which was located south of the Amiri Diwan (a reception and administration complex for the ruler), in between Al Bidda and Doha where he was 'quartered with the Commander, a major' and described 'Three neighbouring towns are distinguished. Doha, with the garrison, and Al-Bidaa, and As-Solata. The garrison consisted of 1 *tabur* (an armed unit of 250 men appx) with two old cannon. Soldiers, military officers, and administrative officers with their families dwell in miserable mud houses, and the state of health is not good; particularly common are eye diseases. At one time scurvy was also common; better nutrition for the soldiers has eliminated this disease completely'. He continued 'in reality the Turkish influence extends no further than the reach of rifles and canon' in the fort.

Robert Cheesman worked in Iraq from 1920-23 as an assistant to Sir Percy Cox, the High Commissioner of Iraq in the British administration. In 1921 Cheesman travelled through Saudi Arabia and, from the port town of Al Uqair in modern Saudi Arabia, he used the organisation of Abdul Aziz Al Qusaibi the ship-owner and Abdulaziz Al Saud, who ruled the central and eastern areas in what is now Saudi Arabia. Cheesman boarded a '*Baghala*' type of Dhow, in April near Al Uqair and crisscrossed between the western shore of Qatar and the eastern shore of the Saudi coast in the Gulf of Salwa, describing how shallow the water was - as the boat needed to be pushed despite being 1/4 mile (400meters) from shore. He wrote, 'Here the Qatar coast is a sandy shore; scrub grows close to the sea and across one to two miles of undulating sand-dunes until the hills are reached, which appear featureless and level-topped, running parallel with the coast and rising from 200 to 300 feet'.

9

THE AL THANI FAMILY RULERS OF QATAR

The Al Thani family can be traced back to a branch of the Maadhid tribe whose eponymous originator, Maadhid bin Musharaf, claims descent from the tribal confederation Banu Tamim, one of the largest in Arabia. From the 17th century AD, the family lived in Ushayqir, a settlement 170km north-west of Riyadh. At some time around the start of the 18th c, they were settled at Yabrin (Jabrin) oasis 280km south-east of Riyadh in present-day Saudi Arabia. During the 1740s they moved to the south of Qatar near Sikak, then to Al Zubarah, Fuwayrit and finally, under their leader Sheikh Mohammed bin Thani, the family settled in Doha around 1848. The family takes their name from the father of Sheikh Mohammad, Thani bin Mohammad bin Thamir who died around 1860 and was apparently a 14th generation descendent of Maadhid bin Musharaf who lived in Yabrin oasis.

The move into Qatar resulted in the family becoming involved in Pearling and trading, which required the families to settle in a permanent base, rather than having their previous clearly peripatetic lifestyle. After Sheikh Mohammed's death, his son Sheikh Jassim became ruler in 1878, developing the

Pearl trade and expanding trade links to India and East Africa. Sheikh Jassim's accession date on the 18th November is now the National Day for Qatar. Consolidating the rule of the Al Thani family Sheikh Abdullah Bin Jassim Al Thani, who succeeded his father in 1913, signed the Anglo-Qatari Treaty on 3rd November 1916. This treaty followed the Anglo-Ottoman Convention, which resulted in the withdrawal of the Ottoman Sultanate from Qatar. It was under his rule that the first oil well was drilled in Qatar in 1938.

Sheikh Abdullah abdicated in 1949, and his son Sheikh Ali bin Abdullah became ruler. It is from this period that oil was first exported from Qatar, and the subsequent flow of money enabled development in Qatar to accelerate. In 1960, Sheikh Ahmad Bin Ali Al Thani became ruler; during his administration, Qatar's independence was declared on 3rd September 1971. The following year Sheikh Khalifa became Amir on 22nd February 1972 and ruled until his son, H.H. The Father Amir Sheikh Hamad bin Khalifa Al Thani became ruler on 26th June 1995. During Sheikh Hamad's rule, the economy of Qatar grew dramatically with increased oil revenues and the development of Qatar's vast gas fields. Sheikh Hamad was successful in gaining the 2022 World Cup for Qatar.

Sheikh Tamim bin Hamad Al Thani

Sheikh Hamad abdicated on 25th June 2013, and his son His Highness **Sheikh Tamim bin Hamad Al Thani** became Amir of Qatar (often Emir is used). Sheikh Tamim bin Hamad Al Thani was born on 3rd June 1980 in Doha, Qatar, and after completing secondary school attended the British military academy at Sandhurst, graduating in 1998. Sheikh Tamim is a multi-linguist, fluent in

English and French, in addition to Arabic. The increasing educational role of the Qatar Foundation has grown under his administration as has Qatar's substantial cultural engagement in areas not only including Qatari culture, but the broader Islamic world.

10

GOVERNMENT

Qatar is a Monarchy whose head of state bears the title of Amir (sometimes spelt Emir) and honorific title Sheikh. Unlike, to an extent, the United Kingdom and the United States of America, the head of state in Qatar is to be treated, written and talked about with considerable respect, as viewed from within the very deferential Qatari society. The Amir is also executive head of the Government policies & function and commander of the Armed Forces.

A Prime Minister chairs the Council of Ministers; their Ministries deal with their respective functions. Other Government and semi-government bodies also administer and execute the policies of Government.

A Shura Council (Consultative Assembly) was established in 1972, with 45 members who act as individuals rather than members of a political party (which are not permitted). From 2021 there will be 30 who are are elected and 15 appointed. There are both Male and Female members. Most Female and Male Qatari nationals aged 18years and older can vote.

11

TOWNS AND MAJOR DIVISIONS

Al Khor الخور : GPS - 25.680 , 51.496 ; location – there is about a 50km drive from central Doha to Al Khor to its north. Public transport -: Bus 102, 102x, 201 & 727 at least every hour between 04:00-23:50 from Al Ghanim (Karwa) Bus Station : a 50 minute journey . Focused around a sea-lagoon with patches of mangrove there are a variety of natural habitats. The harbour is a fishing harbour, with dozens of dhows and a small retail fish market. Though there are a few historical sites, these are not a 'must see'. Probably the one of most interest today is the house of the grandfather of Sheikh Tamim bin Hamad Al Thani, his mother's father Abdullah Bin Nasser Al Misnad. The old house is south of the small harbour, just west of a children's play area on the junction of Al Khor Rod and Al Arab St. Within Al Khor are restaurants and accommodation. The town includes housing at Al Khor Community, to the north of the main town, for employees of Qatar Gas and other employers at Ras Laffan 20km to its north. Outlying areas include Al Thakhira and Ash Shafallahiyah.

Al Ruwais الرويس : GPS - 26.131 , 51.200 ; location -

one of the longest drives in Qatar is the 90 minute, 130km drive between Al Ruwais, in north-west Qatar and Doha. Public transport -: Bus 100, 101, 201 - at least every hour between 04:10-19:10 from Al Ghanim (Karwa) Bus Station : a 90 minute journey . Near Qatar's northern tip, Al Ruwais is a port town with a new port that was established in 2011 to replace the now abandoned old port in the town's south. The port principally serves to receive regional cargo including fruit, vegetables and livestock. These shipments have substantially increased since the Qatar boycott. The port also serves as a fishing port. To the north of the town are sandbar type islands and along the coast, south-west of Al Ruwais are a number of ruined towns including, Al Jamal, Al Khuwair and 24 km south-west, Al Zubarah. The older town of Al Ruwais is just to the modern port's east, with mangrove to the town's east. Offshore are usually dozens of small fishing boats. There are limited accommodation and dining options.

Al Wakrah الوكرة : GPS - 25.177 , 51.604 ; location - it's just over 20km between Doha and to its south, Al Wakrah by car. Public transport -: Bus 109, 119, 129 serving the main road at least every half hour from Al Ghanim (Karwa) Bus Station : for the 35 minute journey - and to the souq it's a 1500 metres walk. There is a Metro station, Al Wakrah, on the Red-Line, though as with the buses it's a long walk to the souq, in this case 3km (use the MetroLink bus and it's a shorter walk from the bus-stop and the souq). Al Wakrah is one of the older, still occupied, settlements in Qatar, dating to at least 1845; today is it being rapidly subsumed by Doha.

Doha الدوحة : GPS - 25.291, 51.533 . By far the largest city in Qatar, probably all the other towns largely serve as suburbs, dormitory or service towns for Doha. Most of Qatar's key attractions are in Doha including Souq Waqif, Museum of Islamic Art , Msheireb Museums, National Museum and Katara. Doha's places of interest are listed separately under their names.

West Bay Doha

Dukhan دخان : GPS - 25.420 , 50.794 ; location - Dukhan is about 20km drive west of central Doha Public transport -: Bus 104, 104a, 137, 137a at least every hour from 04:30-20:30 from Al Ghanim (Karwa) Bus Station : for the 90 minute journey . Dukhan is a 2nd World War town, established to service the nearby Oil Fields. As a 'company town' access is against permit. The area to its north includes Zekreet and the area around 'Film City'.

Lusail لوسيل GPS - 25.417 , 51.503 ; about 20km north of central Doha. Public transport is Lusail Metro which has a MetroLink feeder bus service M110 and Lusail Tram. Lusail was empty sabkha and desert less than 20 years ago. Coastal landfilling and excavation has resulted in not only a new town, but a new coastline. The development is still at a relatively early stage, however it does have the 2022 World Cup main stadium, the Lusail Multi-purpose Arena and Lusail Circuit. Place Vendome will be yet another massive shopping mall, the marina area will service sea based leisure craft as well as up-market housing. Qetaifan Island will have a range of hotels, including floating hotels. Perhaps the most iconic building will be Katara Towers, a crescent-moon shaped building largely given over to a hotel.

Mesaieed (Also Umm Said) مسيعيد : GPS - 24.990 , 51.549 ; location - south of Doha by some 40km. Public transport -: Bus 109 every half hour from 04:09-23:09 from Al Ghanim (Karwa) Bus Station : a 90 minute journey . Mesaieed is a major town founded after the 2nd World War. Receiving piped crude oil from Dukhan and gas from Ras Laffan and islands near Idd Al Shargi, this is a major industrial area. This flow of gas supports fertilizer, steel and aluminium plants. A major artificial industrial port services other exports. The town has substantial housing projects within it, enabling much of the workforce to have a short commute. Recreational facilities include cricket & football and there are restaurants, though the closest hotels are in Sealine about 20 km south of Mesaieed and Al Wakrah, about 20 km north of Mesaieed.

Ras Laffan رأس لفان : GPS - 25.892 , 51.560 ; location - Ras Laffan is some 80km north of Doha. Public transport -: No public transport . Ras Laffan is a major industrial development and is the major employer in northern Qatar; forming part of Qatar's massive energy industry. LNG tankers anchor about 20km offshore, waiting for cargo. To its north-west is Al Jassasiya's Rock Carvings.

The Pearl اللؤلؤة GPS 25.368 , 51.551 is an extensive man-made development to the north of Doha. There is public transport including Legtaifiya station on the Red Line – with free MetroLink 110 buses (05:50-22:00 daily) running into the development. It is largely made up of a series of islands, principally of apartment housing, though hotels, retail and restaurants abound. The style is a modern take on a European Mediterranean town, reminiscent of the atmosphere of Venice, with waterways. Many of the properties are available to purchase or long lease. Other areas in Qatar that also have similar purchase options including Al Khor Resort, Msheireb, Old Ghanim and more. The most visited sections of The Pearl are Porto Arabia, Viva Bahriya and the Qanat Quarter, each of which are enclosed lagoons with a Pearl-like island in their centre.

12

POPULATION AND GDP

During the 21st century, Qatar's population (figures given by the United Nations and Qatar's government) has increased almost as rapidly as its economy (from IMF).

Year Population GDP in Billions of Dollars

1950 - 25,000

1960 - 47,000

1970 - 108,000

1980 - 222,000 - 17.63

1990 - 474,000 - 6.27

2000 - 591,000 - 18.09

2010 - 1,699,435 - 119.17

2011 - 1,732,717 - 167.78

2012 - 1,832,903 - 186.83

2013 - 2,101,288 - 198.73

2014 - 2,172,065 - 206.23

2015 - 2,235,355 - 161.74

2016 - 2,291,368 - 151.73

2017 - 2,338,085 - 161.10

2018 - 2,674,320 - 183.34

2019 - 2,687,871 - 175.84

2020 - 2,684,329 - 146.09

. . .

As of the end of 2020 the population (in official Qatari figures) was 2,684,329 of which males are 1,936,214 and females 748,115. This overwhelming skew towards males is a result of the large numbers of single male migrant workers employed for their labour and skills. It is thought that Indian nationals make up very approximately 25% of the total, Bangladeshi 12 %, Nepalese 13% and Pilipino around 10%. Nationals of Qatar probably account for less than 13% of the total population and British nationals around 1% and those from the USA lower than 0.5%.

Much of this rise in population has been as a result of the economic impetus provided by Natural Gas and to a lesser extent oil with massive urban development, large-scale investment projects and rising government expenditure. The increase in wealth and population has been the engine for infrastructure development such as the Port, Airport, and Metro system. Along with these communication systems, high profile events including the 2006 Asian Games, 2011 Arab Games, FIFA Arab Cup and upcoming 2022 Football (Soccer) World Cup require an increased workforce. This very substantial rise in demand for labour and skills means that population growth is expected to continue until 2070 when it may reach 3,400,000 and gradually drift slightly lower after that.

In 2015, the regional break up of population (according to Qatar's Planning and Stastical Authority, QPSA) by administrative region shows Doha, Al Wakrah to its south and Al Dayyan to Doha's north on the central east coast have a combined population of 50% of the total population in Qatar. The east coast band of perhaps 15km inland, from Mesaieed/Al Wakrah to Al Khor/Ras Laffan is by far the main population area. Given that much of Qatar is within 60 minutes drive of the Corniche in Doha, the country's towns and villages are within the commuter belt of Doha.

Municipalities
Doha
956,457
Al Rayyan (south-west Qatar)
605,712
Al Wakrah (south-east Qatar)
299,037
Umm Salal (central Qatar)
90,835
Al Khor (north-east Qatar)
202,031
Al Shamal (north Qatar)
8,794
Al Dayyan (east central Qatar)
54,339
Al Shahaniyah (central west Qatar)
187,571

13

ECONOMY

Qatar's oil and natural gas resources are the country's main economic engine and government revenue source, they comprise around 60% of GDP, 85% of exports, 70% of total government revenue (depending on the fluctuations of oil and gas prices). Key export destinations are Japan, India, South Korea and China, though Qatar is looking to supply Germany through the Zeelink LNG pipeline from Zeebrugge Belgium, as an alternative to Russian gas imports into Germany. Imports are overwhelmingly from the USA and China.

As the government receives much of its income from oil income, rather than taxation, its spending drives Qatar's high economic growth and per capita income levels. Robust state spending on public entitlements and booming construction spending, particularly as Qatar prepares to host the World Cup in 2022, looks set to maintain overall economic growth for many years. Lower oil and natural gas prices have, in recent years, led the Qatari Government to tighten some spending to help stem its budget deficit.

Country	IMF est. GDP 2021 US$billion	IMF est. GDP Per Person 2021 US$
Qatar	166.03	59,140
Luxembourg	84.07	131,780
Switzerland	824.73	94,690
United States	22,675.27	68,300
United Kingdom	3,124.65	46,340
United Arab Emirates	401.51	35,170
Saudi Arabia	804.92	22,700

Looking at the GDP per person figures in The Gulf, they include the very low paid immigrant workers and the non-earning children, which in a typical Qatari family will be more than in the UK or USA. This means that the GDP (per capita) per wage earning Qatari will be very substantially higher than the raw figures suggest.

The income from oil and gas that flows into the government is in effect a profit sharing with the production companies. The spending of this income by the Government is the critical engine of the economy.

Budget	2018 Billion Dollars	2019 Billion Dollars	2020 Billion Dollars	2021 Billion Dollars
Total revenue	48.10	57.96	57.81	43.86 (planned)
Oil Revenue			46.03	
Non-oil revenue			11.78	
Total expenditure	55.82	56.78	57.67	53.34
Surplus/Deficit	-28.1	4.3	0.14	-9.48

Some figures are omitted

Expenditure all figures rounded	2018 Billion Dollars	2019 Billion Dollars	2020 Billion Dollars	2021 Billion Dollars
Government employees Salaries and Wages	14.36	15.68	16.16	15.86
Current Expenditure	14.72	15.41	15.89	16.63
Small projects	1.236	1.07	0.96	1.10
Major Projects	25.52	24.61	24.66	19.75
Total Expenditure	55.82	56.78	57.67	53.34

Major expenditure headings	US$ total
Defence & Security	11.57
Public Finance	10.93
Municipality and Environment	6.93
Education	4.75
Health	4.53
Culture & Sports (this includes the World Cup stadiums)	3.57
Transportation and Communication (this includes Hamad International Airport, the Metro, Lusail Tram and various IT projects)	3.15

Qatar's reliance on oil and natural gas is likely to remain for the foreseeable future. Proved natural gas reserves exceed 25 trillion cubic meters - 13% of the world's total and the third largest in the world. Proved oil reserves exceed 25 billion barrels, allowing production to continue at current levels for about 56 years. Despite the dominance of oil and natural gas, Qatar has made significant gains in diversification into non-oil sectors, such as manufacturing, construction, and financial services, leading non-oil GDP to rise in recent years towards half the total.

Much of the diversification away from oil and gas however also relies on 'added value' products making use of that oil and gas. These include Petro-chemicals (ethylene and methanol extracted from gas by super steam heating) which are fundamental to the plastic industry. Fertilizers (ammonia also created from gas, combined later with nitrogen and urea that uses ammonia and CO_2) and finally using gas as a power source for iron and steel smelting.

The major industrial area is Mesaieed Industrial Area south of Al Wakrah. The primary industries here are based on the utilisation of Qatar's oil and gas with Qatar Petroleum, a refinery, lubricants, fertiliser (as a joint venture with by Norsk Hydro using gas as a raw material), fuel additives, vinyl, and chemicals. Using gas as an energy source are aluminium and steel smelters (another joint venture with Norsk Hydro). A major electricity production unit uses natural gas as a power supply. Construction aggregate is both locally sourced and imported, for example, gabbro, an igneous rock similar to basalt, is imported from Oman. North of Mesaieed is the **Hamad Port**, a man-made commercial container port and also coastguard and adjacent military port constructed from 2010 in a former area of *sabka*. It handles general containers, machinery, vehicles, imported grain and livestock. Associated with Hamed Port is a port and commercial district, **Um Alhoul**, a Free Zone to support smaller scale manufacturing, warehousing & logistics, business services and commercial – retail, services, offices and it will offer hotels. Um Alhoul also is home to a major electricity and water desalination plant that will produce 2.52GW electricity and 514 million litres of water, per day.

North of Doha is **Ras Laffan** which is Qatar's original petrochemical complex, supporting several natural gas liquefaction (LNG) plants. Ras Laffan is Qatar's export facility for LNG from Qatar's North Field.

Transport with a focus on air routes served through **Hamad International Airport**, supports the development of Qatar as an international communications hub. Qatar Airways with 205 passenger jets and 34 cargo only jets, uses the airport as its hub and spoke centre serving over 83 countries and 146 destinations. To the south of Hamad

International Airport is **Ras Bufontas**, a free trade zone which is focused on light industry, emerging technologies and service businesses. Tourism is also a partner to the Airport and Airline development.

Tourism is a significant focus of diversification. The number of visitors was planned to increase from 2.9million in 2016 to 5.6million in 2023, grow expenditure from US$ Billion 4.75 in 2016 to US$ Billion 10.99 in 2023, an increase in direct contribution to GDP from 3.5% to 4%. Supporting this is an ongoing major redevelopment of **Doha Port** adjacent to the Museum of Islamic Art . This will be a leisure port, a destination for cruise ships and leisure marine operations in general.

14

OIL & GAS

The history of exploration for oil in Qatar is inextricably linked with oil exploration generally in the Middle East. Qatar is within the historical commercial contract called the 'Red Line Agreement'. This 'Red Line Agreement' grew from an arrangement by Calouste Gulbenkian, who was Armenian born in Ottoman Turkey in 1869, but in 1902 became a British citizen. He was well connected with the Ottoman Sultan Abdul Hamid II, who had just ascended to the throne.

Gulbenkian had promoted the prospects for oil in Mesopotamia (Iraq), which at the time was ruled by Ottoman Turkey. Such were the apparent prospects that the Ottoman sultan had large areas of land in Mesopotamia transferred from government ownership directly to his personal control, as the '*Liste Civile*', which also nullified previous exploration agreements. Over time, German interests obtained small concessions from him in modern Iraq. During this period most of the territory in adjacent Persia was signed for exploration under a 1901 agreement with a Briton, William K. D'Arcy, who later unsuccessfully also sought exploration rights within Ottoman domains.

The Young Turk revolution in 1908 altered the economic

situation in favour of British interests. In 1910, the National Bank of Turkey was established to support British interests in the Ottoman Empire with Calouste Gulbenkian as a director. He negotiated an agreement between various interested parties and in 1912 Turkish Petroleum Co was founded with shares allocated as 25% Deutsche Bank (which was also involved in the Berlin-Constantinople-Baghdad Railway project), 25% by a subsidiary of Shell (Anglo-Saxon Petroleum) and 50% for National Bank of Turkey, of which Gulbenkian controlled 15%, excluded was D'Arcy. The outcome of the agreement was a non-compete clause that the partners would only work in cooperation with each other within the territory agreed, in effect a form of cartel. The territorial boundaries of the agreement were formed when a map was produced with a red-line drawn through it, marking the boundaries of the concession area. The red-line ran from Turkey to the south, covering the Levant, Iraq and the Arabian Peninsula (except Kuwait). This agreement collapsed after World War II and the establishment of Saudi Arabia.

Despite all this manoeuvring, no company was granted an exploration agreement. Finally, it was agreed that D'Arcy (then known as Anglo-Persian) would obtain 47.5% of Turkish Petroleum Co, Deutsche Bank 25%, Anglo-Saxon Petroleum Co would obtain 22.5%, and Calouste Gulbenkian would receive 5%, after which he became known as 'Mr 5%'. Shortly after this, the Ministry of Finance in Turkey granted a concession lease. World War I paused final negotiations and also resulted in German shares being transferred to the French Government's Compagnie Francaise des Petroles.

The cessation of war, in 1918, also resulted in the United States of America wanting to obtain oil exploration rights in the region, with several USA companies co-operating as the 'Near East Development Corporation' NEDC. During several years of negotiations an eventual agreement was reached that the USA could join the cartel with shares for Anglo-Persian

Oil Company, Royal Dutch/Shell, the Compagnie Francaise des Petroles and NEDC at 23.75 % each and Gulbenkian still at 5%, he was clearly either essential to the success of the operation or a superb negotiator. The agreement was signed in July 1928 and the company named Petroleum Concessions Ltd. Qatar was included in this general situation through a new subsidiary, Qatar Petroleum Co.

In Qatar, the initial negotiations for exploration took place in 1922. The Anglo-Persian Oil Company (of that cartel) surveyed in 1926, but no oil was found. After a viable oil discovery in Bahrain in 1932, a further concession for Qatar was signed on 17 May 1935 with Anglo-Persian representatives for 75 years in return for 400,000 rupees on signature and 150,000 rupees per annum with royalties; Britain agreed to provide enhanced security. In October 1938, the first oil well was sunk in **Dukhan** and oil was found in 1939, however due to World War II exports did not begin until 1949.

Though labour for the oil industry in Qatar initially was foreign, during the early 1950s, Qatari nationals were increasingly employed. This increase in the number of Qatari nationals being employed in the oil industry resulted in improved labour rights and higher wages for the workforce.

Offshore-oil was explored by the International Marine Oil Company, and Shell Qatar acquired these fields in 1952. Following this, oil was discovered in 1960 at Idd Al Shaqi, (the concession was later acquired by Occidental Petroleum of Qatar). These offshore fields store and export their oil from Halul Island, just under 100km north-east of Doha which was developed by 1966.

Qatar joined OPEC in 1961, a year after the organisation was formed. In 1973, the Qatari government obtained 25% of the shares in Qatar Petroleum Co and in February 1977, the company became wholly owned by Qatar's government.

In 1971, Qatar discovered the **North Dome Gas Field**

(**South Pars**) in The Gulf; the field straddled the maritime border between Iran and Qatar. Production started in 1981 which, eventually, turned out to be the largest gas field in the world. Since 2007, the UAE and Oman receive 21billion cubic meters of gas annually from these fields via the Dolphin Gas Project, which was established in 1999.

The Qatar Government withdrew from OPEC on 1st January 2019, explaining that it wished to increase gas production by 43%. Oil production in Qatar is some 1,530,000 barrels per day (2020) and 171 Billion cubic meters of gas a year.

15

CULTURE

Culturally Qatar is full of contrasts, jaw-droppingly modern, yet deeply conservative; remarkably insular yet potentially open.

Although most people living in Qatar are not Qatari nationals, this section gives an overview of Qatari nationals unless noted otherwise.

There are two fundamental, almost inextricably linked, areas in Qatar that impact its culture, the role of religion, Islam and that of the family, both nuclear and extended.

The Qatari nuclear family, Grandparents, Parents and Children, forms the key social unit in Qatar. The extended family, which includes first cousins and other cousins, creates further units and the tribe offers a known form of identity to other nationals.

Marriages are generally made with the agreement of the parents of both the husband and wife and in a substantial proportion of marriages, it has been arranged or organised by the family. Marriage is most likely to be from within the extended family, as reported within a Qatari Government Ministry of Development Planning and Statistics (MDPS – now the Qatar Planning and Statistics Authority QPSA) 2016 statistics report. This report shows these consanguineous figures at 42% with 24% of the total as first cousins. Typically, according to the MDPS report, male Qataris are 26 when they first marry, and females are 24. Polygynous marriage is permitted in Qatar, and the MDPS figures show 8 % of marriages were polygynous. Fertility rates (the number of children a woman has during her life) has declined from 4 in 2007 to 2.6 in 2019 for Qatari females according to MDPS & later QPSA figures.

Traditionally, socialising takes place from within the extended nuclear family, with male members and female members forming separate groups during the week, usually after working hours if they work. Social activity, during the week, centres on coffee shops and modern malls, along with informal groups in parks and beach side locations.

At weekends, the nuclear family is the focus, though as can be imagined first cousins of both a husband and wife may be included as they are also the brother or sister of a spouse.

The Tribe is a major source of an individual's identity in Qatar. A tribe is a group of people who share a common identity that, in many instances, is the belief they are descended from a single man, and by implication, his wives. It may be that a tribe is a historical accretion of smaller units which today share a collective identity.

Names & titles

Historically the head of a tribe and also major sections within a larger tribe will have the honorific/title Sheikh (a daughter or wife will be a Sheikha, which might also be a given first name, in which case check what is the family name to see which of the two possibilities you have). In Qatar, this title is now reserved exclusively for members of the ruling Al Thani family with the word Amir, which means, in this example, prince, reserved for the ruler. A Tribe's members will have the tribal name as their family name/surname, for example, Al Kubaisi (Al means 'the', one of the members of the tribe). A member of this tribe might be called Mohammed bin Ali bin Abdullah; here his first name, Mohammed, is followed by '*bin*' which means son (of), Ali (his father) who is the son of Abdullah, who therefore is Mohammed's Grandfather. A female has a similar name line-up, for example, Sheikha bint Ali bin Abdullah Al Kubaisi; here the first name is Sheikha (often used as a female first name) bint Ali, the word '*bint*' means daughter (of Ali). On marriage, both the man and woman retain their birth names; however, children have their first name, followed by their father's name and so on.

Marriage

Marriages are often regarding as an agreement between the bride's and groom's families and a contract, *Melcha* (*Milka*), is drawn up and witnessed by suitable people, ideally including the Imam (religious leader) of the major local mosque. Typically, a dowry is paid by the male's family to the female's, after agreement what it should be.

A celebratory event, *Shabka,* might be held by the families for gifts to be presented. This celebration is followed by agreeing on the date for the marriage, which might be weeks or months away. Before the actual night of the wedding, a '*henna* party' may be held for the females of the families, often nowadays in a hall specially built for weddings or hotel's ballroom. An event on the night of the marriage is held; the bride and females will have a separate venue from the groom and men. For the bride's party only female guests can attend, perhaps with a strict no camera rule, however as guests will receive a gift, the memory will be enhanced. At all celebratory events, the chief participants are at one end of the room and guests always formally greet them.

The men's event is complete with sword dancing and traditional music until, perhaps in a chain of hooting cars, the men's party leads the groom to his new bride. After marriage, typically at least one of the male children and his wife and family will remain living with his parents.

Town and Country

There are two intermingling cultures in Qatar; a *bedouin* one, which is the traditional nomadic society where historically a tribe may have had a territory, which was acknowledged as their collective land within which other people could enter with permission. Traits such as bravery alongside generosity, epitomised though hospitality, is core to the culture of *bedouins*. Alongside this culture is that of the *hadhr,* which is a culture of settled people, in Qatar this is mainly on the coast. The fixed location for these families allowed for educational establishments to develop. However although the family was settled, male members might be away for weeks, months or occasionally years at a time as they worked in Pearling or commerce overseas. This obliged women to be involved in many areas in society that men might have otherwise occupied.

Social Greetings

Greetings between members of the same sex is a matter of tradition, perhaps a 'cheek kiss', once on each cheek if you know of each other, maybe twice on the same cheek if you are more than acquaintances, a multiplicity if you are friends and haven't seen each other for a long time. A nose kiss may be given if they are perhaps from the same family. Occasionally a person may kiss the forehead of another person; this is a sign of deference to that other person. Usually during these greetings the right hand is held, or the right hand is placed on the left shoulder of the other person.

Verbal greetings in Qatar are often formulaic and lengthy. Qataris make enquiries about the other person's health and family, and the other person reciprocates these. If between men, these enquiries are never about a man's wife, as this is considered disrespectful.

Between a Qatari and non-Qatari, a normal handshake will be used, often the hand is held for a long time of the people who are friends.

Often, even if you have invited a person or group of people for coffee or a meal in a restaurant, there will be a good-natured disagreement after the meal amongst everyone as to who will have the 'honour' of paying for the meal. Do not misunderstand this, each person will happily pay, especially if you are the only foreigner, however if you have invited people do insist; and accept the reciprocal invitation.

Within most population groupings, decisions are top down, whether in major choice making or in smaller issues such as what restaurant to visit. Where the culture is Arab and to an extent, other Asian cultures, this is the form of decision making in many businesses. In businesses and area such as meetings for work, a person is addressed using the type of their university degree or job title, followed by first name, Engineer Ahmed or His Excellency Khalid. To some extent, this explains some of the importance of achieving certification. It may be that a man is called *abu* Mohammed or *abu* Miriam; *abu* means father, and here he is being acknowledged as a father and also it is an indication that he is known well by the person who addresses him, as they also know his child's name. A similar range of address terms are used for women though the term *umm*, which means mother, is used.

Qatari Clothing

Clothing for both sexes is expected to be modest. Qatari men wear the white *thobe* (in winter it may be a dark colour), either with a small stand up collar (Mandarin style or western formal shirt collar), both have cuffed sleeves often worn with cuff-links. The *thobe* is usually tailor-made for the wearer incorporating choice of material quality, shade of material, overall design and fit. Under the *thobe* lightweight long *sirwal* pants are worn, and also a vest (undershirt). The *ghutra* headdress is usually a heavily starched white cloth (it may be Kashmiri embroidered design), formed from a square of material and folded once across two corners to form a triangle, the longest edge forms the front with the apex of the two shorter edges down the back. It is worn in various styles according to the wearer's preference; very distinctive to Qatar is what is known as a 'cobra' style, which you will know when you see it. Under the *ghutra* is a small *ghafiya* cap that provides some grip for the *ghutra* and stops the hair touching the *ghutra*. The black circle, *agil,* of rope on the *ghutra* (often with a long tasselled cord at the back that is very Qatari style) was in the past used to hobble the front legs of a Camel; some religious men do not wear this on the *ghutra*. The men wear formal sandals, or possibly shoes, and in addition to the cufflinks wear a stylish watch and frequently a pen in the *thobe's* chest pocket. Worn for prestige on special occasions such as weddings, is a *bisht* - a traditional long, white, brown or black lightweight Arabic cloak trimmed in gold thread.

The man's ensemble makes an unmistakable statement of the wearer's identity, he is a Qatari.

Qatari women typically wear a black (it might be another colour) cloak *abaya* that is worn over the shoulders and reaches just above the ground. Over her head and covering the hair and neck is a scarf *shayla,* also known as a *hijab*. Under this *abaya* and *shayla* may well be the latest fashion from New York, London, Paris or Milan, elaborate Lebanese style fashion or only jeans and T-shirt, along with western style underwear.

DO'S and DON'TS

Criticism

Things that would cause embarrassment and loss of face to a Qatari should absolutely be avoided. Criticism might be given indirectly, circumspectly, and never in front of others to avoid that loss of face, perhaps after seeking advice through a person known to you both who is more senior to the person you want to address.

Pointing with a single finger, making a fist or banging a desk to make a point are not acceptable behaviours. Wearing footwear in a home, showing the soles of the feet (even if covered by socks/tights) or footwear's sole should be avoided; though this is not a critical issue as inevitably in a large group somebody's feet will be in the general direction of another person. In traditional meals, food might be eaten with the hand. Here avoid using the left hand to handle food, as this hand is used for personal cleansing; this still applies even if you are left-handed. Also, hold a drinking glass in the right hand.

Discussing Politics and Religion

Although conversations between groups of friends and family members include politics and religion, these topics are unlikely to be discussed in front of people they are less familiar with. Indeed, if you are a foreign national in Qatar, conversation about politics and religion should absolutely be avoided; discussion about the ruling family should also be circumspect. In all cases, a positive admiring viewpoint is usually the most appropriate attitude.

Never discuss your own religion, proselytizing is prohibited by law and your positive viewpoint of your own religion might be misconstrued as proselytizing.

Interaction between non-family males and females takes place within an environment considered acceptable within Islam. Naturally, there is some variance; however in this area caution is ideal. Culturally it is inappropriate for a female to be alone with an unrelated male, this includes being in a vehicle (clearly taxis are an elastic area where sitting in the rear is best if you are a female passenger), elevator, room and so on. These situations should be avoided as misinterpretation can easily be made by either the other person or those who are aware of it.

Greeting members of the opposite sex is also an area where traditions play a role. Physically touching a member of a different sex is usually considered inappropriate, for example a male and female would not typically shake each other's hands.

In very conservative Islamic society, touching the flesh (hand) of the opposite sex is considered an intimate act. In these situations, the female would take the lead in either offering or withdrawing her hand from being shaken, and she should try to assess how conservative the male is. Generally, if you are the female consider the circumstances, if it is a business meeting a handshake might be more appropriate compared to casual social interaction.

General Language

Language that might be considered abusive, or gestures that can be construed offensive can attract police action, even if made within the 'privacy' of your car towards another road user. Penalties include prison and fines.

Clothing

For non-Qatari men and women, clothing should not be too transparent, revealing or tight. Normally acceptable for Women are loose fitting trousers or knee length skirt/dress with a high neck and covered shoulders or sleeved loose – fitting T-Shirt should generally be suitable. Tight 'hot-pants' and 'strappy' top, or tops which reveal the naval, chest or back should not be worn. In general, dress conservatively to avoid unwanted attention, which may include by law-officers. Men should not wear shorts in town, choose loose fitting long trousers and always wear a shirt or T-Shirt of a non-offensive design. Playing sports, men can choose normal shorts / football shirt and women similar to that in most western countries, except looser fitting, perhaps with leggings. Wearing clothing with seemingly innocuous text such as 'I Love Dubai', or sports team's clothing whose sponsor is an airline of countries who boycotted Qatar, these include Emirates and Etihad, is inappropriate given the previous political situation. On a public beach, men should choose loose swim-shorts in preference to Speedo-type swimwear;. Women should never wear a bikini on a public beach. Indeed this could be considered provocative and therefore subject to police action.

Private hotel pools are the place to consider wearing Speedo or bikini style swimwear, if you must.

Physical Intimacy

Avoid Public display of affection with members of the opposite sex, even holding hands, including with your spouse or older children, and do not kiss, hug or engage in any other display of affection with them in public. These might attract complaints and therefore police involvement.

LGBT+

Homosexuality is absolutely prohibited in Qatar, penalties include several years imprisonment, physical lashing and potentially death. LGBT+ symbols and their display are an area where caution is suggested. Same sex marriage is not recognised. Consider that public homosexual sexual activity will bring a higher punishment than for similar heterosexual activity. Additionally, 'cross-dressing' in the case of men, is likely to result in arrest. Do review your own government's advice (see below).

Islam and Culture

Islam is a crucial part of Qatar's culture. It determines activity during the day due to the importance of prayer times. As has been said, it also is critical in the social interactions between males and females. Clothing and modesty are also impacted by the religion, even details of how far above a person's ankles a garment should be. The foods that cannot be eaten, such as pork, how an animal should be killed and the views on alcohol are all covered by the Quran or sayings of the Prophet Mohammed.

Churches, Christianity & other religions.

There are several churches which have premises in Doha, most especially to the south of the F-Ring Road, at the junction with the Doha Expressway. Their congregations include Coptic Egyptian, various denominations from India and the Philippines – including Catholic and Protestant. The principal day for services is Friday (the day off for most workers); services are also held on Sunday.

Churches are required to avoid prothletising – as should you. Blasphemy is also a crime, insulting Islam also has attracted action by the government.

Do read your own country's foreign ministry's advice regarding Qatari culture www.gov.uk/foreign-travel-advice/qatar/local-laws-and-customs https://travel.state.gov/content/travel/en/international-travel/International-Travel-Country-Information-Pages/Qatar.html

16

LANGUAGE PHRASES

Below is a simplified range of words and phrases and doesn't include the various gender-specific suffixes and prefixes.

English transliteration Arabic

hello - marhaba - مرحبا

how are you - kayf halik - كيف حالك

I am fine - ana bikher - أنا بخير

what's your name?- ma ismik - ما اسمك

my name is .... - ana ismi - انا إسمي

welcome - ahlan wa sahlan- أهلاً وسهلاً

good morning - sabah alkhair - صباح الخير

good evening - masa alkhair - مساء الخير

yes - naam - نعم

no - laa - لا

welcome/
help yourself - tfadhal - تفضل

thanks - shukran - شكراً

goodbye - maa assalama - مع السلامة

sorry - asif - آسف
please - minfadhlak - من فضلك
about / almost - yaani - يعني
where is the... - ayn al - اين ال
company - ash-sharika - الشركة
hospital - mustashfaa - مستشفى
hotel - alfunduq - الفندق
restaurant - mataam - مطعم
supermarket - subermarket - سوبر ماركت
museum - mathaf - متحف
this is expensive- haadha ghaali - هذا غالي
no it's cheap - la inaha rakhisa- لا إنها رخيصة.
thobe - thoob - ثوب
ghutra - ghutra - غترة
aqal - agaal - عقال
black cloak - abaya - عباءة
(for women)
headscarf - shayla - شيلة
(for women)
veil covering face -niqaab - نقاب
face mask - birqa - برقع
furniture - athaath - أثاث
chair - kursi - كرسي
table - attawlah الطاولة
bed - assirir - السرير
carpet - sajada - سجادة
jewels - mujawharat - مجوهرات
gold - dhahab - ذهب
silver - fudha - فضة

are these made - hal hadhih masnuwiat -هل هذه مصنوعة
of real gold - min aldhahab alhaqiqi- من الذهب الحقيقي

. . .

vegetables - kodhrawaat - خضروات
onion - basila - بصلة
cabbage - alkarnab - الكرنب
tomatoes - tamatim - طماطم
cucumbers - khiar - خيار
radishes - fijul - فجل
beans faswlaya فاصوليا
potatoes - bitata - بطاطا
fruits - fawakah - فواكه
watermelon - albatikh - البطيخ
lemon - liamun - ليمون
orange - alburtaqali - البرتقالي
dates - tamar - تمر
banana - mawz - موز
peaches - khukh - خوخ
grapes - aanb - عنب
walnuts - jooz - جوز
I want to drink - ared an ashrab - أريد أن أشرب.
juice - aasir - عصير
orange juice - aeasir alburtuqal -عصير البرتقال
apple juice - aasir altafahu - عصير التفاح
coffee - qahwa - قهوة
tea - shai - شاي
bread - khabaz - خبز
rice - aaruz - أرز
cheese - jbin - جبن
one egg - bidha - البيض
how much is a dozen eggs? - كم هو دزينة من البيض؟ kam hu dazinat min albida?
meat (beef) - lahm - لحم
lamb - lahm kharuuf - لحم خروف
chicken - dijaaj - دجاج
fish - samak - سمك
shoes - jooti - جوتي
clothes - malaabis - ملابس

shirt - qamis - قميص
traditional pants- sirwaal - سروال
trousers - bantaloon - بنطلون
suit - badhla - بذلة
a dress - fistan - فستان

17

ISLAMIC RELIGION IN QATAR

In AD628 Prophet Mohammed sent an envoy Abu Al Alaa Al Hadrami to Munzir ibn Sawa Al Tamimi, the Sassanid governor of Qatar and the surrounding area. Similar requests were sent to all rulers of lands abutting the Hijaz where Mecca and Medina, the two core towns under Prophet Mohammed's rule, are located. The letter asked for his allegiance to the Islamic faith, which he and some of his subjects did. After more correspondence, Mohammed advised that those who did not become Muslims should pay *Jizya* a tax levied on non-Muslims. After the death of the Prophet Mohammed in 632, a widespread revolt occurred throughout the Islamic world. Abu Al Alaa Al Hadrami was sent by the new Caliph to defeat the rebels. From this date, Qatar increasingly became an Islamic country, mostly Sunni.

Though Christianity was well established in Qatar during this period, Islam gradually became the dominant religion, and by the 10th century, probably the entire area was Islamic.

From 1787 and the Al Saud incursions, Qatar has increasingly followed the Wahhabi version of Islam that is based on the Hanbali school of Islam, as is dominant in Saudi Arabia. As with Christianity, there are different schools of thought within Islam, these often develop a distinct identity. The Hanbali school follows the law and culture as given in the Quran, the Prophet Mohammed's sayings, customs and records by the companions of the Prophet Mohammed. This approach is much the same way as the Bible, sayings and traditions of Jesus and accounts made by his disciples inform the behaviour of Christians. Unlike some other Islamic schools, the Hanbali school does not accept legal or cultural interpretations from other Islamic schools of thought.

The name Hanbali comes from an Iraqi academic Ahmed bin Hanbal who died in AD 855. This school of thought was followed by Imam Muhammad ibn Abd Al Wahhab Mosque (the State Grand Mosque in Doha has his name), who lived from 1703-1792. He was a student of several Hanbali theologians, who espoused ideas at the extreme of Sunni Islamic thought. Imam Muhammad ibn Abd Al Wahhab Mosque gained the support of local rulers to the north of what is now Riyadh in modern Saudi Arabia, these eventually included the ruler of a town, Diriyah, also near Riyadh, Sheikh Muhammed bin Saud. These two men collaborated to expand their political and religious territory, which by 1818 covered large areas of Arabia including the Qatar peninsula, that state is now called the First Saudi State. After the fall of this state in 1818, a Second Saudi State developed from 1824 which further increased the influence of Wahhabism in Qatar.

The basis of Islam is what has been called the **Five Pillars of Islam** that are incumbent on each Muslim.

- *Shahadah* - testimony of faith each Muslim must state, in the form: 'There is no God but Allah, and Muhammad is His Prophet'.
- *Zakat* – annual charitable giving, based on a proportion of ones wealth
- *Sawm* - fasting during the month of Ramadhan.

- Making the *Haj* pilgrimage to Mecca at least once during one's lifetime, if possible.
- *Salat* prayers five times a day.

Imam Muhammad ibn Abd Al Wahhab Mosque

The mosque is the first and quintessential Islamic building. In Arabic, the name is *masjid* which means 'place of prostration'. The Prophet Muhammad's house, which was a typical 7th-century AD Arabic style house, with an internal courtyard giving access to the rooms around it acted as the first mosque. The ceilings of the rooms were supported by columns, creating what is now called a hypostyle (meaning under columns) mosque and larger mosques in Arabia followed this style.

The critical function of a mosque is a place of prayer to Allah (God), though it is acceptable to worship elsewhere. Prayers are held five times daily based on solar time (the position of the sun in the sky) therefore the time of worship varies throughout the year and will also depend on the location on the globe. The first prayer is about 10 minutes before sunrise; second at solar noon; third late afternoon (initially based on a calculation of the time that a person's shadow became a specific proportion of their height); fourth when the entire solar disk has sunk below the horizon; fifth when, according to some Islamic schools of thought, the sun would be between 12 & 18 degrees below the true horizon, this is around 90minutes after the 4th prayer. Today, technology has, fortunately, immeasurably simplified knowing when prayer is due.

In Islam, it is preferred that for the midday Friday prayers men gather as a community in a *masjid al jumaa* (congregational mosque) with an Imam to lead prayers. Most mosques do not have a particular Imam (prayer leader); however, in urban areas there is a major mosque to serve a district, the *masjid al jumaa*, which does. The word *jumaa*, which in this instance means congregation, comes from the same Arabic 'root' word as for Friday and University. Many of these *masjid al jumaa* are named in memory of an individual, such as Imam Muhammad ibn Abd Al Wahhab Mosque, the State Grand Mosque of Qatar.

On entering almost all mosques, a visitor faces the *mihrab* (prayer niche) which faces towards Mecca, which in Qatar is towards the south-west. This direct relationship between a mosque's main entrance and the *mihrab* is the preferred one. Though a mosque's purpose is to accommodate prayers, it is possible to prayer in any clean, respectable place and for that, a small prayer rug can be used, to ensure a clean surface on which to pray. Some major mosques in Qatar have prayer space for women and a mezzanine floor enabling them to hear the prayer service if they attend, without being themselves overlooked by men.

Ramadhan

Ramadhan is the holy month, when Muslims abstain from eating, drinking and smoking between sunrise and sunset during the entire month. Non-Muslims are affected because it is prohibited to be seen eating, drinking (of any liquid) or smoking in public places during daylight hours in Ramadhan. As a result, most restaurants are closed (though large hotel's main restaurants usually function for non-Muslims), all bars are closed, and hotels are not permitted to serve alcohol publicly. Working hours are shorter, with later starts and earlier finishes. Ramadhan is looked forward to and enjoyed by Qataris, as it is a time for self-restraint, spiritual reflection, and visiting friends and family after evening prayers, when social activity tends to go on late at night. During Ramadhan, government offices are open from 09:00-14:00, Saturday to Thursday; commercial offices that deal directly with the public will have shorter hours than normal but longer than 09:00-14:00. Banks may work from 10:00-14:00 / 21:00-23:00 (check specific timings). Other businesses and smaller shops will also have altered hours with short timings during the day and later closing at night. Major supermarkets may have unaltered timings. As Ramadhan follows the lunar calendar, it moves forwards each year (falls earlier) by about ten days.

18

EDUCATION

Before 1949, Qatar had simple schools that focused on teaching the Quran. A general school for boys was established in Doha in that year following the increasing income from oil exploration. From then other schools were established in 1954, and the first girl's school started in 1956. By 1976 there were 130 schools in Qatar with an equal split between boys and girls schools. In 2019 the number of schools has risen to 290, says QPSA.

Today education for Qatari nationals and foreign employees of the education ministry is free, within the government system. There are three streams of education in Qatar; elementary school for children aged 6 to 12, preparatory school for children aged 12 to 15 and secondary school for children aged 15 to 18. Up to aged 15 education is compulsory. Qatari government schools are single-sex with English taught as a foreign language.

From 1964, there has been a variety of fee-paying International schools in the country, catering primarily for children of non-Qatari nationals, although Qatari's can and do attend. There is a wide variety of national curriculum followed at various grades, including USA (32 schools), UK

(131) and Canadian (3). In private schools, the history of Qatar is taught in addition to their national curriculum along with Arabic and Islam if the student is Muslim. International schools may be coeducational or single-sex. The Qatari government supports Qatari nationals attending these, with up to QAR 28,000 as a grant.

The major Qatari university 'Qatar University', was founded in 1973; there are now seven Qatari university-level educational institutions. Within Qatari government universities there are scholarships available to non-Qatari nationals. Additionally, there are 19 foreign university-level establishments in Qatar, mainly from the USA, with campuses predominantly at Education City; the first international university was Virginia Commonwealth University. Most of the international academic level establishments offer a limited range of courses based on their parent body supplying material and tutors. There is some segregation of the sexes at classroom level at several universities. Overall, according to the QPSA, about 70% of students (in both government and private universities) are female with around 67% of all graduates being female. These percentages, where female numbers in Qatar have been increasing annually, are comparable throughout The Gulf. The figures for the UK (2018) are 57% female students and in the USA (2019) 56%.

The education system is under the authority of several bodies; the Supreme Education Council which oversees the education system at all levels from pre-school through university; the Ministry of Education which is gradually being subsumed by the Supreme Education Council; finally and in effect an autonomous body the Qatar Foundation (for Education, Science and Community Development) which aims to place Qatar at the cutting edge of Education with an especial emphasis on the inclusion of foreign Universities.

PUBLIC HOLIDAYS AND RELIGIOUS PERIODS

New Year's Day 2022/23/24 - January 1 **New Year's Day** (Banks only, not official government holiday)

2022/23/24 - February second Tuesday in February **National Sports Day**.

2022/23/24 - March the first Sunday in March**Bank's holiday**, not an official government or other private company holiday)

2022 April 03/ 2023 March 23/ 2024 March 10 **Ramadhan** (see p91&95) dates are dependent on the lunar new moon sighting and the start is officially announced, possibly the day before. The end of Ramadhan is dependent on the beginning of Eid Al Fitr

2022 May 03/ 2023 April 22/ 2024 April 10 **Eid Al Fitr**, this is an Islamic Holiday and dates are dependent on the lunar new moon sighting and the start is officially announced possibly the day before. The number of day's holiday are around 5 and these may start before that actual date of Eid – and with a weekend this means government and business are closed for a week+.

2022 July 10/ 2023 June 29/ 2024 June 18 **Eid Al Adha**, this is an Islamic Holiday and dates are dependent on the lunar new moon sighting and the start is officially announced possibly the day before. The number of day's holiday are around 5 and these may start before that actual date of Eid – and with a weekend this means government and business are closed for a week.

2022/23/24 December 18 **Qatar National Day** – (Founder's day - public holiday). This is an official holiday on the same date each year. Typically, celebratory events are held on the Corniche - the road is closed.

ARRIVAL INTO QATAR

As regulations can and do change with rapidity, you should check for the current entry requirements from the Qatari government – websites below. Many nationalities (80+ countries) can obtain a free tourist visa-waiver on arrival in Qatar with a current passport that should be valid for a minimum period of 6 months from the date of entry into Qatar. Place-of-stay in Qatar details and presentation of an outbound airline ticket may also be required. The typical visa-waiver period is 30 days, this includes for nationals of the UK & USA. This 30 day waiver, may be extended for a further 30 days at the Ministry of Interior immigration office at Hamad International Airport check-ins counter number 8, on payment of QAR100 payable by credit/debit card. **https://portal.moi.gov.qa/qatarvisas/** has details and this should be checked for up-to-date information.

While the pandemic is active Qatar applies other conditions of entry, these may well continue for some time and might become permanent. During the **pandemic** a negative PCR test before departure that is less than 72 hours old on arrival into Doha is obligatory for everyone travelling to Qatar. Registration on **www.ehteraz.gov.qa** is required. The registration requests details of vaccine used and an upload of the following attachments:

Copy of passport

Copy of certified vaccination certificate

Copy of Negative PCR test result

Copy of hotel quarantine reservation for unvaccinated people or those coming from high-risk countries.

Application needs to be made no more than 72 hours prior to arrival time and at least six hours before arrival, making sure to submit the required documents.

The registration on Ehteraz is without charge.

The **Ehteraz app** is to be active when using public transport and for entry in many places in Qatar. Fines for non-availability on a phone were levied.

Astra Zenica, Moderna & Pfizer, all 2 jab, & Johnson & Johnson, 1 jab, vaccines are acceptable to the Qatari government. Travelers who are fully vaccinated with the above vaccines require an antibody test upon arrival, if the result is positive, they are exempt from the quarantine requirements; if the result is negative, the passenger will undergo a charged quarantine, based on the classification of the departure country. **https://covid19.moph.gov.qa/** should be checked for current information.

For customs, check the airport information **https://dohahamadairport.com/airport-guide/at-the-airport/security-customs**. Prohibited items include, but are not limited to, weapons, firearms and ammunition/ alcoholic beverages/ pork products/ narcotic drugs (drugs include codeine). If you take prescription drugs, consider bringing your doctor's prescription. Check with the Qatar embassy in your country for official details.

For up-to-date information check with your own country's foreign ministry

www.gov.uk/foreign-travel-advice/qatar/entry-requirements

https://travel.state.gov/content/travel/en/traveladvisories/traveladvisories/qatar-travel-advisory.html

and the Qatar government

https://portal.moi.gov.qa/qatarvisas/

https://covid19.moph.gov.qa/

https://dohahamadairport.com/airport-guide/at-the-airport/security-customs

www.ehteraz.gov.qa

Qatar Airways

ARRIVAL BY AIR

Airlines serving Doha include **British Airways** (Heathrow), **Oman Air** (Muscat), **Pegasus Airlines** (Istanbul), **Qatar Airways** (from innumerable airports including Austria - Vienna; Australia - Adelaide; Canberra; Melbourne; Sydney; Perth; Belgium - Brussels; Canada - Montréal–Trudeau; China - Hong Kong; Shanghai–Pudong; Denmark - Copenhagen; Finland - Helsinki; France - Nice; Paris–Charles de Gaulle; Germany - Berlin–Tegel; Frankfurt;

Munich; Greece - Athens; India - Mumbai; Ireland - Dublin; Italy - Milan–Malpensa; Pisa; Venice; Rome–Fiumicino; Japan - Tokyo–Haneda; Tokyo–Narita; Netherlands - Amsterdam; Norway - Oslo–Gardermoen; Poland - Warsaw–Chopin; Portugal - Lisbon; Singapore - Singapore; South Africa - Durban; Cape Town; Spain - Barcelona; Madrid; Sweden - Gothenburg; Stockholm–Arlanda; Switzerland - Geneva; Zürich; UK - Birmingham; Cardiff; Edinburgh; London–Heathrow; London–Gatwick; Manchester; USA - Boston; Chicago–O'Hare; Dallas/Fort Worth; Houston–Intercontinental; Los Angeles; Miami; New York–JFK; Washington–Dulles.

Allow plenty of time for immigration procedures and especially for emigration. You should also ensure that you have ample time when using transfer services.

Many airlines apps not only offer flight information, but also very usefully will update with your checked baggage information including what luggage carousel you should find it on. An app is useful as in the unfortunate event that your luggage is delayed, you should know shortly after landing, if you have internet access. Lost property Hamad International Airport: Phone +974 4010 6666/4462 6531

Airport hialostproperty@hamadairport.com.qa llqas@qataraviation.com

Flight status https://dohahamadairport.com/airlines/flight-status

Check with the Qatar embassy in your country for details

Tobacco allowance: 400 cigarettes.

Personal items and gifts up to a maximum value of QAR 3,000.

Imports of alcohol and narcotics are prohibited; as is anything to do with vaping, its liquid etc.

Inside the luggage area is an information area, **ATM machines** (ideal to use here as this area is less busy than outside in the arrival meeting hall), **currency exchange** operated by www.travelex.qa (rates are not as reasonable as those in the city). After immigration and customs, exit immediately into the arrivals hall, which has toilets, ATM machines, currency exchange, lost property and coffee shops.

Inter-Terminal Transfer

There is an automatic shuttle internal train within Hamad International Airport, connecting the north & south nodes of the airport.

SIM Cards

Consider using a Qatar SIM card. At the airport **Ooredoo,** the Qatari communications company, has kiosks immediately after immigration. Pre-paid SIM cards with an initial value of QAR35 are also available, with top-ups available throughout the country. Qatar also has Vodafone as a mobile network.

WhatsApp may not function, without a VPN.

GETTING FROM HAMED INTERNATIONAL AIRPORT INTO DOHA

METRO

The Doha Metro system's Red Line, also known as the Coast Line, has three termini including Hamad International Airport. The metro connects the airport with Msheireb interchange near Souq Waqif and onward to other stations including West Bay and Legtaifiya near The Pearl (about a 30minute journey). The Metro operates on a travel card system. A standard carriage, single journey is QAR2, a full day travel is capped at QAR6/- & each person above 5 years needs a valid travel card. A standard travel card costs QAR10/- and credit must be added for valid travel; they are also available for the Lusail Tram (but not buses). Other values, and Gold Club carriage services (card costs QAR100 and needs credit added and charges are capped at QAR30 daily), are available, obtainable at Metro stations. Journeys are timed for charging, the maximum time given per journey is 90mins.

The Metro operate 06:00 to 23:00 from Saturday to Wednesday; 06:00 to 23:59 on Thursday and 14:00 to 23:59 on Friday – this may well change.

Look for any signage that says family section, this is not to be used by men travelling without a women and/or children.

MOWASALAT (KARWA) Bus Services

The Mowasalat (Karwa – Mowasalat is the organisation – Karwa is increasingly used for the name of their transport bus/taxi service) Bus Station 25.259, 51.612 at Hamad International Airport is signed west (turn right after you exit immigration) of the arrival area.

Bus 747 timings 04:42-23:42 from Airport to Souq Waqif near Corniche (travelling near Al Ghanim (Karwa) Bus Station: and many hotels)

Bus 727 timings 04:00-23:50 from Airport to Al Khor (north of Doha - skirting far west of city centre on D Ring Road)

Bus 737 timings 24 Hours from Airport to Al Marat St (west outside City Centre Mall)

Bus 757 timings 24 Hours from Airport to Al Mansoura St (in general area of City Centre Mall)

Bus 777 schedule 05:00-24:00 from Airport to West Bay (City Centre Mall) and The Pearl via Corniche

Bus 109 timings 04:04-23:04 from Airport south to Mesaieed (via Al Wakrah south of Doha) and north near Souq Waqif (in city centre) check direction of the bus.

Mowasalat (Karwa) buses have the front section for women only.

These bus routes are less than QAR7 and must be paid with exact change or with a KARWA smart-card (tap on boarding the bus and tap on exit). Buy the KARWA card at ticket vending machines including at Hamad International Airport, Al Ghanim (Karwa) Bus Station, The Pearl Qatar and

Qatar Mall. Cost QAR30 valid long term and can be topped up; QAR20 unlimited journeys in 24hours; QAR10 for two trips in 24hours.

Immediately outside the south exit (straight after immigration) are the hotel buses for complimentary services.

TAXI

From the Airport the Taxi Kiosk is the easiest option to get a taxi. This is signed at the end of the arrivals on the left side (east). The Karwa taxi service (run by Mowasalat) from here is metered with a minimum fare QAR25 and QAR 1.20 per kilometre between 05:00 & 21:00 and QAR1.80 from 21:00-05:00. Cash payment only in Qatari Rials (get cash from the arrivals ATM machines). It's possible to flag a taxi down in a street. Bookings in other locations 800-TAXI (8294) or by App. Some taxis have options for reduced mobility passengers; call +974 4458 8888, providing as much advance notice as possible. Mowasalat also have a franchise versions which have the Karwa turquoise body and different roof colours; Al Million (purple roof), Al Ijarah (blue roof), Profit Trading (yellow roof) and Capital Taxi (black roof).

Uber also operates a taxi service in Doha. From the airport to West Bay, Sheraton/W Hotel area a UberX may cost QAR36 and UberXL QAR46.

Hamad International Airport does have free wifi - HIAQatar Complimentary WiFi network and free internet kiosks and desks around the airport. – and reasonable assistance to get connected.

CAR HIRE

There are about 20 car rental services available at the Airport exit, south of arrivals (immediately ahead - and it's on the other side of the road with pedestrian crossings available), including Europcar www.europcarqatar.com/; Avis www.avisqatar.com/;Hertz www.hertz.com/rentacar/reservation/;And local including Al Mana (a major Qatari group) http://www.almanaleasing.com/;

Mustafawi http://www.mustafawi.qa/; Strong (http://www.strongrentacar.com/) Rates are from QAR100/ per day. If you use an international car-hire company, consider downloading their app, which may make any booking a better experience.

To rent a car for up to seven days if you have a licence from various countries, including the EU / USA, your full driving licence should be acceptable, given the license's validity of vehicle type and period validity. For more than seven days, you will need an 'International Driving Permit 1968' (this is the version accepted by Qatar – you should check on application that you are obtaining one valid for Qatar) or a license issued from a GCC (Gulf Cooperation Council) country. Also required will be your credit card with a minimum of three months validity; your passport will be photocopied, and fines will be payable before departure (or charged to your credit card after departure). You should be 21 years + (some companies require 25+) and have held a full licence for 1 year+. Carry at all times your valid driver's licence, and make certain copies of the vehicles registration documents and insurance documents are in the car. Make certain you know exactly where to return the car as the staff need quick access to the vehicle to receive it. The location is usually the short-stay – check which one - there are west and east – both on three levels and note that Qatar Airways and other airlines are in different locations in the airport.

Ensure you are familiar with the operation and safety features of the vehicle with the hire office staff; this is especially important if you will drive off-road with a 4x4.

5*hotel information desks are available; exit south of arrivals (immediately ahead - and it is on the other side of the road over the pedestrian crossings) and here you can get details of hotel shuttle bus services.

ARRIVAL BY SEA

There are Cruise Lines that call into Doha – principally on a circular cruise, similar to a Mediterranean or Caribbean cruise, with Dubai as the terminus. Currently, AIDA, MSC and TUI (Mein Schiff) call variously into Abu Dhabi/Dubai/Oman/Bahrain/Doha in the winter months. Other cruise lines which visit Doha are on around the world cruises, these include Seabourn. In Doha, shore excursions include a short city tour and sand-dune safari.

ARRIVAL BY LAND

The border crossing into Saudi Arabia is at Abu Samra, in the south-west of Qatar. The name of the Saudi side is Salma, this is the only land border into Qatar. You should ensure that all documentation for all people in the car are up-to-date including any exit / entry health requirements. Vehicle documentation also needs to be current and the insurance policy should include Qatar, in addition to the registration country. There are kiosks for GCC nationals and separately other nationalities. Exit requirements from Saudi Arabia need to be met, including any exit visa, if required. If travelling from outside Saudi Arabia, you also need to consider the need for a Saudi visa and vehicle insurance. SAPTCO, the Saudi bus company in the past operated a Riyadh-Doha service, though currently this does not operate.

EMBASSIES

Some Qatar embassies overseas

Canada Ottawa (embassy)
http://ottawa.embassy.qa/en
Embassy Qatar
150 Metcalfe Street, 8th floor
Ottawa, Ontario
K2P 1P1
+16132414917
+16132413304
Email: ottawa@mofa.gov.qa
http://ottawa.embassy.qa/en

. . .

United States of America Washington, D.C. (embassy)
Embassy of the State of Qatar
2555 M St, NW
Washington, DC, 20037
+12022741600
+12022370682
Email: washington@mofa.gov.qa
http://washington.embassy.qa/en

United Kingdom London (embassy)
Embassy of the State of Qatar
South Audley Street
W1K 1NB
London - UK
020 7493 2200
Email: london@mofa.gov.qa
http://london.embassy.qa/en/services
Cultural Attaché
21 Hertford Street - London
Tel: 0207 495 8677

Australia Canberra (embassy)
Embassy of the State of Qatar
Q10 Akame Circuit
O'Malley ACT 2606
Canberra – Australia
+61261528888
Email: canberra@mofa.gov.qa
http://canberra.embassy.qa/en

France Paris (embassy)
Embassy of the State of Qatar

1, rue de Tilsitt 75008
Paris France
+33145519071
Email: paris@mofa.gov.qa
http://paris.embassy.qa/en

Germany

Berlin (embassy)
Embassy of the State of Qatar
Hagenstr 56
14193- Berlin
Germany
+4930862060
Email: berlin@mofa.gov.qa
http://berlin.embassy.qa/en

Foreign embassies in Qatar

Australia

21st Floor, Tornado Tower
Majlis Al Taawon St
Doha
Qatar
Phone: +974 4007 8500
Fax: +974 4007 8503
Email: embassy.doha@dfat.gov.au
Phone: +974 4007 8500
https://qatar.embassy.gov.au/

Canada

Tornado Tower,

Corner of Majlis Al Taawon Street and Al Funduq Street,
Doha, State of Qatar
Telephone: (974) 4419 9000
Hours of operation
Sunday to Wednesday
8:00 am to 4:30 pm
Thursday
8:00 am to 1:30 pm
Email:: dohag@international.gc.ca
https://www.canadainternational.gc.ca/qatar/

France

Diplomatic St
West Bay, Diplomatic area,
P.O. BOX: 2669 DOHA
Hours 08:00-16:30 (not Friday)
In case of emergency: (+ 974) 66 84 50 83
Email: contact@ambafrance-qa.org
https://qa.ambafrance.org/-English-

Germany

Fereej Kulaib
Hours 08:00-13:00 (not Friday)
6, Al Jazira Al Arabiya Street
P.O. Box 3064
Doha
Qatar
Telephone (+974) 4408 2300
Fax (+974) 4408 2333
Email: info@doha.diplo.de
https://doha.diplo.de/

. . .

United Kingdom

West Bay Dafna Area, Onaiza Zone
66, Al Shabab Street
P.O. Box 3
Doha
Qatar
Telephone (+974) 4496 2000
08.00-15.30 (not Friday)
Email: embassy.doha@fco.gov.uk
Email: consular.dohaa@fco.gov.uk
https://www.gov.uk/world/qatar

United States of America

22nd February Street
Al Luqta District
P.O. Box 2399
Doha, Qatar
Phone: (974) 4496-6000
Fax: (974) 4488-4298
https://twitter.com/usembassyQatar
https://qa.usembassy.gov/

Check your government's travel advice to Qatar. This advice will update periodically and will have an impact on areas such as holidays booked through travel agents and insurance validity.

https://www.gov.uk/foreign-travel-advice/qatar
https://travel.state.gov/content/travel/en/traveladvisories/traveladvisories/qatar-travel-advisory.html

https://smartraveller.gov.au/countries/middle-east/pages/qatar.aspx

. . .

Children

Qataris love children, so you will find yours get a warm welcome. An important issue for everyone especially children will be sunburn, at any time of year, and heat. If you intend hiring a car or will use a chauffeur drive type, enquire in advance about the availability of child car seats for your children and as always with any service request in Qatar follow this up once confirmed before you arrive. Hotels and many restaurants are usually pleased to have children; however high chairs are a rarity, so again if needed factor this into your choice.

Clothing

Loose fitting polycotton mix is a good choice of material as the cotton will absorb sweat, and the man-made fibre helps keep the shape. If you have breathable or fast-dry that's also a good choice as the relatively high humidity will reduce sweat evaporation. In general loose fitting non-transparent clothing is an ideal style. Shorts for men should be avoided, except for sports, and ideally for comfort a looser fit for trousers and shirts (not sleeveless). Women should avoid strappy tops, short sleeves, crop-tops and low-cut tops, skirts or trousers should reach below the knee. Leggings for either sex should not be worn in place of trousers. Avoid bikini or speedo type swim-wear and in public beaches, when not swimming, consider a loose 'cover-all'. The law in Qatar allows the police to take action against people wearing revealing or indecent clothes. If you look at the cover-all garments worn by Qatari men and women – the local definition of revealing or indecent clothes may not be the same as yours. A social media hashtag campaign is #Reflect_Your_Respect (check for the latest version).

For most occasions, when eating out a 'smart casual' is all you will need, it's only in the more formal 5* hotels that you may need to 'button-up' – check with the specific hotel regarding this.

Doha has a largely well-paved street network so shoes that you find comfortable to walk around town should be ok. However, out of Doha, in the desert, you will need shoes that can manage with rough loose surfaces. Here sandals are not ideal as they don't protect toes from stones, thorns and bites.

Other

Qatar will have all the little things you need, such as pharmacies, good doctors, toiletries and personal care, including sanitary towels etc. for women. Prices are broadly comparable to European prices.

Electricity

Qatar runs on 240v, and 50Hz electricity supply with sockets a mix of mainly square 3 Pin with some round 3-Pin; some electrical equipment is sold with a 2-pin plug. The UK is 230v and 50Hz, so Qatar power is usually compatible with UK standards though you may need a socket adaptor. The USA and Canada run on 120v and 60Hz; therefore you will need an adaptor for power and plug sockets. Australia runs on 230v and 50Hz so you may not need a power adaptor but will need an adaptor for plug sockets. Your hotel may have adaptors for your devices; they certainly are widely available in Doha at low cost.

21

HEALTH AND ACCESSIBILITY

The quality of healthcare in Qatar is generally very high. According to QPSA, there are 19 major hospitals, with 3,134 beds. With about 890 persons per bed; this is roughly double the UK's 460 persons per bed and the USA's 410 persons per bed.

There are pharmacies, with English speaking staff, throughout Doha city and beyond, including some which are open 24 hours. Larger pharmacies in Qatar are well stocked and include the UK Boots brand franchise. Many of your requirements or a suitable substitute should be available at these pharmacies if you run out for any reason.

If you travel with medicines, you should bring the original prescription (ideally with signed and stamped letter from the prescription's issuer giving details) and the medicine should remain in original packaging with enclosed use literature, as narcotics or psychotropic substances are on banned import lists and surprising medicines, such as Codeine and Valium, will therefore be included. Do not bring more than a month's supply. Herbal medicines, in general, are included on these lists. For the UK government's take on this, read more https://www.gov.uk/foreign-travel-advice/qatar/health. Should you need additional medicine it's also helpful to show the prescription to a local Qatar healthcare provider, as you may require a prescription for new medicine.

Ensure you have proper insurance to cover you for medical treatment, making certain you are covered for existing conditions, as you will be required to pay for medical treatment in Qatar, and emergency evacuation in case of serious accidents needs to be considered. Typical travel health threats need to be considered, such as deep vein thrombosis (DVT).

The temperature and effect of the sun may well be the primary health issue that most visitors will need to consider. In mid-summer, the sun's angle in London is lower than it is in spring or autumn in Qatar, and therefore protection against sunburn should be taken throughout the year; most especially for children. Drinking rehydrating liquids is essential as outside air-conditioned buildings, the heat causes water loss, and inside the drying effect of that air-conditioning will also affect the body's water content. Consider the impact of heat exhaustion and heat stroke if you hike outside, their symptoms including red, dry or damp skin, headache, and dizziness. Water from the tap in Qatar is likely to be safe, certainly to brush teeth etc. In Doha, the water is desalinated seawater that leaves the Water Desalination Station safe to drink, though with a noticeable taste. However travelling through the water-pipe system and perhaps being stored in a tank, does mean that its safety, as in all other countries, may be compromised.

As this book is not an authority on health safety, you should review your own government's travel advice to Qatar, as they are experts in their specific field.

www.fitfortravel.nhs.uk/destinations/middle-east/qatar

https://wwwnc.cdc.gov/travel/destinations/traveler/none/qatar (note the unique prefix)

It is important to consult with your health care provider about your own personal health requirements and their opinion about your needs when travelling to Qatar as that is the only way to ensure you get the correct advice. They may review hepatitis A; hepatitis B; Rabies; tetanus vaccines as options. Your health care provider may also discuss with you how the heat may affect you and how you can be aware of symptoms, especially in younger and older people such as dry or damp skin, muscle cramps, nausea, headaches and confusion, particularly as some medications may increase the effect. Other areas they may discuss, most especially in younger and older people who are more vulnerable to viral and other health issues, might include preventing contracting Leishmaniosis, which is spread by sand flies, which can cause itchy bumps or rash and lesions and glands swelling. Other insect-spread issues they may discuss are malaria and dengue fever and West Nile virus, which are spread by mosquitos. Ask your healthcare provider about their recommendation to repel insects, including the effectiveness and suitability for you of Deet and Permethrin if you will travel outside towns in Qatar. Some health providers may mention, MERS-CoV virus (a Camel spread infection, including through drinking un-pasteurised Camel milk) that is related to SARS pneumonia and Crimean-Congo haemorrhagic fever (a tick-spread disease), though the incidence of these is very low.

Check also with your government's website (as above) and with www.masta-travel-health.com or www.passporthealthusa.com for vaccinations.

Special Needs Travellers

Though a modern country, Qatar does not have the range of facilities required by many travellers with special needs. Speak with your health-care provider and specialised organisation for their knowledgeable advice in your particular instance. There are some low floor buses in Doha with designated seating for people with special needs, however, most buses do not have these. Major shopping malls and 5* hotels will have the best facilities; many have lifts and broad corridors and, critically, special needs toilets. Souq Waqif has reasonable accessibility, and special needs toilets, however the uneven 'ancient' streets might cause problems. The Museum of Islamic Art has good access and wide corridors in galleries and special needs toilets. The National Museum is very much worthwhile visiting and again has good access and wide corridors in galleries and special needs toilets. Mathaf Museum has reasonable access, some steps on the outside, along with special needs toilets. Most other museums have limited facilities. The Corniche has a reasonable surface along with very wide pedestrian access. Camel race tracks and other sports facilities have limited access.

22

SAFETY

Qatar, for most visitors and residents, is a safe country, with few physical assaults or robberies. In general, safety standards are comparable to most western countries.

Although crime rates are low, crimes do happen in Qatar, though rarely reported. Take normal precautions regarding your valuables to ensure your visit remains a positive one.

However 'health and safety' passive safety features are less common, and therefore you should be more alert regarding your immediate environment and the impact it may have on your safety.

Having appropriate insurance when you visit Qatar is important and do remember to note all possible health issues you have or have had. Insurance is especially important as third-party liability within Qatar is adjudicated under a very different legal system to many western countries. Any claims awarded in Qatar that are successful may attract a very much smaller monetary compensation than in most western countries. Claims against you will also be handled differently while you are in Qatar. Your insurance policy should include air-ambulance repatriation.

As this book is not an authority on foreign safety, you should review your own government's travel advice to Qatar.

https://www.gov.uk/foreign-travel-advice/qatar

https://travel.state.gov/content/travel/en/traveladvisories/traveladvisories/qatar-travel-advisory.html

The use and handling of your Credit card should be examined to ensure its security, as you would do within your own country, most particularly in public places and if handled by third-parties. Do advise your bank that you will be travelling in Qatar to make certain that it can be used. Personal belongings, most especially those of value such as passports, should be held in a safe and secure place including when travelling to your destination. Copies of essential items should be made and then stored in a location separate from the original.

Severe penalties are carried out for possession & use of prohibited **drugs**, as does trafficking in them which if a person is convicted can carry the death penalty. Drinking alcohol in public and in non-designated locations (designated locations include restaurants serving alcohol) is also prohibited. Alcohol may not be carried into Qatar, there is however a Duty-Free at the airport, enabling you to buy alcohol on departure. Being intoxicated in a public place or when driving etc, is within a zero-tolerance area of Qatar's law enforcement – attracting, perhaps, a jail term of 3-years and large fines.

Language that might be considered abusive, or gestures that can be construed as offensive can attract police action, even if made within the 'privacy' of your car towards another road user. Penalties include prison and fines.

Avoid public display of affection with any other person, even holding hands with your spouse or older children, and do not kiss, hug or engage in any other display of affection with them in public.

LGBT+

Homosexuality is absolutely prohibited in Qatar, penalties can include several years imprisonment, physical lashing and potentially death. Do review your own government's advice.

Media

Pornography is prohibited, and the internet is very effectively monitored and censored for what is considered offensive or subversive.

Road Safety

The most common safety impact on individuals is by road traffic, including dangerous driving, sometimes with little consideration to pedestrians or other road users, both within urban areas and out-of-town. If you drive, adopt a mode of 'defensive driving', most especially staying alert to the actions or potential actions of other road users. Ensure you wear seat belts, and that suitable additions are available for children. Outside Doha, straying animals may be encountered on roads, and these add to dangers when driving. Off-road driving increases the risk in all respects, especially at speed.

If walking on a roadside pavement, remain alert to the general traffic and try to walk facing the traffic so that awareness of oncoming vehicles is possible. Drivers can be inconsiderate, as well as considerate, but it's the inconsiderate drivers you should remain alert for.

Photography & Video

Do be cautious of where you take photographs. Any government building, palace or military and security (police etc) location is a security area and not to be photographed. Most mosques, in general, should not be photographed. The focus by western media on working conditions in Qatar does mean that construction sites (stadiums while under construction etc) should not be photographed. Avoid photography of people without their permission, especially women.

In some areas away from Doha, on the edge of small

settlements, there may be feral dogs which can be intimidating.

Do read your own country's foreign ministry's advice regarding Qatari culture https://www.gov.uk/foreign-travel-advice/qatar/local-laws-and-customs https://travel.state.gov/content/travel/en/international-travel/International-Travel-Country-Information-Pages/Qatar.html

23

INTERNAL TRANSPORT

Except in limited areas like Souq Waqif, the Corniche and The Pearl, Doha is not a city to walk in, main roads have few crossing options and even in winter the temperature, for many visitors, precludes walking any distance. In Doha public transport provides reasonable access to many areas of interest. The Metro is supported by a MetroLink bus service, where an individual bus route feeds into a Metro station. The bus network spreads throughout the city, though it concentrates on main routes and especially towards Doha's south-west where a light industrial area is located and there is accommodation for construction workers. App based taxi services offer an option to augment public transport, for example from a Metro station to a final destination. They can be flagged down on the road. All transport is air-conditioned.

Driving

Qatar drives on the right-hand side of the road (driver sits on the left in the vehicle as in Europe and much of the world). There is a mix of traffic light controlled road junctions, roundabouts (*rotary*) and flyovers. Signage's text is in Arabic and English with speed and distance signs in kilometres with numbers only in the Hindu/Arabic number system (as used in the west). Vehicles are typically automatic, with large engines and air-conditioning. In essence driving regulations are comparable to most western countries, including not leaving the scene of an accident (see below), fines for illegal parking, penalties for not wearing seat belts, using phones etc. The maximum speed is 120kmph, with lower speeds in places down to 60kmph. There are some 100 petrol stations in Qatar, offering a variety of services, including shops and car wash. Petrol (gasoline/fuel) prices are set by the Qatar Petroleum (based on oil prices) and recently have varied between QAR 1.200 – 2.050 per litre. Service is by an attendant, and they are low paid, so a small tip/rounding up helps, especially if for example your windscreen was cleaned while the vehicle is refuelled.

A road network of five, four and three-lane motorways serve Doha, which, despite the 120kmph speed limit, encourage speeding by being broad and relatively traffic free out of town. Fixed location and mobile speed radar with still and video cameras include sophisticated recognition systems including number plate; these allow the imposition of fines. Vehicle number plates have the name Qatar in English and Arabic and only Hindu/Arabic numerals (the numbers used in the west). There is no regulation requiring any warning of a specific speed-trap camera. Speed bumps and 'speed tables', with limited notice and visibility also attempt to slow traffic, if you hit one at speed damage may occur to your vehicle's chassis. Trucks are prohibited from using roads in Doha from 06:00 -08:00 / midday - 15:00; 17:00 p.m. - 22:00 due to the volume of traffic, you will find roads especially heavily congested during these hours.

The original core of Doha, that is focused on Souq Waqif, is now surrounded by a series of ring-roads. The inner one is now named Al Diwan St, then moving outward is B Ring

Road, C, D, E (D & E combine to the west and become the Doha Expressway) F and G (which leads to the Salwa/Lusail Route. A less easily oriented series of roads form a network north and west of West Bay, with the north-south Lusail Expressway and west-east Onaiza St (which becomes Al Khafji St) being the key routes.

For many short-term visitors, there will be a crucial couple of roads. Firstly the Corniche which follows Doha Bay and gives immediate access to The National Museum, Museum of Islam Arts, Souq Waqif and West Bay. The Corniche is a very scenic drive or walk but at 7km is a walk for the cooler period of a day. It is also a direct route for public transport (bus route 76 & 777) connecting many of Qatar's principal tourist attractions.

The second key route is a driving route leading from the port. This route is formed by the B Ring Rd, Al Khaleej St, Al Istiqlal St and Lusail Expressway that acts as an inner ring road skirting south of Souq Waqif and leading to Katara and The Pearl.

CAR HIRE

Qatar has numerous car hire companies including

Europcar www.europcarqatar.com/; Avis www.avisqatar.com/;Hertz www.hertz.com/rentacar/reservation/;And local including Al Mana (a two-hour group) http://www.almanaleasing.com/; Mustafawi http://www.mustafawi.qa/; Strong (http://www.strongrentacar.com/) Rates are from QAR100/ per day.

If you use an international car-hire company, consider downloading their app that may make any booking a better experience.

To rent a car for up to seven days from several countries, including the EU / USA, your full driving licence should be acceptable, with suitable validity of vehicle type and period validity. For more than seven days, you will need an 'International Driving Permit 1968' or a license issued from a

GCC (Gulf Cooperation Council) country. Also required will be your credit card with a minimum of 3 months; your Passport will be photocopied, and fines will be payable before departure, or will be automatically debited from your credit-card.

Accident Reporting

To register a minor road accident, you can use Metrash2 app https://www.moi.gov.qa/site/english/metrash2/. You may obtain and activate Metrash2 Service through SMS or Self Service Kiosk or helpdesk@moi.gov.qa : there must be a mobile number a registered in the applicant's name

Speak with the car hire company while receiving the vehicle regarding this app and accident regulations as requirements can change.

In the event of an accident speak with the car hire company immediately to seek their updated advice as they may handle the below for you.

Irrespective of the circumstances or blame remain calm and polite to other people involved.

In the event of injury

1/Phone 999 – Ambulance

2/Advise your location

3/Answer any questions from the emergency service

4/Follow their advice

For accidents, you can

1/ Supply no more than four pictures of each vehicle. One photograph should show the vehicles number plates clearly.

2/ Move your vehicles from the scene and park away from the road.

3/ Ensure the location services of your phone are enabled.

4/ Sign in to Metrash2, select 'Traffic Services', open the 'Accident Report' option.

5/ Enter details of both vehicles and note the Vehicle

number plate, driver's identification card number & driving licence, (all residents of Qatar have an identification card), and mobile phone number – dial it to ensure it is correct.

6/ Attach photos of both vehicles and click on the agreement on the validity of the data.

7/ Submit the report for the traffic investigation police.

8/ A notification SMS (text message) will be sent to you asking to wait for another message to complete the procedures.

9/ After reviewing the accident photos by traffic investigators, an SMS will be sent to both parties with instructions to go to your insurance company for vehicle repair approval. The vehicle repair police report can be printed from the Ministry of Interior's official website, or through the insurance company concerned.

As always these regulations can change – its ideal to contact the car rental company and request that they deal with everything; as is clear it's a bureaucratic process.

Karwa Taxi at Soul Waqif

TAXI

There are a variety of taxi services available, including Karwa taxi service (run by Mowasalat / Karwa) which is metered with a minimum fare QAR10 and QAR 1.20 per kilometre between 05:00 & 21:00 and QAR1.80 from 21:00-05:00. Cash payment only in Qatari Rials. It's possible to flag a taxi down in a street. Bookings 800-TAXI (8294) or by App. Some taxis have options for reduced mobility passengers; call +974 4458 8888, providing as much advance notice as possible; or download the Karwa app. Uber also operates a taxi service in Doha. From the airport to West Bay, Sheraton/W Hotel area a UberX may cost QAR36 and UberXL QAR46. Cashless payment is used.

METRO

The Metro operates on a travel card system; for standard carriage, single journey is QAR2 a full day travel pass is capped at QAR6/- & each person above 5 years needs a valid travel pass. A standard travel pass costs QAR10/- and credit must be added for valid travel; they are also available for the Lusail Tram (but not buses). Other values, and Gold Club carriage services (card costs QAR100 and needs credit added and charges are capped at QAR30 daily), are available, obtainable at Metro stations. Journeys are timed for charging, the maxim time given per journey is 90mins.

Doha Metro - Red Line standard carriage

The Metro operates 06:00 to 23:00 from Saturday to Wednesday; 06:00 to 23:59 on Thursday and 14:00 to 23:59 on Friday

The Doha metro system has three lines (Red, Gold, and Green) and 37 stations open by 2022 (more stations and an additional line may open after this). They are partially underground and partially overground. The **Red Line**, also known as the Coast Line, has three termini including **Hamad International Airport**. Two interchanges, Al Bidda GPS 25.290, 51.520 and Msheireb GPS 25.282, 51.526 are within walking distance (max 1.2 km) to Souq Waqif. The line travels through West Bay and onto Lusail. The east-west **Gold Line** (Historic Line) stretches from Ras Bu Aboud to Al Aziziya. It includes the interchange at Msheireb and the stations at Souq Waqif GPS 25.287, 51.534 also for the Museum of Islamic Art) and National Museum GPS 25.255, 51.610. The **Green Line** from Al Mansoura, in southern Doha, also passes through the two interchanges, Al Bidda and Msheireb and on west to Al Riffa.

TRAM

Within the Msheireb area is a tram system, with 9 stops (Sahat Al Nakheel: Wadi Msheireb – for the Metro: Galleria – for the Souq Waqif underpass: Msheireb Prayer Ground : Heritage Quarter – for the museums: Al Baraha : Sahat Al-Masjid : Al Kahraba Street : Al Mariah Street Station) in a loop. It operates between 09:00-midday & 16:00-21:00 (Fridays 16:00-21:00).

A tram service is planned to operate from 2022 focused on Lusail town, with interchange options onto the metro Red Line at Lusail and Legtaifiya

BUS

Mowasalat (Karwa) Buses (a distinctive turquoise colour) in Qatar have a Karwa payment card system, with a tap on entry and exit. The cards are available in two 24hour options (QAR10 for 2 journeys within 24 hours of purchase and QAR20 for unlimited travel within 24 hours of purchase). A long term rechargeable card is QAR30. Ticket Vending Machines are available at Hamad International Airport - they are also available from Doha Bus Station, Karwa Bus Stations, through Ticket Vending Machines, select merchants, and Ooredoo (mobile phone network provider). Larger supermarkets such as Lulu and Carrefour also sell them

The Mowasalat MetroLink bus service is intended to provide a last kilometre service to a Metro station and operates from 06:00 through to 21:00 Sunday to Wednesday and finishing later on Thursday & Saturday and starting later and finishing later on Friday. The services which operate several times an hour are circular routes in a local close to the below stations.

Use the Karwa app for more information. Bus routes and the Metro they service are below.

M105 - DECC Station: M110 - Legtaifiya Station: M114

- Al Doha Al Jadeda Station: M115 - Al Doha Al Jadeda Station: M118 - Umm Ghuwailina Station: M121 - Al Matar Al Qadeem Station: M122 - Al Matar Al Qadeem Station: M123 - Oqba Ibn Nafie Station: M124 - Oqba Ibn Nafie Station: M125 - Oqba Ibn Nafie Station: M128 - Al Wakra Station: M132 - Al Wakra Station: M134 - Al Wakra Station: M139 - Umm Ghuwailina Station: M140 - Free Zone Station: M143 - Corniche Station: M145 - Lusail Station: M202 - Education City Station: M203 - Education City Station: M208 - Al Messila Station: M209 - Al Messila Station: M313 - Al Aziziyah Station: M316 - Ras Bu Abboud Station.

From the airport bus station GPS 25.259 , 51.612 Bus Route 109 serves Mesaieed to the south and Al Ghanim (Karwa) Bus Station GPS 25.285 , 51.536 in central Doha. Route 777 travels along the Corniche to West Bay and 747 travels along Al Matar St into Al Ghanim (Karwa) Bus Station:.

A practical paid, shuttle coach services the general West Bay area and runs every 15mins between 06:00-21:00. One 'circular' route travels from the General Post Office GPS 25.309 , 51.517 via City Centre shopping Mall GPS 25.325 , 51.530 and Doha Exhibition Centre GPS 25.322 , 51.527 , to the ‘W Hotel’ GPS 25.328 , 51.529 zig-zagging with several stops along the route. Friday is for families only.

There are free shuttle bus services within the industrial area (west of Doha city centre) 88 will go between streets 1 (Salwa Road and Industrial Area) and street 52 (Abu Hamour Road and Industrial Area) and buses 16, 18, 61, and 81 will crisscross the area. These are principally targeted at workers in the industrial sector.

From Doha Al Ghanim (Karwa) Bus Station there are some longer distance national bus journeys, principally catering for immigrant labour and schoolchildren.

Route 100 operates three times a day 09:30/15:30/21:30 -

return 12:35/18:35/05:05 for the three hours innumerable stop journey. Route 101 is more frequent and is an hourly service from 04:10-19:10 and similar return timings, from Doha Al Ghanim (Karwa) Bus Station : to the north Madinat Al Shamal.

Routes 102/102X every half hour between 04:00-22:30 from Doha Al Ghanim (Karwa) Bus Station : to Al Khor taking an hour and 10 minutes and from Al Khor route 201 for Madinat Al Shamal with a service every 90mins from 04:00-22:00 - and returns similar times.

Routes 104 & 104A travel from Doha Al Ghanim (Karwa) Bus Station west to Dukhan, every hour from 04:30-20:30 along with route 137 Three times a day at 13:30/17:30/21:30 and other direction from 08:36

There are a useful couple of services to Doha's south. One service, 109, serves Mesaieed (via the Airport) south of Doha every half hour from Doha Al Ghanim (Karwa) Bus Station : starting from 04:09-23:09 with a half hour journey. One, route 136 travels south-west to Bu Samra (04:03-08:03-12:03-16:03-20:03 and similar returns for a two-hour trip).

These bus routes are less than QAR9, with a KARWA smart-card (tap on boarding the bus and tap on exit). Buy the KARWA card at ticket vending machines at Hamad International Airport, Al Ghanim (Karwa) Bus Station, The Pearl Qatar and Qatar Mall and elsewhere.

A private tourist service, The 'Doha Bus', offers a Hop on – Hop off type service (see tour operators below).

Less common as daily transport for western expats in Doha is using a bicycle. Carbon Wheels at The Pearl GPS 25.376 , 51.545 midday-21:00 (not Friday) offers products and repair service. Cycle riding can be made at Lusail Circuit GPS 25.487 , 51.449. There are residents of Doha who cycle on the expressway road routes; however, for a visitor it would be prudent to ride with more locally experienced riders. There are some leisure cycling options in Aspire Park or Al Bidda Park.

The previous annual cycle Race, Tour of Qatar, operated by Tour de France from 2002 has not happened after 2016. It was held in early February over 5 days.

24

MEDIA

Qatar, as an Arab country, is open to Arab language media from around the world, in much the same way as English language media from the USA is available in London and British media is available in New York. Some of this media is based within an Arab country, while others, that have a 'pan-Arab' approach, especially if they have a critical approach to Arab governments, may be based in a non-Arab location, for example in London.

In Qatar, the relatively small population of Arab speakers required that local media received a subsidy (whether direct or by advertising & other support) through the government. This subsidy resulted in censorship, whether from the government or self-censorship. This also was the situation with English language newspapers. This support and overt government censorship was largely removed in 1995. Currently there are two Arabic papers Al Sharq, Al Watan.

English language papers include the Gulf Times www.gulf-times.com, The Peninsula www.thepeninsulaqatar.com and Qatar Tribune www.qatar-tribune.com.

Al Jazeera News Studio

There are several Television stations including Taalam and Baraaem, both aimed at children, Al Jazeera news and current affairs www.aljazeera.com/live/ also in Arabic and Arabic only Qatar Television (a government operation). Al Jazeera's news programs are claimed to be free of government political censorship, certainly it has replaced other channels in Qatar and other Arab countries as peoples preferred choice to source news.

There are a few magazines, including Expat Woman Qatar www.qatarexpatwomen.com, Time Out www.timeoutdoha.com.

Radio stations include Al Jazeera (Arabic and English) www.aljazeera.com/live/, Sout Al Khaleej (Arab and English www.soutalkhaleej.fm.

25

UNESCO LISTINGS

Qatar has a single UNESCO World Heritage Site, **Al Zubarah**, (p227) a coastal town that was listed in 2013 as 'outstanding testimony to an urban trading and Pearl-diving tradition which sustained the region's major coastal towns'.

On the north-west coast of Qatar, Al Zubarah was a Pearling and trading centre that flourished from around AD1760-1811.

The town is on a ridge of slightly higher ground, with the sea to its west and sabkha to the east. The landscape was established during the mid-Holocene period when the seawater levels in The Gulf were up to three metres above its current level. During this period, the sea was over a kilometre inland at Al Zubarah, after which it has retreated, stabilising around its current position about 1,500 years ago with sabkha replacing the sea.

The entire plain on which Al Zubarah is located is currently without tree cover, testimony to the heat, wind, lack of rain and the high salinity of the soil, coupled with the impact of roaming livestock. Windblown sand and debris cover much of the entire town area, which is occasionally excavated and therefore finds are continually being made.

The town's establishment was probably a result of tribal migration from the area of southern Iraq through to Kuwait. Iraq during this time was ruled by Mamluks from Georgia, under the Ottoman sultans. They imposed a centralised rule in the region and supressed tribal resistance in the Basra region, emigration from Iraq took place during this period. An initial settlement of Al Zubarah was probably established from 1732 by people from the Al bin Ali family and the Al Khalifa family (currently rulers of Bahrain). These peoples are part of the large Utub tribal confederation, which includes the current rulers of Bahrain and the ruling family of Kuwait.

In the early 1770s Basra was hit by the plague, which must have impacted its trade and allowed other centres to develop. Further migration into Al Zubarah from the Basra area occurred during the Ottoman–Persian War of 1775–1776. During the period that Al Zubarah was inhabited, there were several smaller settlements in north-west Qatar. Most seem to have been impacted by the rise and decline of Al Zubarah, either negatively or positively. Al Zubarah follows the legacy of similar towns that developed around The Gulf, many of which traded with Mesopotamia in ancient times and then the Abbasid and subsequent rulers based in Baghdad. These small towns often served a small hinterland as well as trans-ocean trade.

Following an unsuccessful attack on Al Zubarah by the Persian governor of Bahrain island in 1783, Al Zubarah's ruler, Sheikh Ahmed bin Muhammad bin Khalifa, invaded Bahrain from Al Zubarah and captured the island, which his descendants have ruled since. Al Zubarah was attacked from Al-Diriyah, near modern Riyadh, by Al Saud forces from 1787 and subsequently paid tribute to them; however the effect of the Al Saud occupation of the Al Ahsa oasis, 140km south-west of Al Zubarah, in eastern Arabia increased the appeal of Al Zubarah, and many people fled into the town. In 1809 Al Zubarah was occupied by the Al Saud forces, however during

Egyptian (Ottoman) attacks from 1811 against the Al Saud in their capital at Al-Diriyah, the Al Saud forces in Al Zubarah were reduced to support Al-Diriyah. Taking advantage of the general military situation, the Sultan of Oman attacked Al Zubarah in 1811 with the result it was largely destroyed. This destruction and the Al Saud confrontation at Al-Diriyah created an opportunity for the Al Khalifa of Bahrain to reoccupy the town, though the occupants then lived in a much smaller area.

From 1868 the Al Khalifa were gradually excluded from the Qatar peninsula during a period of confrontations. Disputes between the Al Khalifa and the Al Thani family from Doha was complicated by the assertion of British power in the Gulf and decline of the Ottoman influence in the region, despite the Ottomans having several occupied forts and a governor located at Al Zubarah. Nonetheless, in 1878 Sheikh Jassim bin Mohammed Al Thani captured the town, though subsequently, his hold was tenuous and there was an ongoing dispute with Bahrain over the rule of the town.

Al Zubarah Fort

Despite the town's decline, its proximity to Bahrain resulted in the building in 1938 of Al Zubarah Fort, following which Britain decided in 1939 that Al Zubarah was indeed part of sovereign Qatari territory. By 2001, the ongoing territorial dispute was settled by the International Court of Justice in The Hague who adjudicated that Al Zubarah was Qatari territory, while at the same time Hawar Islands (off the west coast) were Bahraini territory.

The short period of Al Zubarah's occupation means that an authentic insight into the organisation of 18th & 19th century towns in the region can be gained. Windblown sand covered Al Zubarah, which concealed cemeteries, courtyard houses, walls, fishermen's huts, mosques, palaces, and narrow streets. Outside the town's walls are a canal and two screening walls, Al Zubarah Fort and separated from Al Zubarah Fort by a road, is the site of another fort, Qalat Murair.

The town walls of Al Zubarah are the original outer wall and a smaller inner wall built after the town's 1811 destruction. The outer wall is around 2500metres long, with 22 bastions at regular intervals. To the north, the wall extended into the sea and formed part of a harbour. This wall, along with the town's overall grid-like layout, suggests a planned town layout. The smaller inner wall is built over previous structures and also made use of older building's material.

The outer town wall enclosed up to 600 separate buildings, suggesting over 6,000 people. Neighbourhoods in demarcated areas have been identified; again, most appear to have been planned. Most parts within the town have the courtyard style housing which was common throughout The Gulf until an oil economy grew; some houses seem to have had the iconic wind towers that are found throughout the region. Many of the buildings have gypsum decoration suggesting a degree of wealth enabling these decorative touches.

In the southern area of the town is a large fortified square palatial compound of just over one hectare with nine interior courtyards and a tower on each corner. Functions identified for some of the rooms include bathing areas and date processing rooms *madbasa* with the long troughs to collect date syrup that is pressed out from dates stored in sacks stacked on top of the channels.

A smaller compound to the north-east of the fortified square palatial compound has been partially excavated. This compound is just over half the size of the larger compound with towers on each corner. Both these compounds may have had an upper floor. One of two mosques so far identified is close to these two residential buildings. Early 20th century photos show it had substantial columns and arches supporting what is believed to be a multi-dome roof, all covered in plaster. Public squares are also found in this area of the town.

In the central area of the town, 80 metres east from the beach was a souq that not only engaged in import & export but also appears to have been involved in a range of activities including glass manufacture and the processing of dates for syrup. Close to it, on the beach, a small fort marked an area of deeper water to its south.

Huts that are believed to be associated with fishing and Pearl diving have also been identified from post-holes by the beach. Though here these are contemporary with Al Zubarah, this type of hut structure and its function remains prevalent throughout the region.

A couple of wall barriers, perpendicular to the original wall extend for a kilometre towards the more recent Al Zubarah Fort. These are thought to have directed traffic towards the town and also to act a defensive shield for the water carriers moving between the town and Qalat Murair to the town's east. Also here is a water canal, that leads towards Qalat Murair, stopping about 500metres to its south-west. Though originally functional as a small boat canal it appears to have been abandoned and partially infilled, probably due to its functional or economic failure during Al Zubarah's existence. In places, the barrier walls run over the canal.

Al Zubarah Fort was built by the ruler of Qatar, Sheikh Abdullah bin Jassim Al Thani in 1938 as a police outpost. It was used as a military fort until the early 1970s. There is a photographic exhibition within the fort, about the old town. The construction followed a period of confrontation with Bahrain over the area and the Hawar Islands when a Bahraini police fort was built on those islands in 1937. The single-story Al Zubarah Fort is of a type common throughout the Arabian Peninsula, with a large open courtyard within which is a water well and rooms opening off the courtyard.

Qalat Murair (Murair Fort – Qalat is the Arabic for fort) (GPS 25.974, 51.043) was built in 1768 by Sheikh Mohammed bin Khalifa along with water wells and a surrounding area of housing. Agriculture and livestock pens were to the fort's south and south-west. Its purpose appears to have been as a defence for the water canal that served Al Zubarah. Today most of the remains are below the surface, and since it was occupied until the early 20th century, the stones may have been re-used for building the adjacent Al Zubarah Fort.

About 1,600metres north-east of Qalat Murair is a small fort Qalat Shuwail (GPS 25.979, 51.056) that was noted in 1850 by Francis Warden, Chief Secretary to the Government of India at Bombay. It is thought this fort is also contemporary with Al Zubarah town.

Both Al Zubarah and Qalat Murair are on ground that is above the current *sabkha* and previous sea levels, shown by wave-cut platforms (levelled areas of rock or coral) offshore. The area around Qalat Murair was the location of the fresh water supply for Al Zubarah; this water supply 'floats' over sea water that intrudes inland.

There are areas of scattered mangrove *Avicennia marina* along the shoreline and on the mud flats and the general inland areas salt tolerant plants close to Al Zubarah. In the sea occasional sightings of Dugong and common Bottlenose Dolphin *Tursiops truncates* are made. Socotra Cormorant *Phalacrocorax nigrogularis* are seen on Um Jatila Island, just off Al Zubarah, and Greater Flamingo *Phoenicopterus roseus* can be seen in winter, most easily close to the shore during high tide. Both Green Turtle *Chelonia mydas* and Hawksbill turtle *Eretmochelys imbricata* have been seen in the water.

Some agriculture associated with Al Zubarah was developed 5km south-east of the town and at Al Jumail 18km north on the coast.

Under the Law of Antiquities of Qatar, it is a criminal offence to excavate or remove any antiquities without permission from Qatar Museums or deface or otherwise damage any parts of a historical site.

Qatar also has three UNESCO inscriptions on the **Representative List of the Intangible Cultural Heritage of Humanity.**

Falcon

Falconry (p169/188/239) as a sport is included in a UNESCO inscription. Falconry in Arabia is an ancient hunting practice mention by the Prophet Mohammed. The building between AD680-83, of falconry hunting lodges by Umayyad caliphs in the deserts of Syria and Jordan, is a testimony to the sport's prestige. Treaties on falconry were written, with Peregrine *Falco peregrinus* and Saker Falcons *Falco cherrug* appearing to be the favoured birds and these continue to be the most favoured today. The history of falconry in The Gulf is little known as it was not, until recently, a written practice. Classically three species were a quarry for falcon hunting: the Houbara Bustard *Chlamydotis macqueenii*, the Stone Curlew *Burhinus oedicnemus*, and the Arabian Hare *Lepus capensis*. The introduction of guns from the 16th c reduced the pressure to hunt with falcons and also reduced the wildlife generally. Today falconry is no longer what it must have been for originally, which was to obtain food, and is a sport. Wild falcons are trapped during migration between September-November and then trained over the following weeks. In Qatar, captive falcons can be seen in Souq Waqif or near the Sealine Hotel south of Doha. There are various pieces of equipment associated with Falconry in The Gulf, the *burqa* (head hood) used to keep the bird calm; a *wakar* which is the stand on which the bird sits, *subuq* the tethers attached to the ankles, and of course a glove for the man called a *dass*, *kaff* or the more modern *mangaleh*. World Falconry Day is celebrated annually on 16 November, and Qatar holds a falconry festival, the Marmi Festival, annually in January which exhibits Falcons, Saluki hunting dogs and hunting demonstrations.

Arabic Coffee as a demonstration of generosity and hospitality is included in this Intangible Cultural Heritage of Humanity list. The Coffee uses green Coffee beans, historically from Yemen. The process of preparing the Coffee was traditionally done in front of guests. The beans are roasted lightly over a fire, pounded with a metal pestle and put in large copper Coffee pot *dallah al logmah* with water and boiled. To add to the flavour, cardamom, cloves or other spices are added. After the Coffee has brewed, it is poured into a small Coffee pot *dallah al manzal*, from which it is poured into small cups *finjan*, that look like large thimbles. Usually, the most honoured guest is served first. Arabic Coffee is often accompanied by dates, which are eaten first. When you have had enough Coffee, after two or three cups is polite, return the cup to the person who serves you with a slight shake of the cup in your right hand to signify, enough.

The third of these UNESCO inclusions is the system of holding a ***Majlis***, a meeting of people while sitting. A *majlis* is a formal space, either as a specific room in a building or, in *bedouin* society, it may have been outside. It forms a number of functions including a reception for outside guests, a celebration meeting or as a discussion area. Today a *majlis* is either a physical space, within a home or public building or is used a term to indicate a personal meeting between a number of people. In traditional society, a *majlis* is a single-sex meeting.

Arabic Coffee serving and the *majlis* can be very formal occasions with guests assigned an often unobtrusive but noted hierarchy.

FIFA WORLD CUP 2022

The event will be held in Qatar from 21 November – 18 December 2022. 32 Teams will play – initially in eight groups of four. There are eight stadiums spread along the eastern side of Qatar - Lusail Iconic Stadium, Al Bayt Stadium, Al Janoub Stadium Al Wakrah, Al Rayyan Stadium (Ahmed bin Ali Stadium) , Al Thumama Stadium, Education City Stadium (Qatar Foundation Stadium), Khalifa International Stadium , Ras Abu Aboud Stadium (see below for locations details).

The first match will take place in Al Bayt Stadium at Al Khor – with Qatar's team playing as part of Group A. Games will be played at 15:00 & 19:00 local time (GMT +4). The semi finals will be held in Lusail on 13 December @ 19:00 & Al Bayt on 14th December @ 19:00 & the play off for 3rd place will be held in Khalifa Stadium on 17 December @ 15:00. Doubtless the country will want Qatar to play in the final at Lusail on 18 December @15:00 – as it's Qatar's National Day (perhaps this explains the choice of date).

Information regarding tickets –

www.fifa.com/tournaments/mens/worldcup/qatar2022/tickets

.

27

MAPS

QATAR LOCATIONS

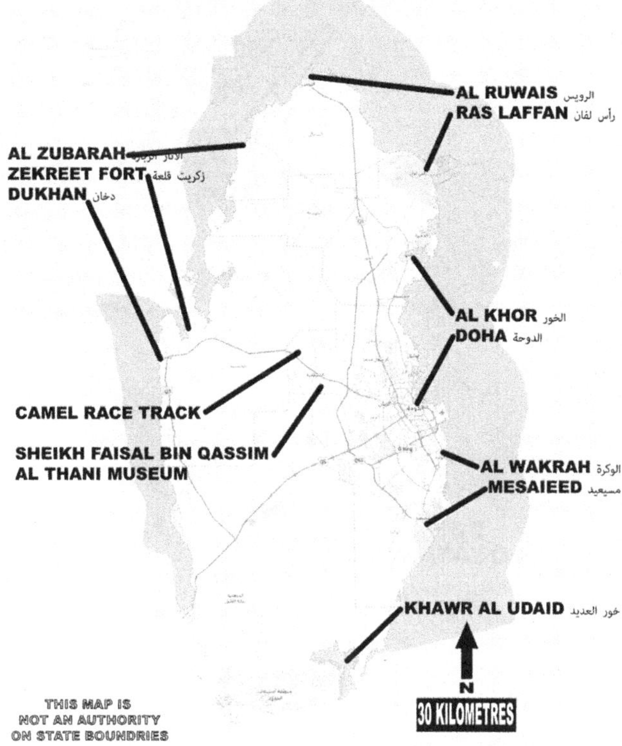

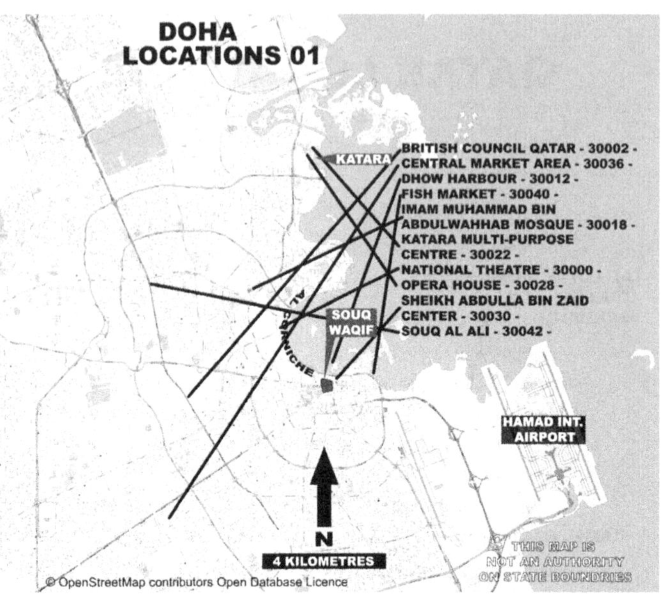
DOHA
LOCATIONS 01
KATARA
BRITISH COUNCIL QATAR - 30002 -
CENTRAL MARKET AREA - 30036 -
DHOW HARBOUR - 30012 -
FISH MARKET - 30040 -
IMAM MUHAMMAD BIN
ABDULWAHHAB MOSQUE - 30018 -
KATARA MULTI-PURPOSE
CENTRE - 30022 -
NATIONAL THEATRE - 30000 -
OPERA HOUSE - 30028 -
SHEIKH ABDULLA BIN ZAID
CENTER - 30030 -
SOUQ AL ALI - 30042 -
SOUQ
WAQIF
AL CORNICHE
HAMAD INT.
AIRPORT
N
4 KILOMETRES
THIS MAP IS
NOT AN AUTHORITY
ON STATE BOUNDRIES
© OpenStreetMap contributors Open Database Licence

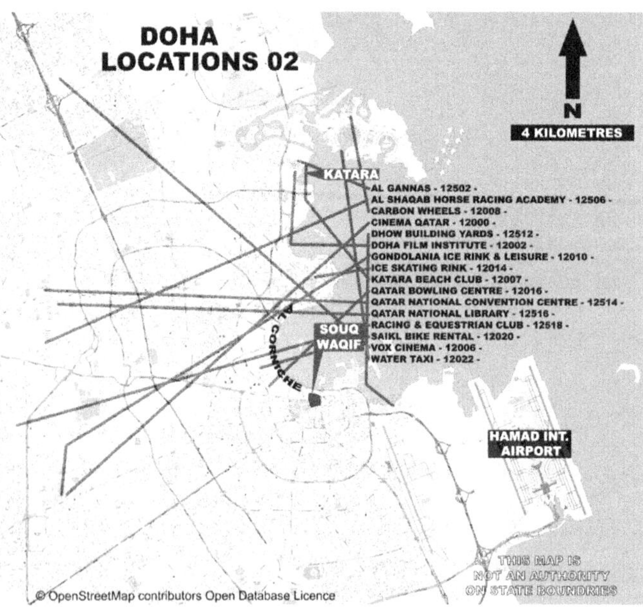
DOHA
LOCATIONS 02
N
4 KILOMETRES
KATARA
AL GANNAS - 12502 -
AL SHAQAB HORSE RACING ACADEMY - 12506 -
CARBON WHEELS - 12008 -
CINEMA QATAR - 12000 -
DHOW BUILDING YARDS - 12512 -
DOHA FILM INSTITUTE - 12002 -
GONDOLANIA ICE RINK & LEISURE - 12010 -
ICE SKATING RINK - 12014 -
KATARA BEACH CLUB - 12007 -
QATAR BOWLING CENTRE - 12016 -
QATAR NATIONAL CONVENTION CENTRE - 12514 -
QATAR NATIONAL LIBRARY - 12516 -
RACING & EQUESTRIAN CLUB - 12518 -
SAIKL BIKE RENTAL - 12020 -
VOX CINEMA - 12006 -
WATER TAXI - 12022 -
SOUQ
WAQIF
AL CORNICHE
HAMAD INT.
AIRPORT
THIS MAP IS
NOT AN AUTHORITY
ON STATE BOUNDRIES
© OpenStreetMap contributors Open Database Licence

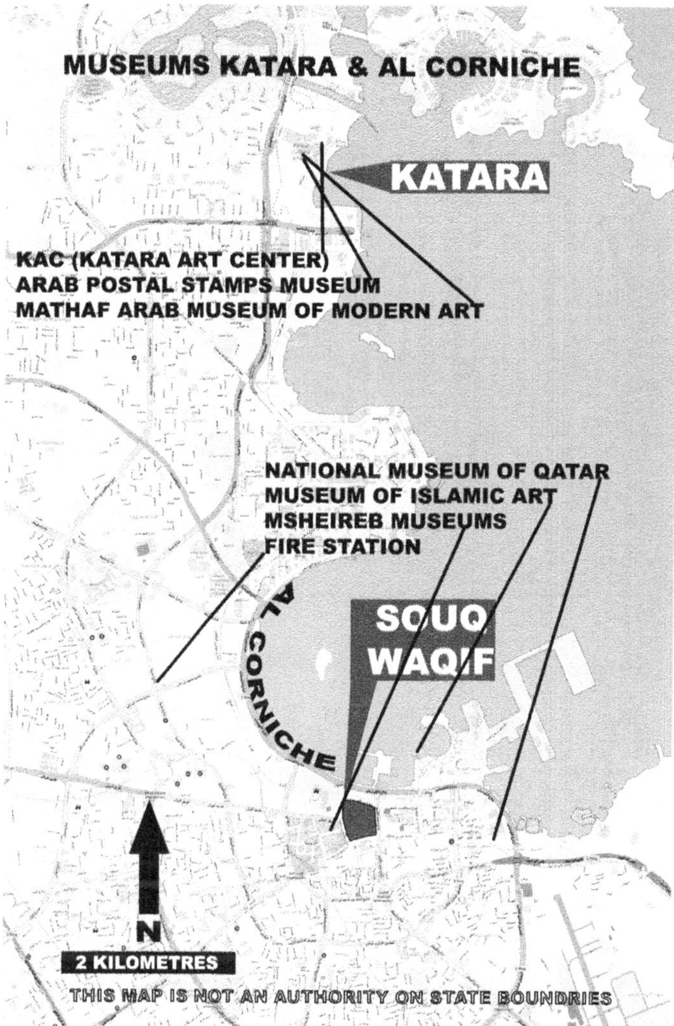
MUSEUMS KATARA & AL CORNICHE
KATARA
KAC (KATARA ART CENTER)
ARAB POSTAL STAMPS MUSEUM
MATHAF ARAB MUSEUM OF MODERN ART
NATIONAL MUSEUM OF QATAR
MUSEUM OF ISLAMIC ART
MSHEIREB MUSEUMS
FIRE STATION
AL CORNICHE
SOUQ
WAQIF
N
2 KILOMETRES
THIS MAP IS NOT AN AUTHORITY ON STATE BOUNDRIES
© OpenStreetMap contributors Open Database Licence

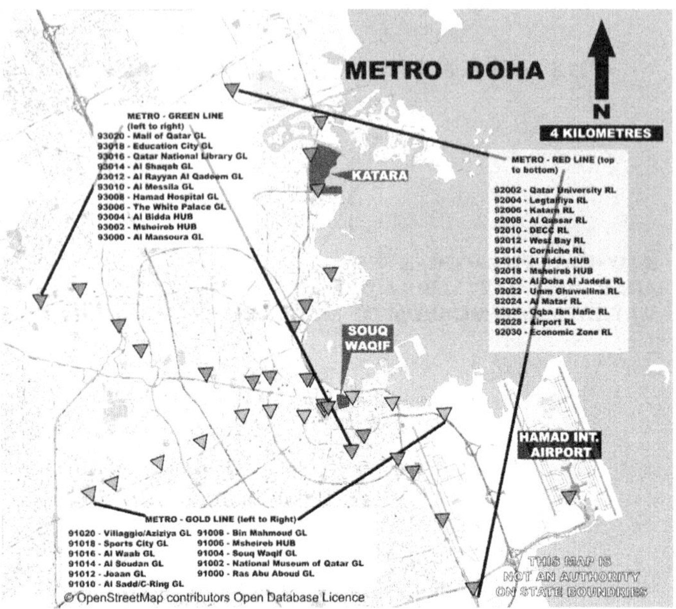
METRO DOHA
N
4 KILOMETRES
METRO - GREEN LINE (left to right)
93020 - Mall of Qatar GL
93018 - Education City GL
93016 - Qatar National Library GL
93014 - Al Shaqab GL
93012 - Al Rayyan Al Qadeem GL
93010 - Al Messila GL
93008 - Hamad Hospital GL
93006 - The White Palace GL
93004 - Al Bidda HUB
93002 - Msheireb HUB
93000 - Al Mansoura GL
KATARA
METRO - RED LINE (top to bottom)
92002 - Qatar University RL
92004 - Legtaifiya RL
92006 - Katara RL
92008 - Al Qassar RL
92010 - DECC RL
92012 - West Bay RL
92014 - Corniche RL
92016 - Al Bidda HUB
92018 - Msheireb HUB
92020 - Al Doha Al Jadeda RL
92022 - Umm Ghuwailina RL
92024 - Al Matar RL
92026 - Oqba Ibn Nafie RL
92028 - Airport RL
92030 - Economic Zone RL
SOUQ WAQIF
HAMAD INT. AIRPORT
METRO - GOLD LINE (left to Right)
91020 - Villaggio/Aziziya GL
91018 - Sports City GL
91016 - Al Waab GL
91014 - Al Soudan GL
91012 - Joaan GL
91010 - Al Sadd/C-Ring GL
91008 - Bin Mahmoud GL
91006 - Msheireb HUB
91004 - Souq Waqif GL
91002 - National Museum of Qatar GL
91000 - Ras Abu Aboud GL
THIS MAP IS NOT AN AUTHORITY ON STATE BOUNDRIES
© OpenStreetMap contributors Open Database Licence

VISITING QATAR - KEY WEBSITES

VISITING QATAR

Key Websites

https://www.moph.gov.qa/english/Pages/default.aspx

https://www.visitqatar.qa/en/home

https://www.qatarairways.com/en-gb/visa-and-passport-requirements.html

https://dohahamadairport.com/airport-guide/at-the-airport/visas-immigration

https://london.embassy.qa/en

https://washington.embassy.qa/en

https://canberra.embassy.qa/en

29

EASY ITINERARIES

Culture vultures half day in Doha

Start with a visit to the impressive Museum of Islamic Art [p160]. This visually imposing building is placed on a man-made island, which is accessed by an avenue of Date Palms. To the east is a park and the rear overlooks the harbour in Doha. The five floors hold an impressive collection of, as it says, Islamic art.

From the museum, take a 1.5-kilometre walk west along the Corniche into Souq Waqif [p166]. About half way is the dhow harbour which is worth a detour if you have time. This souq was the original trading hub of Doha and today is a labyrinth of small shops, cultural sites and restaurants [p241] ranging from budget to luxuriously expensive, where you can refuel after your walk

Corniche and Sheikh Abdulla Bin Zaid Al Mahmoud Islamic Cultural Centre

Museum full day in Doha

If you have a full day free in Doha, and want to immerse yourself in history and culture, this is for you.

The National Museum [p156] is an ideal place to begin. This was opened in 2019 and its focus is, in general, on the history and culture of Qatar. The design is based on the crystal 'desert rose' formation, though it could be also likened to a jumble of flying saucers. The interior is spacious and surprisingly immersive.

Walk, or call a taxi, for the 2km journey to the Museum of Islamic Art [p160]. The route cuts west and then north past the Movenpick hotel on Ali bin Amur Al Attiya St. This museum is spread over five floors, with especially collected exhibits, the museum includes various temporary exhibitions and dining choices.

Stroll along the Corniche for lunch in Souq Waqif [p166], where a great choice of options is listed [p243]. After lunch, Souq Waqif is an intriguing maze of shops and sights, including the Falcon Souq.

From Souq Waqif it's a short walk to the west, of less than 800metres to the Msheireb Museum's complex [p172]. These four buildings offer in insight into the cultural and social changes seen in Doha, over its recent history. Take the Metro from Msheireb Station, at the end of the day.

Dune bashing and a stroll through Katara full day.

South of Doha are the dunes bordering The Gulf. To experience this make a booking with your choice of tour operator [p235]. The drive from Doha is initially along expressways, before arriving into the powder like white dunes that spread like a carelessly tossed blanket. Check with your operator about any lunch options by the sea.

Returning to Doha, organize for you to be taken to Katara [p182]. Here within a distance of only 500metres is the Postal Stamp Museum , a centre devoted to Falcons and hunting, restaurants and a plethora of sights.

30

PLACES TO VISIT

Here the places to visit are grouped in a geographical order, rather than by type. In Doha, for instance, they are in a linear direction from east to west. This means that starting, for example, at the National Museum the next entry in the book is also the next tourist place to its west; the Fish Market then the Islamic Art Museum, Riwaq Gallery and so on. From Doha, the guide heads to different areas in Qatar. You can choose to visit these places in the order listed, or choose the ones that interest you, check the index for their entry. You need to take into account your own fitness, general health, heat on the day you visit and so on, in making the decision whether to walk or take transport, only you or your health advisor can decide this. Heat and humidity will be the key consideration, always have drinking water to hand and also if you are losing electrolytes, their replacement may be needed. GPS details are as a general reference, not for exact location or navigation by as your own device may record details differently.

Restaurants are also grouped geographically and then in price order. They are chosen to offer a reasonable option in that location, for example in Al Ruwais Iskender Pasha is included, however if it were in Doha there are other restaurants that would squeeze it out. The focus is on restaurants that offer something different as well as 5* hotel restaurants that are more interesting. If you prefer a more international dining experience, closer to that in a western city, choose a restaurant from within the better hotels. In general local restaurants, outside hotels, offer freshly cooked food, and especially in the lower cost options away from tourist areas they cater for the local population and have often extremely authentic cuisine. The downside is that general hygiene may not be as high as McDonalds or 5* hotels and the service may be haphazard, after all they do not have layers of management and head offices to lay down consistent standards – and the price does reflect that.

Hotels are also listed geographically. Here the intention is simply to show some choices. Prices vary seasonally and you may have a loyalty card with an international chain that might make the decision for you. Qatar is boosting the number of hotels, for the hoped for influx of fans in the World Cup. This means that capacity at normal times is far in excess of demand, bargains are to be found especially if you are a walk-in client who is prepared to walk-out if a room price does not suit you. In general, brand name 'international' hotels do offer the most consistent service. In the lower price range, especially hotels that are not part of an international group, service may be patchy and in these hotels that are more than a few years old, lack of maintenance starts to impact their quality.

Major hotels, and the restaurants within them, will usually have alcohol available (minimum age is 21 years old); Ramadhan may affect availability; elsewhere alcohol is not available.

All hotels and restaurants rely on staff who work on a contract of say a couple of years within Qatar. This means that the constant change in staff will affect how well they can manage their business, which may result in changes of service levels and overall quality.

Hotels are stared by the dollar price (charges will be in QAR) of their cheapest room, out of their peak season.

US$ 0-60 *
US$ 61-90 **
US$ 91-125 ***
US$ 126-190 ****
US$ 191-250 *****
US$ 251+ ******

Restaurants are stared by the dollar price (charges will be in QAR) of typical lower cost meal for a single person in that restaurant.

US$ 5-9 **
US$ 9-13 ***
US$ 13-19 ****
US$ 19-25 *****
US$ 25 + ******

CORNICHE, SOUQ WAQIF & CENTRAL DOHA

Bear Lamp (Hamad International Airport) - This giant sculpture of a Teddy Bear and lamp by Swiss artist Urs Fischer acts as a mascot to the airport and acts as a hub in the Duty Free area.

Rough GPS - 25.262 , 51.613 Street - Duty Free - Hamad International Airport / مطار حمد الدولي Public Transport - Bus 109, 727,737,747,757,777 Metro Red Line Hamid International Airport

Small Lie (Hamad International Airport) - Small Lie the oversize wooden marionette by Brian Donnelly is in Hamad Airport departures area E (below the moving walkway).

Rough GPS - 25.262 , 51.613 Street - Departures E - Hamad International Airport / مطار حمد الدولي Public

Transport - Bus 109, 727,737,747,757,777 Metro Red Line Hamid International Airport

Dhow Building Yards / مصنع السفن - Easily reached on the eastern part of the Corniche is a small Dhow Building Yard. This is a private operation, however a smile and a request to look is usually answered with a 'welcome'. This is prime real estate and may sooner rather than later disappear in favour of a boutique hotel.

Typical hours - appx 08:00-17:00 Sun-Thurs Entry charge – no charge

Rough GPS - 25.285 , 51.560 Street - Ras Al Aboud Expressway just east of Oasis Hotel. - Corniche / الكورنيش Public Transport - Bus 109,777 Metro Gold Line National Museum

National Museum Qatar

National Museum Of Qatar / متحف قطر الوطني - The National Museum of Qatar is intended to bring to life the story of Qatar. The modern museum, which opened in 2019, is a multi-level building, with the collections held on what amounts to a single floor, which weaves around the structure for around 1,500m. The exterior structure is fibre-reinforced concrete discs, 539 in all, supported by a steel structure.

Jean Nouvel drew his inspiration for the exterior

appearance, which ultimately impacts the interior due to its geometry, on the 'desert rose' evaporative crystallization of mineral-rich sands in a previously saline environment. These take many forms including, as in this museum, a multi-pane interlocking structure. Scattered around the grounds a several small gardens, and activity area for children. Artwork by Jean-Michel Othoniel, sits in the lagoon. This work is 114 fountain sculptures, representing Arabic calligraphy.

The entrance is hidden within the structure, rather than being an obvious pathway.

The building's interior is subdued, probably without any right-angles, flat surfaces or absolutely vertical walling. An immersive, multi-dimensional sound and video system offers an engaging experience throughout the galleries.

Payments are made in the lobby and after that and taking in the giant silver-coloured sculpture Motherland, a 'baṭṭulah' face mask, by Hassan bin Mohammed Al Thani, take the escalator up from the lobby into the area with 11 galleries. Within the galleries, the illustrative videos were produced by Doha Film Institute in up to 21,600 x 4,000 resolution.

The first gallery illustrates the formation of Qatar, from a geological viewpoint starting 700million years ago; it includes meteorites and fossils with an audio-visual backdrop to illustrate the evolving natural environment. It concludes with the modern environment of Qatar as The Gulf, with its geography today.

Moving through to the second gallery where Qatar's natural environment today is covered, with an ecological focus. Taxidermied animals in realistic settings and set against a very engaging audio-visual screening of Qatar's nature.

Galley 3 is the archaeology of Qatar, with stone tools set up generally in a traditional museum style. Explanatory videos support understanding of the skills involved in producing stone tools and pottery. Some of Qatar's archaeological sites are included in video. The galley has a broad-based view-point of archaeology and includes more modern exhibits, not just prehistoric.

National Museum Qatar

The people of Qatar are the focus of Gallery 4 and 5. The Cirebon Wreck, a 10th century ship probably built in the Straits of Malacca which was carrying Chinese and Asian finished goods, that were supposed to have been intended for delivery into Basra, the port for the Abbasid Caliphate city of Baghdad is used to illustrate trade links available to Qatar into the far east during that period. Nomadic life and sea and land is illustrated with ship's navigational equipment and videos of a form of transhumance. Naturally the use of camels in Qatar is portrayed, along with equipment and accessories and their 'wasms' (brands to identify the owner and their tribe). Traditional weaving is shown, including floor coverings and tent equipment. Moving into Galley 7, the world of pearls is covered. A remarkable item is the Pearl Carpet of Baroda, which was commissioned by the Maharaja of Baroda to hang in the Prophets Tomb in Medina (it therefore is more probably a wall hanging). Auctioned in 2009 for US$5.5 million, it is intended to display the luxurious use of Gulf pearls, however it also shows the flow of wealth between Qatar and India (and beyond) during the 19th, 20th & 21st centuries .

The final galleries cover Qatar today, with the essential impact of oil on the country, and gives a perspective to the use of the wealth it brings.

Finishing the visit to the new National Museum, a visit into the old National Museum, which was the palace of Sheikh Abdullah bin Jassim Al Thani, is possible. This is an early 20th c structure, which was enlarged and recreated over the century. Inside is a range of buildings, which are refurbished in the style of the early 20th c.

It's worth dropping into the gift shop, with its remarkable ceiling and see if there is a souvenir for you. On the roof is the excellent Jiwan restaurant, serving a modern take on Qatari and Gulf cuisine, with French style

Typical hours - doors open Sat-Thurs 12:30 to 20:00 - Fri 13:30 to 20:00 Sun closed Entry charge - QAR 50 (non-residents of Qatar) Online booking https://qm.org.qa/tickets/select-tickets/ -

Rough GPS - 25.287 , 51.548 Street - On Museum Park St near the east Corniche extension - Corniche / الكورنيش Public Transport - Bus 76, 109 Metro Gold Line National Museum Contacts - +974 4452 5555 infonmoq@qm.org.qa www.nmoq.org.qa

Fish Market / سوق السمك - On the eastern end of the Corniche this small open-air market is a great stop early in the morning, to see fresh fish being landed directly off small boats.

Typical hours - best in morning Public Transport - Bus 76, 109 Metro Gold Line National Museum

Rough GPS - 25.291 , 51.548 Street - Corniche / الكورنيش Public Transport - Bus 76, 109 Metro Gold Line National Museum

Council of Ministers Secretariat General / الامانة العامة لمجلس الوزراء - In the exterior atrium between the two sections of the Council of Ministers Secretariat General building is the '**Reflective Flow**' chandelier. This was designed by Beau McClellan and at 18 tons the chandelier is listed by Guinness World Records as the largest chandelier in the world. It's difficult to see during the day, but at night the lights come on so you can enjoy them

Typical hours - not open to public -

Rough GPS - 25.291 , 51.544 Street - Corniche / الكورنيش Public Transport - Bus 76, 109 Metro Gold Line National Museum

Museum Of Islamic Art / متحف الفن الإسلامي - The Museum of Islamic Art is a major centre for the collection, display and study of Islamic art from around the world. The museum, which opened in 2008, is a five story, purpose built building on a man-made island for the collection, with a geometric exterior design and spacious interior. A public park surrounds it to general area to the south and east, while the dhow harbour is to the north and west. I. M. Pei, the architect, drew his inspiration for the exterior from the 'sabil', an ablution and drinking water fountain within the courtyard of the Ibn Tulun Mosque in Cairo. The sabil features an angular façade and is set as the focus within an large courtyard, both features referred to on the façade of the museum and its isolated location within Doha.

An avenue of date palms leads visitors up towards the entrance, which holds within its atrium a cafe, with a range of drinks, snacks and light meals; perhaps take a snack after visiting one floor - before you move onto the next.

There is an enforced dress-code of conservative dress, for both men and women, this includes wearing non-figure hugging opaque clothing, longer sleeve tops and loose trousers or well below knee skirts for women and smarter style shirts and long trousers for men. After security checks at the entrance an imperial style staircase in the atrium leads up to floor 2. Elevators are available. To the right of the entrance is the publicly accessible library. As with the library, the focus is on Islamic Art, with books in both Arabic and English. The library does not lend books.

Museum of Islamic Art

The two floors with permanent galleries are a horse-shoe shape around the atrium, which extends up through the entire building, and the galleries follow naturally one after the other as a linear flow, starting at a gallery either side to the north (by the glass-walling) and continuing around to the gallery opposite the starting point.

This is a museum in the style of a traditional museum, with pieces set in display cases. The focus on Islamic Art is specific, compared to general collections held elsewhere, such as the V&A. The items were often specifically purchased for the museum and the spacious rooms with their excellent lighting and cases, display each piece in a way that older museums would struggle to do.

Floor 2 focuses on Islam's science with astrological devices, navigation equipment, and a substantial collection of calligraphic material, including illuminated pages. Repeating geometric patterns are a staple of Islamic decoration and woodwork from the 14th century, on this floor are several examples. Navigation equipment includes astrolabes, from the 10th c. Ceramic tilework pieces from central Asia feature decorative calligraphy. Calligraphy is also a feature in illuminated books and the museum has a fine example, The Shahnameh, by the acclaimed Persian poet Ferdowsi, is beautifully illuminated, along with the calligraphy of his epic 100,000 line epic about Persia.

Floor 3 is a multi-national collection from the core areas of the Islamic world (Central Asia, Persia, Syria, Egypt, India and Turkey) rather than its wider span. This is best viewed starting from the eastern side (left of the glass wall) as there is a rough chronological order from early, to late Islamic art. Mamluk glass demonstrate the skills of a whole group of grafts people needed to create a glass vase, decorated and also inscribed with calligraphy. Look for an extraordinary bejewelled container for a coffee cup, used in Turkey. A 19th c gold devotional necklace from Tamil Nadu although in gold, with silver and rubies, also show that value has many forms as nuts are also a feature of this piece.

Floor 4 has two non-connected galleries which hold temporary exhibitions. Concerts of various types are held here with information & some ticket sales from www.qatarphilharmonicorchestra.org. Before you leave - there is a gift shop, perhaps something for you or friends

The exterior of the museum has the Museum of Islamic Art Park. It's a superb place to stroll through – with the museum and West Bay as remarkable backdrops. Cultural events are held occasionally – adding to the park's appeal. This can be accessed from the museum's entrance door after a short walk and taking an elevator down. The walk from the museum to the 7 sculpture by Richard Serra is about 1 kilometre; golf style buggies offer a complimentary shuttle service. Along the route are coffee shops and landscaped gardens. The walk's terminus includes another metal sheet sculpture by Richard Serra, who also made a sculpture East-West in Zekreet western Qatar and mounds from which to view the harbour and the West Bay skyscrapers.

Typical hours - Sat-Wed 09:00-19:00 Thurs 09:19:00 Fri 13:30:19:00 Entry charge - QAR 50 (non-residents) - https://qm.org.qa/tickets/select-tickets/

Rough GPS - 25.295 , 51.539 Street - Eastern end of Corniche - Corniche / الكورنيش Public Transport - Bus 76, 777 Metro Gold Line Souq Waqif -

Museum of Islamic Art

Contacts - +974 4422 4444 Check www.mia.org.qa

Al Riwaq Gallery / متحف الفن الإسلامي Just next to the Museum of Islamic Art, Al Riwaq Gallery holds temporary exhibitions. Check the website for current exhibitions. It has hosted artists such as Takashi Murakami and Damien Hirst.

Typical hours - 09:00-18:00 Sat-Thurs - Fri 14:00-19:00

Rough GPS - 25.293, 51.543 Street - Eastern end of Corniche - Corniche / الكورنيش Public Transport - Bus 76, 777 Metro Gold Line Souq Waqif Contacts - https://qm.org.qa/en/visit/museums-and-galleries/

7 (Seven) - 7 by Richard Serra represents the multiplicity of meanings the number 7 has in Islam. It also makes a fitting terminus to the park behind the Islamic Museum and an ideal location to watch the skyscrapers light up at dusk.

Rough GPS - 25.298 , 51.540 Street - Museum of Islamic Art - Corniche / الكورنيش Public Transport - Bus 76, 777 Metro Gold Line Souq Waqif

Corniche / الكورنيش - Probably the most seen 'tourist attraction' in Doha, simply because it's not only incredibly scenic but a route between main tourist areas. The sweep of the Corniche takes in the National Museum, Museum of Islamic Art, Dhows, Souq Waqif Al Bidda Park and evening views of the almost psychedelic illuminations of West Bay. Walking from east to west follows the attractions above ending in the Sheraton's park, and is the route suggested by this guide; it also provides the best views of West Bay. There are numerous 'photo' stops on the walk of around 7km - allow a couple of hours plus for a leisurely walking only time. A few cafes are along the route - with lots in Souq Waqif. A bottle of water in hand is ideal, along with your camera.

Rough GPS - 25.291 , 51.534 Street - Corniche - Souq Waqif / سوق واقف Public Transport - Bus 76, 777 (Airport), Metro Gold Line Souq Waqif

Dhow Harbour / ميناء الداو - Here are a few Dhows, anchored off the jetty along with modern boats. A number of sea excursions leave from the jetty including from the

Anantara reception to the Banana Resort Island, there is a small car park if needed. The general jetty (called a harbour) this offers a great opportunity to see Dhows close up as well as get a different angle for photographs of Doha. The small island in the centre of the harbour was, until 2006, a small resort hotel, it must be waiting a new development, possibly a water fountain.

Rough GPS - 25.295, 51.535 Street - Off Corniche near Souq Waqif - Corniche / الكورنيش Public Transport - Bus 76, 777 Metro Gold Line Souq Waqif

Pearl Monument

The Pearl Monument / اللؤلؤة - On the Corniche, just after the Islamic Art Museum is a fountain in the shape of an open Oyster shell with a Pearl inside. It's a useful 'place mark' along the Corniche together with the helical minaret on the Qatar Islamic Centre.

Rough GPS - 25.291 , 51.534 Street - Corniche - Souq Waqif / سوق واقف Public Transport - Bus 76, 777 (Airport), Metro Gold Line Souq Waqif

Sheikh Abdulla Bin Zaid Al Mahmoud Islamic Cultural Centre / مركز الشيخ عبد الله بن زيد ال محمود الثقافي الإسلامي - This centre, also called Al Fanar, explains and promotes Qatar's culture, the Arabic language and Islam. Inside are prayer rooms and lecture halls. Arabic language lessons are offered. The centre is useful if you wish authoritative information about Islam in Qatar. The helical minaret of the building is a useful prominent landmark when walking in central Doha. It takes its design from the Malwiya Minaret of Great Mosque in Samarra Iraq.

Typical hours - 05:00-20:00 Sun - Thurs Entry charge - No Charge -

Rough GPS - 25.289 , 51.536 Street - Junction Abdulla bin Jassim St and Hamid Al Kabir St - east of Souq Waqif. - Souq Waqif / سوق واقف Public Transport - Bus 76, 177 Metro Gold Line Souq Waqif - Contacts - +974 4444 7444 binzaid@islam.gov.qa www.binzaid.gov.qa

Souq Waqif

Souq Waqif / سوق واقف - Souq Waqif سوق واقف combines tradition with modern requirements in an excellent setting in the heart of Doha. Its core is the rectangular market area, though there are adjacent areas that create a larger square area of commerce, dining, entertainment and hotels of around 20 hectares (about 500x440m).

If you have time to visit only one place in Doha, this is it.

Souq Waqif (which means the standing market) was set up close to the sea, on either side of a wadi (Wadi Msheireb), which in dry weather provided an open space for people to walk between stalls. In origin, the date for the souq must be similar to the origin date for Doha, which grew from the 1820s. The souq served Doha, as the town grew it also served Qatar in general and the ships which anchored offshore. Until the early 1970s the souq was on the edge of the sea, and heavy rains would cause Wadi Msheireb to flow through the souq. Conversely at very high tides, if the wind was blowing in the right direction, sea-water might also be pushed inside the souq - in either case both the shop-keepers and their customers had to stand - it was the standing souq hence the name.

The Ottomans built Al Koot Fort in 1880, which must have increased trade for the souq's merchants to its east. In 1927 the Amir of Qatar rebuilt the fort, establishing this area as the centre of Doha. The growth of the oil industry after World War 2 naturally increased overall trade, especially after its dramatic price increases in the early 1970. However new department stores (such as The Centre in 1978) shopping malls (such as The Mall in 1997 and City Centre in 2001) resulted in the loss of trade.

In 2003 a fire destroyed large areas of Souq Waqif, and its fate seemed sealed. However Sheikh Hamad bin Khalifa Al Thani and his wife Sheikha Moza bint Nasser Al Missned decided that the souq would be restored. This happened in two phases, one was a general rebuilding in 2006 and in 2008 all buildings built after 1950 were demolished and the old buildings were renovated so that all these buildings maintain their traditional style with modern supporting infrastructure.

A key element in the rebuilt souq is its multi-use; there are retail shops selling a mix of every-day requirements for the local population as well as visiting tourists; cafes and restaurants which encourage shoppers to linger; frequent entertainment events based on Souq Waqif Square and peripheral sites including a cinema, mounted horse security;

finally there are hotels, that replace the original residents of Souq Waqif with temporary guests.

Today Souq Waqif is a largely pedestrianised area, and the former car park to its east has been replaced by a multi-story car park under Souq Waqif Square. The original street layout has been retained and in this guide the route to enter is from the Corniche cutting into the main pedestrian route. This is Al Souq Street (GPS 25.289, 51.530), in the north of Souq Waqif, 100m south of Abdullah bin Jassim St (less than 100m west of Souq Waqif bus stop on Grand Hamad St).

Majlis Al Dama

Al Souq Street is full of restaurants and cafes, including the exotic **Parisa** (a Ritz Carlton restaurant), which despite its name is a Persian dining experience. A good alternative restaurant is the less glamorous **Al Shurfa** (the Tivoli Al Jomrok Boutique Hotel, restaurant), just to the west of the entrance passage has an excellent location for its Arab dining experience. Al Shurfa's balcony has uninterrupted views over the Corniche to West Bay. A couple of good cafes to sit in, have a coffee and snack and enjoy the atmosphere are **Shay Al Shoomos** (at the north entrance passage noted above) - a small cafe run by a Qatari woman; serving authentic Qatari food that is especially good for breakfast - & **Majlis Al Dama**, hidden in the passageways south of the Bird Souq. Majlis Al Dama takes its name from Al Dama, a board game similar to draughts/checkers, but with each player having 16 pieces it has a decidedly Qatari twist. The game is often played between customers inside the coffee shop.

Camels Souq Waqif

The **Pet and Bird Souq** is to the west of Al Souq Street in an open-roofed section of Souq Waqif. Here are innumerable domestic pets, wild birds (budgerigars etc) as well as wild animals. The main souq is also in this western area. This is a fantastic area to wander through, though it's impossible not to get disorientated. This is a traditional style of a covered souq, with a myriad of small shops selling fabrics, traditional clothing, spices, gifts, perfumes and lots more. Farther to the west is the **Camel** pen area off Al Jasra St (GPS 25.2891, 51.531) and also horse stabling (GPS 25.289, 51.530), the Falcon Souq (GPS 25.288, 51.530) is between Al Jasra St & Al Asmakh St.

The **Falcon Souq** 25.288, 51.531 opens roughly 09:00-12:30 /17:00-21:00 (Fridays only in the afternoon). There are individual shops - just walk into your choice and say hi. The best time to visit is in the afternoon, ideally Thursday, when potential buyers visit to check out the birds, but visit any time and the birds are all sitting waiting for

Falcon Souq

you. For a nice souvenir, why not buy a falcons hood, (a rufter or locally it's called a burka). Just to the north of this is the Falcon Hospital, which though a key element of this falcon area is not normally open for casual visits.

To the south-east of the souq (southern end of Al Souq Street) are the **Gold and Crafts Souqs**. Opening Hours – 09:00-12:00 / 15:00-21:00 Sat-Fri. Here are gifts and gold in a colourful setting. The gold is generally ornate Gulf style at 19 carat plus, though if you search you may find simpler designs. Prices can be negotiated down by 5-10%. If you are buying handicrafts, bargain a lot more.

Tivoli hotels (https://www.tivolihotels.com/en/souq-waqif-doha) have a number of boutique hotels in Souq Waqif, along with some of the better restaurants in Souq Waqif.

The core of the souq is less than three hectares while the larger area is under twenty hectares. To put this into context, the core area is comparable to the building space of the Palace of Versailles and the larger area about 25% of the ornamental gardens immediately next to Versailles. This does mean that as a location, it is comfortable to explore and enjoy.

Typical hours - The souq is made up of individual businesses with their own hours. Most shops open between 10:00-12:00/16:00-22:00 and Restaurants from 10:00-22:00 - Ramadhan timings will vary. Entry charge - No charge to enjoy the atmosphere. -

Rough GPS - 25.289 , 51.534 Street - Junction Abdullah bin Jassim St and Hamid Al Kabir St - south of Pearl Monument on Corniche St and jetty for Dhows. The Gold Line Souq Waqif Station and Msheireb Central Metro Station are within 350m and 800m. - Souq Waqif / سوق واقف Public Transport - Bus 76, 177 Metro Gold Line Souq Waqif

Tourist Information (& the Police) / المعلومات السياحية (والشرطة) - An ideal stop for tourist information in Souq Waqif. The police even dress in a heritage style. Phone –

Call Centre +974 4406 9921 - www.visitqatar.qa An ideal stop for tourist information in Souq Waqif.

Typical hours - 08:00-midday 15:30-19:00

Souq Waqif

Rough GPS - 25.289 , 51.534 Street - Junction Abdullah bin Jassim St and Hamid Al Kabir St - south of Pearl Monument on Corniche St and jetty for Dhows. The Gold Line Souq Waqif Station and Msheireb Central Metro Station are within 350m and 800m respectfully. - Souq Waqif / سوق واقف Public Transport - Bus 76, 177 Metro Gold Line Souq Waqif

Wind Tower House / بيت اللاقف - An authentic Wind Tower House, now set in an incongruous location within the rebuilt Souq Al Najada. Wind towers are found through Persia and were also used on the western side of The Gulf from Kuwait to Musandam (Oman). As here, wind towers are usually four sided structures, though they can be hexagon or octagon, that rise above and are part of a building, usually a house. The upper part of the tower is open on each side and roofed. A barrier within the tower directs the wind down to provide a breeze into the house that adds a cooling effect. Water evaporators, within these type of towers, might add to the cooling effect. This tower is currently not open but previously was a museum. There is a recreated wind tower in the south-west of Souq Waqif.

Rough GPS - 25.285 , 51.533 Street - Junction of Grand Hamid St (Banks St) and Ali bin Abdullah St - inside the courtyard of Souq Al Najada - Msheireb / مشيرب Public Transport - Bus - Al Ghanim Bus Station Metro Red/Gold/Green Lines Interchange Msheireb.

Koot Fort

Al Koot Fort / قلعة الكوت - Just to the south west of Souq Waqif near the underground carpark entrance is Al Koot Fort, This was built in 1927, on the site of a previous Ottoman fort on the north of Wadi Msheireb which dated from 1880. The Ottomans abandoned their fort when they withdrew from Qatar in 1915 and naturally it became dilapidated. The then ruler of Qatar, Sheikh Abdullah bin Jassim bin Mohammed Al Thani rebuilt it, to secure the Souq Waqif. This has been a museum for exhibition of handicrafts however currently it is not open.

Rough GPS - 25.287 , 51.531 Street - south of Souq Waqif - Souq Waqif / سوق واقف Public Transport - Bus - Al Ghanim Bus Station Metro Red/Gold/Green Lines Interchange Msheireb

Msheireb Museums / متاحف مشيرب - The Msheireb Museums hope to tell an untold aspect of Qatar's no so long ago history. Set within four separate, single floor, houses, each building tells a different part of the story. Designed by Ralph Appelbaum, their restoration is sympathetic to their original structure. They are part of the Msheireb organisation chaired by Sheikha Moza bint Nasser Al Missned, the mother of the Amir of Qatar, and is a subsidiary of the Qatar Foundation. Download their interactive, extremely large, app.

The buildings are adjacent to each other on Al Arshef Al Watani St meaning a visitor can choose to visit only one or all four can be. As the museums are less than 500m south-west of Souq Waqif they make an easy add-on to a visit there.

The smallest of the buildings is **Radwani House**, which provides visitors an insight into how family life evolved in Qatar over the years. The house was occupied until 1971 and is an attractive single story courtyard house. The house showcases not only the manner in which it changed over time, but also how domestic family life was transformed in Doha. As with all these museum houses Radwani House was home to the more affluent people in Doha. Almost as an insight into the changes in Doha, Radwani House is enveloped by office blocks, those of the Qatar National Archive and the Amiri Guard.

Company House Set within a house that was once used as the headquarters for Qatar's first oil company, this museum tells the story of the Qatari petroleum industry workers and their families, who helped the flow of wealth that transformed Qatar into a modern society. There are displays of equipment that looks antiquated, even if only a few decades old .

Company House

The **Bin Jelmood House** provides space for reflection on the story of slavery and its trade in Qatar and the broader Gulf, which still is little acknowledged within the region. It comments about slavery in Islam, that it 'regulated the institution of slavery, improving the lives of the enslaved through the Quran's teachings...'. It also has a section on modern slavery. Unique in The Gulf Region, unusual in the world it is a concept for a museum that many capital cities lack.

On the other side of the road (next to Msheireb Mosque) is **Mohammed bin Jassim House** Built by Sheikh Mohammed Bin Jassim Al-Thani, son of the founder of modern Qatar, this heritage house addresses Msheireb's past, its present and what it hopes is a sustainable future.

Typical hours - Sunday: Closed Monday to Thursday: 09:00 – 17:00 Friday: 15:00pm – 21:00 Saturday: 09:00 –17:00

Rough GPS - 25.287 , 51.529 Street - East side of Al Asmakh St - Msheireb / مشيرب Public Transport - Bus 76, 177 Metro Msheireb (Hub) Contacts - +974 40065555 museums@msheireb.com www.msheireb.com

Al Bidda, Al Rumaila, Wadi Al Sail Parks 'Doha Grand Park' / الحدائق البدع و الرميلة و وادي السيل - Al Bidda Park is a substantial landscaped park on the Corniche in central Doha. The total area is around 1.7 sq km (slightly larger than Hyde Park London) and includes water feature, cafes, a children's park 25.303143, 51.514019 and maze. There are designated sports areas including for tennis, cycle paths and outdoor gym. Specific barbeque areas need to be used for cooking while there are several small cafes spread over the area. Toilets and first aid is available. Walkways give access over roads from one area to the next. Underground car parks, (with space for 6,000 vehicles!) are approached from the Corniche (southbound) and Uhud St. This, unsurprisingly, is busiest at the weekend and after 16:00hrs.

Rough GPS - 25.298 , 51.516 Street - West of the Corniche - Al Bidda park area / حديقة البدع Public Transport - Bus 100, 101,102,102X,170,172 , Metro Red Line/Green Line Al Bidda.

Imam Muhammad ibn Abd Al Wahhab Mosque / جامع الإمام مُحمَّد بن عبد الوهاب - This is the largest mosque in Doha and is open to non-Muslims. The mosque is named after the Islamic theologian from the 18th c in Riyadh Saudi Arabia and was opened in 2011. In keeping with the austere version of

Imam Muhammad ibn Abd Al Wahhab Mosque

Islam in Qatar, the mosque is simply decorated. Inside there are separate prayer rooms for men and women and several libraries, with some books in English. The floor space for the men's room is 7,400m and the entire building has three floors. The 93 domes refer to the multi-dome mosques in Makkah and Al Madinah. Guided tours available through the website www.binzaid.gov.qa or visit Sheikh Abdulla Bin Zaid Al Mahmoud Islamic Cultural Centre (Al Fanar). It is preferable for non-Muslims to visit outside prayer times, most especially midday prayers, as you will then be able to move more easily. Though the timings given here do allow for timing variations throughout the year, do check the actual prayer times in Doha on the day you wish to visit before you arrive. Children under 8 are not permitted. Photography is only permitted with mobile-phone, and excluded in the ladies prayer rooms. Men should wear long trousers and long-sleeved shirts, avoiding text on them. Women should be wear concealing clothing that only shows face, hands and feet. The mosque issues, returnable, head-scarf and Abaya to wear if needed. Footwear must be removed before entering. Each sex can only visit the appropriate area in the mosque. An ideal time to visit is before the sunset prayers so that the tour is finished and you can then enjoy the panorama to the east over the city as the skyscrapers are illuminated and the call to prayer is made. Call your Uber style taxi when you want to leave as this is relatively isolate from main routes.

Typical hours - Open to non-Muslims during non-prayer times. 08:00-11:30 / 14:00-15:00 / 17:00-18:00 / 21:00-22:00 Always check newspapers for each days prayer times. Entry charge - No Charge -

Rough GPS - 25.318 , 51.507 Street - Junction Khalifa St and Al Istiqlal St - Al Jebailat / الجبيلات Public Transport - Bus

100,101,102,102x 170 Contacts - + 974 4470 0000 binzaid@islam.gov.qa www.binzaid.gov.qa

Qatar National Theatre / المسرح الوطني - Well located and a well-designed interior, it offers a good venue in Doha for performers. Unfortunately, without a dedicated website finding out about performances is by

Typical hours - Entry charge - as per event -

Rough GPS - 25.305 , 51.516 Street - off Corniche - Corniche / الكورنيش Public Transport - Bus 76, 777 Metro Red Line Corniche Contacts - +974 4483 6118 https://www.-dohafilminstitute.com/venues/qatar-national-theatre

Saikl Bike Rental / سيكل للدراجات الهوائية - Bikes rented for adults and children by the Hour (with helmets) also bike service . Branch in Sheraton grounds

Typical hours - 15:00-midnight daily

Rough GPS - 25.298 , 51.513 Street - Off Al Khaleej St - Al Bidda park area / حديقة البدع Public Transport - Bus 100, 101,102,102X,170,172 , Metro Red Line/Green Line Al Bidda Contacts - +974 5028 0404 info@saiklqtr.com www.saiklqtr.com

Khalifa International Tennis and Squash Complex / مجمع خليفة الدولي للتنس والإسكواش - With over 20 courts plus a main court of 7,000seats this is a major hard-court outdoor tennis complex. It has held WTA & ITF events. Courts are available to book, STA.

Typical hours - as per event Entry charge - as per event -

Rough GPS - 25.312 , 51.515 Street - Majlis Al Taaawon St - Al Bidda park area / حديقة البدع Public Transport - Bus 101,102, 102X, 170 Metro Red Line Corniche (1500metres) Contacts - +974 4440 9666 admin@qatartennis.org http://www.qatartennis.org/

Fire Station / الدفاع المدني - Just west of the Corniche is the old Fire Station, converted into an art centre in 2014 with a gallery, artists incubator for some 20 artists every year and material shop by Cass Art +974 4452 5625. This at its heart is a small incubator to develop artists from Qatar to develop their talent. A finishing exhibition is held. Rotating exhibitions of other art is held. An artists supply shop retails art material. There is a small theatre for public events, and a cafe #999 is open to relax in, next to Al Bidda Park.

Typical hours - Sat-Thurs 09:00-19:00 Fri 13:30-19:00 Entry charge - no charge (QAR50 non-residents of Qatar) check on https://qm.org.qa/en/visit/visitor-guidelines/

Rough GPS - 25.303 , 51.507 Street - junction Mohammed bin Thani St and Al Istiqlal St - Al Bidda park area / حديقة البدع Public Transport - Bus 101,102, 102X, 170 Metro Red Line Corniche (1500metres) Contacts - +974 4422-4222 contact@firestation.org.qa www.firestation.org.qa

Qatar Bowling Centre / مركز قطر للبولينج - With a World Champion Bowling Team - this is the bowling centre in Doha, they hold international events which may affect opening schedules. There are 32 lanes, Billiards and Table Tennis and Cafe.

Typical hours - Sat-Wed 09:00-24:00 Thurs 09:00-02:00(night) Fri 09:00-01:00(night) Entry charge - from QAR 8 per game - shoes included

Rough GPS - 25.292 , 51.516 Street - off Khaleej St - Corniche / الكورنيش Public Transport - Bus 100, 101,102,102X,170,172 , Metro Red Line/Green Line Al Bidda Contacts - +974 4432 9178 qatarbowlingfederation@gmail.com www.qatarbowlingfederation.com

West Bay

WEST BAY

Qatar Sports Club, Suheim Bin Hamad Stadium, Qatar Handball Federation / نادي قطر الرياضي - A sports complex focused on one of Qatar's more successful league teams. Regular local football matches are held, check for a detailed schedule in the media. Parking is very limited so if the match is a major event a taxi, bus or Corniche Metro Station (Red Line).

Typical hours - 08:00-22:00

Rough GPS - 25.317 , 51.514 Street - Junction Al Istiqlal St and Al Markhiya St - Al Dafna / الدفنة Public Transport - Bus 75, 100,101,102,102X,170 Metro Red Line 1500metres walk Contacts - +974 4483 1777 info@qatarsc.com www.qatarsc.com/

City Centre Doha / سيتي سنتر الدوحة - With Carrefour, Debenhams department store, banks & money changer innumerable shops including jewellery, footwear, discount shops, fashion, electronics and restaurants - City Centre s probably the most convenient mall for visitors in Qatar.

Typical hours - 10:00-midnight daily

Rough GPS - 25.326 , 51.530

Street - Conference Centre, Omar Al Mukhtar - West Bay / الخليج الغربي Public Transport - Bus 57,74,76,777 Metro

Doha Exhibition and Convention Center (DECC) Contacts - +974 4493 3355 info@citycenterdoha.com www.citycenterdoha.com/

Doha Exhibition & Convention Center (DECC) / مركز الدوحة للمعارض والمؤتمرات A major exhibition centre in the heart of Doha. With hotels, shopping mall and metro - its probably the best location for exhibitions and conferences in Doha. From 1 up to 5 halls can be configured.

Typical hours - as per event

Rough GPS - 25.323 , 51.529

Street - Conference Centre, Omar Al Mukhtar West Bay / الخليج الغربي Public Transport - Bus 57,74,76,777 Metro Doha Exhibition and Convention Center (DECC) Contacts - +974 4033 1111 https://www.decc.qa/visitors/ info@decc.qa

Ice Skating Rink / ساحة التزلج - Ice Skating within the atrium of a Shopping Mall. It's a peripheral service for the mall; maintenance and management are below the level of similar facilities in other major cities.

Typical hours - 10:00-21:00 Daily (Fri 13:00-23:00) Entry charge - from QAR35 -

Rough GPS - 25.326 , 51.530 Street - Junction of Omar Al Mukhtar Rd and Conference Centre Rd - West Bay / الخليج الغربي Public Transport - Bus 57 Metro Doha Exhibition and Convention Centre (DECC)

Regatta Sailing Academy - Sailboat training with Lasers and Darts - some may be available for individual hire without instruction. With warm seas and a breeze, this makes a good time out.

Typical hours - as per event Entry charge as per service

Rough GPS - 25.354 , 51.529 Street - off Lusail Expressway (south Katara) - Katara / كتارا Public Transport - Metro Red Line Al Qassar Contacts - +974 5550 3484 simon@regattasailingacademy.com www.regattasailingacademy.com

Landmark Mall - The Landmark Mall doesn't have the

franchises that make up so many of Qatar's other malls. It does however have a useful supermarket, Carrefour. This though a franchise isn't a clone of those in France, as the buying is locally made and the products represents the brands of Qatar and the region.

Typical hours - 09:00-22:00

Rough GPS - 25.334 , 51.467 Street - Doha Expressway / Al Markhiya St - Al Duhail / الدحيل Public Transport - Bus 100, 101 Contacts - +974 4487 5222 info@landmarkdoha.com www.landmarkdoha.com

The Pearl

THE PEARL AND KATARA

Doha Golf Club / نادي الدوحة للغولف - West of The Pearl, this popular and well established 72par 18 hole course holds the Qatar Masters in March. The course is large enough to almost make you think it's in the depths of an Arabian lush green countryside, then the skyscrapers of West Bay loom into view and it becomes one of the more remarkably city located golf courses. As to be expected the clubhouse's restaurant is good, it's an Intercontinental hotel operated one. Check that it accepts non-members as during the pandemic it operated as a member-only venue.

Typical hours - 06:00-21:00

Rough GPS - 25.380 , 51.505 Street - off Al Jamia St - West Bay / الخليج الغربي Public Transport - Bus 102X Metro Red Line Qatar University (a short taxi ride) Contacts - +974 4496 0777 info@dohagolfclub.com www.dohagolfclub.com

Katara / كتارا - Katara is a modern cultural centre about 10km north of the Cornice and Souq Waqif area. Although entirely modern in creation, it is a take on an Arab town, with its narrow, winding car-free streets, shaded from the sun.

Katara Mosque

There are a couple of mosques, both worth visiting. South of the outdoor theatre-in-the-round in the heart of Katara is a Turkish influenced mosque. This was designed by Zeynep

Fadillioglu, who designed the interior of the acclaimed Sakirin Mosque in Istanbul. The craftsmen were restorers from the Dolmabahce Palace. On the opposite side of the outdoor theatre-in-the-round is the Golden Mosque, traditional in design but very unusual in its surface treatment. Its polite to ask before entering, '*mumkin a shoof?*' and in case regulations change. Men should wear long trousers and long-sleeved shirts, avoiding text on them. Women should be wear concealing clothing that only shows face, hands and feet, that does include wearing a scarf; footwear must be removed before entering and left outside. Close to the tiled mosque are pigeon-towers. There are others to the east of Al Gannas (the Falcon Club) perhaps the pigeons are hunted. Both these towers are facsimiles of many pigeon towers in the Nile valley; though there are similar ones south of Al Kharj in Saudi Araba. There are a plethora of small retail outlets of art, fashion and more. The area has innumerable restaurants, including lots of small takeaways east of Al Gannas. The main area wraps around the outdoor theatre-in-the-round Workshops, events and exhibitions create a dynamic environment. Annual events include a falconry festival, in September, an Arabian horse show in early February https://kiahf.qa, The beach front adds to its appeal, all-be-it pay to enter. Parallel to the beach area is a promenade that runs south.

Rough GPS - 25.361 , 51.525 Street - off Lusail Expressway - Katara / كتارا Public Transport - Metro Red Line Al Qassar or Katara

Opera House / دار الأوبرا - Surprisingly for Qatar, this is a traditional looking Opera House that wouldn't look out of place in Milan or Paris. The first performance was held in December 2010 and now performances are principally during the winter, including both classical western and other cultures performances. The building is the home for the Qatar Philharmonic Orchestra https://qatarphilharmoni-corchestra.org which held its first performance in October

2008. As with so much in Qatar, the Orchestra's performances are focused on the new. They support rising new Arab performers and composers with performances both in Qatar and worldwide.

Typical hours - as per performance Entry charge - as per event

Rough GPS - 25.360 , 51.525 Street - Lusail Expressway - Katara / كتارا Public Transport - Metro Red Line Al Qassar or Katara Contacts - +974 4454 8185 events@katara.net www.katara.net

Pigeon Towers

Katara Pigeon Towers / برج الحمام - كتار - Three ornate Pigeon Towers to the west and another two to the east of the Amphitheatre. These towers take their inspiration from Pigeon Towers much of the greater Fertile Crescent of antiquity, most especially, for this design, those of the Nile Delta. The original antique towers were specifically built to house pigeons in order to collect their Guano for nitrogen rich soil fertiliser or a supply of birds for Pigeon Pie. Iranian towers may incorporate a Wind Tower design to cool the interior. These Doha ones with their White Doves seem to be ornamental rather than as used originally.

Rough GPS - 25.359 , 51.525 Street - off Lusail Expressway - Katara / كتارا Public Transport - Metro Red Line Al Qassar

Qatar Photographic Society / الجمعية القطرية للتصوير الضوئي - The Qatar Photographic Society holds exhibitions, along with lectures, workshops and competitions to encourage the art of photography in Doha. Despite this interest in photography, and though there are shops selling camera equipment in Doha, batteries, spare parts and accessories are more limited and may be expensive. The society is worth dropping into during a visit into Katara as it may give an insight into Qatar that is unavailable elsewhere.

Typical hours - 08:00-13:00 / 17:00-21:00 with variations for events.

Rough GPS - 25.360 , 51.525 Street - off Lusail Expressway on the west of the cultural area of Katara, next to the easy to find Pigeon Towers & Persian style Katara Mosque. - Katara / كتارا Public Transport - Metro Red Line Al Qassar or Katara Contacts - + 974 4408 1812 qps2628k@gmail.com www.qpsphoto.qa

Arab Postal Stamps Museum / متحف الطوابع البريدية العربية - The Arab world's philatelic history; with stamps from 22 countries this could be a great insight into what each country wants project about itself. The displays are quite traditional rather than an immersive insight; this is a set up by Katara - separately there is an online ordering service for stamp collectors from Qatar Post https://store.qatarpost.qa/webstore/.

Typical hours - 09:00-21:00 Sun-Thurs / 09:00 midday / 17:00-20:00 Sat on Friday closed

Rough GPS - 25.359 , 51.525 Street - off Lusail Expressway on the west of the cultural area of Katara, near the easy to find Pigeon Towers. - Katara / كتارا Public Transport - Metro Red Line Al Qassar Contacts - azayan@hotmail.com https://www.katara.net/en/communities/arab-postal-stamp-museum

Doha Film Institute - Doha Film Institute funds and supports production of local, regional and international films with an Arab focus. It hosts film screenings (check local media or web site - most are at the weekend), educational programmes and workshops. As with so much in Qatar - this is a hub of the Qatar Foundation and its chairperson Sheikha Al-Mayassa bint Hamad bin Khalifa Al Thani.

Typical hours - 08:00-16:00 Sun - Thurs Entry charge - as per event -

Rough GPS - 25.359 , 51.526 Street - off Lusail Expressway in Katara, south of the Multi-Purpose Hall and Theatre - Katara / كتارا Public Transport - Metro Red Line Al Qassar Contacts - +974 4420 0505 info@dohafilminstitute.com www.dohafilminstitute.com

Katara Multi-Purpose Centre / مركز كتارا متعدد الأغراض - A modern multi-purpose function centre, for events, exhibitions, meeting and even weddings. On its 'roof' is an outdoor theatre-in-the-round, almost a Roman amphitheatre with 5,000 seats that has held a variety of performances. Check media for upcoming events here.

Typical hours - as per event

Rough GPS - 25.360 , 51.526 Street - off Lusail Expressway - Katara / كتارا Public Transport - Metro Red Line Al Qassar or Katara.

Katara Art Centre (KAC) / مركز كتارا للفنون - An art gallery, workshop, artists 'incubator', retail outlet for art and interior design. Katara Art Centre acts as a hub for cultural communities to create a critical grassroots base in Doha for contemporary life. Weekends have popular events, adding a vibrancy to Katara, though Katara is vibrant without this addition.

Typical hours - Sat-Thurs 10:00-22:00 Friday 14:00-22:00 (departments do work shorter hours) Rough GPS - 25.361 , 51.528 Street - east of Lusail Expressway - Katara / كتارا Public Transport - Metro Red Line Al Qassar or Katara Contacts - +974 4408 0244 hello@dohakac.com www.dohakac.com

The Force of Nature

The Force Of Nature This statue by Italian artist Lorenzo Quinn, is exactly what it says, a tribute to the force of nature, specifically hurricanes. Made of bronze, iron and stainless steel it overlooks the sea just east of the Amphitheatre. Similar statues to this Katara one another can be seen in Berkley Square London New York and China and a variant in Reston USA.

Rough GPS - 25.360 , 51.527 Street - Katara Amphitheatre - Katara / كتارا Public Transport - Metro Red Line Al Qassar or Katara

Katara Club / نادي كتارا- Karata Club is an upmarket Spa & Gym directly on the northern section of the beach at Katara. The setting is matched by its ambiance and general club service; the restaurants let down the experience slightly.

Typical hours - Sun - Thurs 06:00-22:00 - Fri & Sat 09:00-21:00 Entry charge - membership -

Rough GPS - 25.361 , 51.529 Street - off Shakespeare St - Katara / كتارا Public Transport - Metro Red Line Katara

Contacts - +974 4408 1580 info@katara.club www.katara.club/

Three Monkeys - Gandhi's Three Monkeys (a somewhat sarcastic title) by Subodh Gupta is based on the See no Evil, Hear no Evil, Speak no Evil in a scrap metal military perspective are just outside Saffron Restaurant in Katara.

Rough GPS - 25.359 , 51.527 Street - Katara Amphitheatre - Katara / كتارا Public Transport - Metro Red Line Al Qassar or Katara

Al Gannas / القناص - Al Gannas (The Hunter) is an organisation which promotes the tradition of Falconry or Saluki hunting. Their headquarters in Katara is in the shape of a Falcons 'Burka' (Rufter). They hold an annual Marmi Festival during most of January in the sand desert south-west of Mesaieed (very appx location 24.894, 51.465) with Falcon hunting and Saluki races. (They start at 06:00 & 12:45 appx)Free 4x4 transport may be available from the 'Sealine Roundabout' 24.863, 51.513. For this event it is essential to check with organisers and ideally take their complimentary transport offer.

Typical hours - 07:00-14:00 Sun - Thurs

Rough GPS - 25.362 , 51.527 Street - off Lusail Expressway - Katara / كتارا Public Transport - Metro Red Line Al Qassar or Katara Contacts - + 974-4408 1366 algannas-qtr@katara.net http://algannas.website (also http://algannas.net)

Water Taxi / العبارة - Within The Pearl this public 'water taxi' operates around the enclosed bay area for 20 minutes. It's almost quicker to walk, however as a holiday activity this is a bit unexpected in Doha, its almost, but not quite, La Serenissima. There are several gates - between 25.364, 51.540 (organise tickets here) & 25.366, 51.545. Private hire is possible, against advance booking and charge QAR200/- +. A longer trip that includes the 'Qanat Quarter' (that really is reminiscent of Venice) to The Pearl's north has a charge of QAR50/- for around 40 minutes.

Typical hours - 14:00-00:00 (Public service) Sun - Thurs Entry charge - QAR25/-

Rough GPS - 25.364 , 51.541 Street - Porto Arabia Avenue - The Pearl / اللولو Public Transport - No public transport Contacts - +974 4409 5279 hmo@ronauticame.com www.ronauticame.com

Carbon Wheels - Bike sale and service

Typical hours - 12:00-21:00

Rough GPS - 25.376 , 51.545 Street - Off Pearl Boulevard (near Rialto Bridge) - The Pearl / اللولو Public Transport - No public transport on publication date - expect this to change close to 2022 Contacts - +974 4441 9048 info@carbonwheels.qa www.carbonwheels.qa

Lagoona Mall / لاجونا مول - Lagoona Mall is a modern mall operation within The Pearl. Apart from the expected outlets like McDonalds and Carrefour, it does have a reasonable selection of shops not found in other malls. This is where Doha's Zigzag Towers are located. Also a few major 5* hotels

Typical hours - 10:00-22:00 (Fri 14:00-12:00)

Rough GPS - 25.376 , 51.525 Street - Off Lusail Highway - The Pearl / اللولو Public Transport - No public transport Contacts - +974 4433 5555 Lagoona@darwishholding.com www.lagoonamall.com/

Lusail Racing Circuit

LUSAIL

Lusail Stadium / إستاد لوسيل - The inauguration and final stadium for the 2022 World Cup with 80,000 seats designed by Foster & Partners. From Lusail Metro on the Red Line (and upcoming tram on the Purple Line), it's a 700m walk.

Rough GPS - 25.421 , 51.492 Street - Al Khor Coastal Rd - Lusail (Losail) / لوسيل Public Transport - No public transport on publication date - expect this to change close to 2022

Lusail Multipurpose Sports Arena / ملعب لوسيل الرياضي - Operated by Qatar's Olympic organisation, this is a modern 15,000 seat venue to host indoor sporting and entertainment events. Handball, volleyball, wrestling, badminton and more have a home here; as do musical events and professional wrestling (WWE etc). South of this arena is the Qatar Shooting and Archery complex www.qatarshooting.qa.

Rough GPS - 25.482 , 51.462 Street - Al Khor Coastal Rd - Lusail (Losail) / لوسيل Public Transport - No public transport on publication date - expect this to change close to 2022

Contacts - +974 4494 4777 qoc@olympic.qa www.olympic.qa

The Challenge 2015 - The Challenge 2015 a sculpture by Ahmed al-Bahrani, the Iraqi artist, are 5 giant hands reaching for a Basketball outside the Lusail Multipurpose Hall. Ahmed has several other sculptures in Qatar, including within the National Museum the Flag of Glory a bronze sculpture, again of hands supporting a flagpole with the Qatari flag.

Rough GPS - 25.483 , 51.463 Street - Lusail Multipurpose Hall off Al Khor Rd - Lusail (Losail) / لوسيل Public Transport - No public transport

Lusail Racing Circuit / صالة لوسيل متعددة - Motor race track (5.3km) with track days at least once a month for car, bike, go-carts & who knows, MotoGP and perhaps even Formula 1 - on occasion. It's a floodlit circuit - so also holds stunning night-time events. You should check directly with the track for a schedule. Various dining and hospitality options are available. The track is well north of public transport, the nearest is the Al Manazel Tram stop - a 13km drive away.

Typical hours - 24 Hours Entry charge - per event

Rough GPS - 25.488 , 51.449 Street - Al Khor Coastal Rd - Lusail (Losail) / لوسيل Public Transport - No public transport on publication date - expect this to change over the years Contacts - +974 4472 9151 info@lcsc.qa www.circuitlosail.com

Doha Festival City / دوحة فيستيفال ستي - Large shopping mall, with indoor snow toboggan slope. Midprice retail outlets including IKEA, Riva, Next, Debenhams, Old Navy and large range of Restaurants. Doha Festival City is one of the newest of Doha's large malls and is operated by Al Futtaim, who also run the gulf-wide City Centres, which are managed to a locally high standard, though most are almost indistinguishable from each other.

Typical hours - 10:00-22:00 Sat-Thurs (Friday closed 11:30-13:00)

Rough GPS - 25.386 , 51.443 Street - Junction Al Shamal Rd and - Al Daayen / الضعاين Public Transport - Bus 170, Contacts - info@dohafestivalcity.com www.dohafestivalcity.com- +974 4035 4444 -

Vox Cinema - Multiplex cinema with 3D. Though prices are slightly lower than European prices, the downside is that films may be censored to local requirements, having an impact on a story line and audiences behave as if at home, talking and using phones during screenings.

Typical hours - check film schedule Entry charge - around QAR75 -

Rough GPS - 25.386 , 51.443 Street - Junction Al Shamal Rd - Al Daayen / الضعاين Public Transport - Bus 170, Contacts - https://qat.voxcinemas.com/contact-us qat.voxcinemas.com

Barzan Towers / ابراج برزان - Barzan Towers are a late 19th century early 20th c couple of fortified towers of lime rubble and coral. Like many other buildings of the period in Qatar, these are built by Sheikh Mohammed bin Jassim Al Thani. Though restored 20 years ago, the impact is authentic, including resident pigeons! However, perhaps the main interest of a visit here is the modern housing and opulent palaces, signs of the wealth in Qatar.

Rough GPS - 25.418 , 51.413 Street - west of Al Shamal Rd - Umm Salal / أم صلال Public Transport - Bus 102 (1200metres)

DOHA SOUTH & EAST

. . .

Al Thumama Stadium / استاد الثمامة - In the south of Doha, again not well served by public transport - however Bus 10 does stop on the road outside.

Rough GPS - 25.235 , 51.531 Street - E Ring Road - Al Thumama / الثمامة Public Transport - Bus 10

Dragon Mart and China Mall / سوق التنين - The Dragon Mart / China Mall is more of an alley way rather than a modern shopping mall, but an indoor shopping experience and very focused in its appeal. This is a pile it high - sell it cheap area with Building materials, Fabrics, Electronics and more from the Far East.

Typical hours - Numerous independent shops having individual times around 10:00-22:00

Rough GPS - 25.194 , 51.455 Street - Junction of Industrial Area Rd and East Industrial Street north - Industrial Area / منطقة صناعية Public Transport - Bus 301, 20,21,32,33,57,300,302,304,737

Asian Town / المدينة الاسيويه - This is the general leisure area that serves the large area for expat labour, chiefly from the Indian Subcontinent. Here is a Cricket Stadium 25.190205, 51.461690, open air concert theatre 25.186765, 51.464169, Cinemas, Supermarkets, low cost restaurants. These offer low cost services and products focused on the residents of the vast accommodation 'township' to its east.

Typical hours - A variety of Leisure, Retail and Dining options having different, but very long hours.

Rough GPS - 25.189 , 51.461 Street - Junction of Industrial Area Rd and East Industrial St - Industrial Area / منطقة صناعية Public Transport - Bus 20,21,32,33,57,300,302,304,737

Al Ahli Sports Club / النادي الأهلي الرياض - Qatar's oldest football club is south of the town centre. Al Ahli's football ground is the Hamed bin Khalifa Stadium with a capacity of 12,000 it held the Asian Cup Final in 1988. A variety of public facilities including swimming pool make it worthwhile checking out.

Typical hours - 08:00-22:00

Rough GPS - 25.252 , 51.534 Street - Junction Najma St and D Ring Rd. - Nuaija / نعيجة Public Transport - Bus 10,12, 727 Contacts - + 974 4032 7777 info@al-ahliclub.com www.al-ahliclub.com

Al Arabi Club / النادي العربي الرياضي - Here at Al Arabi Club are several sports facilities, most notably a football stadium, where Al Arabi, which is one of Qatar's most successful clubs, has its home ground. There is a lot more, including basketball and a swimming pool. The club is also home to Qatar's Volleyball Assn

Typical hours - 08:00-22:00

Rough GPS - 25.259 , 51.519 Street - west of Rawdat Al Khail St - As Salatah al Jadeeda / اسلطة الجديدة Public Transport - Bus 12x, 20 Contacts - +974 4467 3666 info@alarabi.qa www.alarabi.qa

Cars 'skiing' down Khor Al Udaid dunes

AL WAKRAH, MESAIEED & SOUTH QATAR

Ras Abu Aboud Stadium / راس أبو عبود - This is practically on the Corniche for the 2022 World Cup, though at the moment it's a walk to reach from public transport.

Rough GPS - 25.289 , 51.565 Street - Ras Abu Abboud St - Ras Abu Aboud / راس أبو عبود Public Transport - Bus 109,777 & Metro Gold Line National Museum

Gulf Youth Bicycle - Sell bikes, mainly cheap aimed at children but usually a few adults in stock

Typical hours - 08:00-12:30-16:00-22:00 (Friday 16:00-22:00)

Rough GPS - 25.214 , 51.580 Street - off Al Wakrah Rd - Barwa Village / قرية بروة Public Transport - Bus 10, 109, 119, 129 Metro Red Line Ras Abu Fontas Contacts - +974 4455 1092

Souq Al Wakrah (Souq Waqif)/ سوق واقف ، الوكرة - Souq Al Wakrah سوق الوكره is a heritage style development a 19km drive south of Doha's centre. At the parking area, golf style buggies are available in the busier evening times to take you into Souq Al Wakrah.

Souq Al Wakrah is comparable in concept to Souq Waqif, though it has a beach front, which is less than a kilometre away, though as with most of Doha's beaches this is not a 'sun-bathing' beach, and is a family only beach 10:00-17:00, with separate male and female changing rooms – do not wear bikinis or speedo style trunks. There is a mix of small shops with a variety of produce including clothing & weapons. The concept is of a residential village, rather than a souq, with 'homes' operating as retail shops and restaurants. Here there are perfume shops, gifts, dried fruit & nuts and sweet shop, cultural shops with things like carpets, swords. A small fish market opens daily but is best early in the morning. A grouping of restaurants on the beach front 25.169225, 51.610372 offer a variety of Middle East cuisines, whole offshore there might be authentic sailing Dhows at anchor offshore. A sea food restaurant is 100m north of the main restaurant area. As with Souq Waqif, Tivoli Hotels have a property, Souq Al Wakrah Hotel; this has five dining outlets and might be an option to consider rather than hotels in Doha, it's a 20 minute drive south of Hamad International Airport.

South of the heritage area is the small port, which usually has dozens of Dhows tied up, the jetty is 1,200m long creating a good evening walk from the beach area.

West of the new heritage area is Abdulrahman bin Jassim Fort 'Al Wakrah Fort' 25.172, 51.605. Currently not open, it has been remodelled with the corner towers reduced in height and with additional buildings.

Typical hours - The souq is made up of individual businesses with their own hours. Most shops open between 10:00-12:00/16:00-22:00 and Restaurants from 10:00-22:00 - Ramadhan timings will vary.

Rough GPS - 25.173 , 51.609 Street - east of Al Wakrah Main St - Al Wakrah / الوكرة - Public Transport Though there is no public transport into Souq Al Wakrah buses 109 & 127, 129 run from Al Ghanim Bus Station to close to it and Al Waqif Metro is the closest station & MetroLink bus M128 route is also close to Souq Al Wakrah – ask at the Metro Station about this or if another service has been introduced as these bus stops are on the wrong side of a road.

Al Wakrah Family Beach / شاطئ الوكرة العائلي - South of Al Wakrah this beach is for women and families only, unaccompanied men are liable for arrest. Unlike hotel beaches maintenance and cleaning is sporadic. The sea is shallow for several hundred meters, so it's difficult to swim in. There are toilets. North is a public beach the sea is relatively shallow off here, with no lifeguard, safety equipment or facilities.

Rough GPS - 25.131 , 51.616 Street - Mesaieed Rd - Al Wakrah / الوكرة Public Transport – as Souq Wakrah

Al Wakrah Park / حديقة الوكرة - The beach area that is over a kilometre north from Al Wakrah Park is used for swimming and barbeques; often by bachelor groups making it unusual for single women to use. It has no lifeguard, safety equipment or other facilities. The bottom is a bit muddy around the mangrove.

Rough GPS - 25.179 , 51.612 Street - Mesaieed Rd - Al Wakrah / الوكرة Public Transport – as Souq Wakrah.

Al Wakrah Fort / قلعة الوكرة - Sheikh Abdulrahman bin Jassim Fort 'Al Wakrah Fort' was probably built in the early 20th century on the site of a previous fort, when Sheikh Abdulrahman was made governor of Al Wakrah. Currently not open, it has been remodelled with the corner towers reduced in height and additional buildings inside. If the gates are open, why not ask if it is possible to look inside.

Rough GPS - 25.172 , 51.606 Street - Al Wakrah / الوكرة Public Transport - Bus 109, 119, 129 Metro Al Wakrah Red Line

Qatar Racing Club / نادي سباق قطر - A track for Motor Bike and Car racing & timed circuits. Events are held mainly Thursday/Friday/Saturday from 18:00 during winter October-April.

Typical hours - as per schedule Entry charge - as per event

Rough GPS - 25.175 , 51.481 Street - north of G Ring Road - Khor Al Udaid / Mesaieed / خور العديد / مسيعيد Public Transport - Bus 20, 32 Contacts - +974-40286000 www.QARc.qa

Al Janoub Stadium Al Wakrah / إستاد الجنوب في الوكر - Designed by the late Zahra Hadid in her sweeping style of building & AECOM, Al Janoub Stadium has 40,000 seats for the 2022 World Cup.

Rough GPS - 25.159 , 51.575 Street - Khat Al Wakrah Rd - Al Wakrah / الوكرة Public Transport - The closest Metro is Al Wakrah which is 7km away, however the MetroLink bus service may offer a service from Metro to stadium. However Bus 119 from Doha does have stops adjacent to the stadium.

Mesaieed Golf Club / نادي مسيعيد للغولف - South of

Doha in Mesaieed, this is at its heart a social club. The golf course is far from international standards, but it is one of The Gulf's last remain courses with 'browns' rather than greens. It is the original course in Doha and part of the Oil Company's facilities. There is also a swimming pool, tennis and the old club house.

Typical hours - 07:00-22:00 Entry charge - membership -

Rough GPS - 24.984 , 51.543 Street - Mesaieed City Rd - Khor Al Udaid / Mesaieed / خور العديد / مسيعيد Public Transport - Bus 109 Contacts - +974 4477 1740 phone contact http://qpic.qa/MesaieedGolfClub/Pages/Home.aspx

Camel & Falcon Activities / أنشطة الجمال والصقور - Arabia doesn't get more Arab than a ride on a camel. Here, opposite the Sealine Hotel, and a bit south along the road near the Sarab Camp (tented accommodation about 500m from a beach +974 6657 3448) are casual Camel Rides and usually Falcon handlers, negotiate the charge. If however you are going to a camp-site near Khor Al Udaid, Camels are available at most (check about this when booking)

Rough GPS - 24.862 , 51.512 Street - Sealine Beach Rd - Khor Al Udaid / Mesaieed / خور العديد / مسيعيد Public Transport - No public transport

Khor Al Udaid / خور العديد - In Qatar's south-east is Khor Al Udaid 'The Inland Sea' and the sand dunes which surround it. The area is on the boundary of Qatar and Saudi Arabia; across the Khor Duweihin (part of The Gulf) is Abi Dhabi.

Khor Al Udaid was designated as a land and sea nature reserve in 2007 and stretches over around 1833 square kilometres. The khor is an inlet of The Gulf and is part of the estuary of the pre-historic river, Wadi Sahba that flowed into The Gulf from the central Arabian plateau. Cascading into the khor are the powder white dunes, which are created from corals and shells. Several sections are locally called 'naqiyat' نقيان meaning pure, a reference to their colour. In the north-west the dunes are scattered, while in the south they are continuous, forming a sea of sand. If you can find undisturbed Sabkha here, and elsewhere, look for the gypsum crystal formation called a 'Desert Rose'. This small formation, usually a few centimetres across, is caused by the evaporated deposits of gypsum or baryte (sulfates) which include some sand. The National Museum's architecture was inspired by this formation. The steeper slopes, most especially undisturbed isolated barchan dunes, might become 'Singing Sands' when the slope collapses and the vibration of the sand passing themselves causes an audible and physical vibration to the dune. This is not a completely empty landscape; small camps have meals available.

Camel rides at desert camp

The dunes are used as a recreational area by 4x4 vehicles, and on the edge of the sea are quite a few permanent camps, that offer lunches or overnight stays. The powder-like nature of the sand does mean that driving on them is particularly challenging as the sand is an extremely soft base for vehicles, so careless driving can cause a vehicle to bog down.

Most local tour operators provide excursions into the dunes. Part of the Qatari / Saudi border runs through the water less than 200m from the land, take care not to swim into Saudi waters as you will be an illegal immigrant.

Rough GPS - 24.615 , 51.365 Street - Khor Al Udaid / خور العديد Public Transport – no public transport & 4x4 is required

Gulf Adventures Camp Beach Camp - On the edge of relatively shallow seas and powdery white sand dunes, this camp run by Gulf Adventures offers a getaway from Doha - ideal if you don't like self-catering camping. The set up allows for dozens of people to enjoy the combination of sun, sea and sand - camels are on call, the only missing ingredient to the Instagram perfect setting is a few coconut palms. There are several alternative camps, run by other companies.

Rough GPS - 24.805 , 51.491 Street - On the East Coast south of Mesaieed مسيعيد - Khor Al Udaid / Mesaieed / خور العديد / مسيعيد Public Transport - No public transport Contacts - +974 4436 1461 www.gulf-adventures.com

Jebel Nakhsh / جبل نخش - Set on the stone desert of southern Qatar, with electricity pylons marching towards the horizon. One of the more distinctive hills in Qatar, due to it rising sharply about 100m above the surrounding plain. Remains of fossil sea creatures from the Miocene period can be seen embedded in the rock. The site is 1km off the road, so it's a 4x4 journey.

Rough GPS - 24.875 , 50.907 Street - West of the Salwa Rd near the Saudi Arabian border. - Salwa / سلوى Public Transport - No public transport

Al Mashabiya and Al Eraiq reserves. / محميه لعريق المسحبيه - The Al Mashabiya Reserve opened in 1997 as a 54 sq km breeding facility, that is partially fenced, for native ungulates especially Arabian oryx; it also has Sand gazelle and Ostrich. The Al Eraiq Reserve was established later to prevent overgrazing. The area is gravel plain, sand sheets, wadis, mesa, etc. The vegetation consists of *Acacia tortilis, A. ehrenbergiana, Lycium shawii, Ziziphus spina christi*, etc. Other species also include Arabian hare along with Spiny tailed lizard; a large number of bird species can also be seen.

Typical hours - NOT OPEN to general public.

Rough GPS - 24.837 , 50.876 Street - east of Junction 5 on the Salwa Rd close to Salwa Beach - Salwa / سلوى Public Transport - No public transport

Qatar National Library

EDUCATION CITY and DOHA WEST

British Council Qatar / المجلس البريطاني في قطر - The British Council is an educational and cultural organisation. A semi-government conduit for British services

Typical hours - 08:00-20:00 Sunday-Thursday

Rough GPS - 25.280 , 51.490 Street - Al Saad / السد Public Transport - No public transport Contacts - +974 800 5501 general.enquiries@qa.britishcouncil.org www.britishcouncil.qa

Dressage

Al Shaqab Horse Racing Academy & Arena / أكاديمية الشقب لسباق الخيل - Dressage and show jumping area with periodic events (see media or website). This is a state of the art academy for riding with extensive, and expensive, stabling for Arabian and Thoroughbred horses. Tours are available against booking. Consider staying in Al Shaqab Hotel, within the grounds, a small hotel with comfortable accommodation and restaurant - a walk from the hotel block. https://www.amlak.com.qa/en/portfolio/al-shaqab-hotel/ Endurance horse racing is also held based from Qatar Endurance Village 24.967, 51.506 at Mesaieed south of Doha. Events are usually on Saturdays with a start in the early morning. The events are 100km+ so they last much of the day (with physical checks during the event). 4x4 vehicle is essential to view. If you contact the event organisers they may be able to offer options to view.

Typical hours - Events as per schedule - normal working hours 07:30-15:30 Sun-Thurs

Rough GPS - 25.306 , 51.440 Street - Al Shaqab St - Al Shaqab / الشقب Public Transport - Bus 42,57 Metro Green Line Al Shaqab Contacts - (+974) 4454 1992 alshaqabtours@qf.org.qa www.alshaqab.com

Central Market Area / السوق المركزي - Until the mid 1990s the Central Markets area was on the edge on the urban area of Doha, an ideal location for a major 75 hectare wholesale market. Today urban sprawl has included towns 8km, and more, west of these market's within Doha's built up metropolis. The markets spread south for 2km along Wholesale Market Rd and included (from north at Salwa Rd to the south) a general market, the 'Omani' Souq (named because of the large number of Omani merchants who set up business there in the 1950s) several fruit and vegetable markets including Dates, a Fish Market, Sheep & Goat Market, Bird Market, Camel Market and separately a slaughter house. The Doha Municipal plant nursery finishes this row of flora and fauna oriented establishments. This area is oriented towards a wholesale / bulk buy customer and the surroundings match the low cost of the produce. For a visitor this is a remarkable insight into shopping for many of Qatar's resident, low paid workers.

Typical hours - 07:00-21:00 daily

Rough GPS - 25.248 , 51.476 Street - at the junction of

Wholesale Market St and Salwa Rd - Abu Hamour (Bu Hamour) / بوهامور Public Transport - Bus 33,33a, 43,136, 136a,137,137a

Aspire Park / حديقة اسباير - Aspire is a public family only park with large grassed areas and relatively mature trees. A lake is the principal feature - beside which is the stature / sculpture Percival. A jogging track of about 3km runs around it. Like many areas in Qatar there is free wi-fi. Some small cafes offer snacks. Very limited car parking for its size. Though open 24 hours a day, the facilities have a more limited opening time.

Typical hours - 08:00-22:00

Rough GPS - 25.254 , 51.436 Street - Aspire / اسباير Public Transport -

Perceval - Sarah Lucas, a British artist who often uses humour in her work, created Perceval a Bronze life size English Shire Horse and Cart (with cement vegetable Marrows), on the western site of the lake in Aspire Park. This sculpture is representative of the small ceramic ornaments found in British homes of the mid-20th century.

Rough GPS - 25.260 , 51.436 Street - Aspire Park - Baaya / Aspire / اسباير / بعيا Public Transport - Bus 31,32,136,136a,137,137a,301 Metro Sports City.

Al Saad Sports / نادي السد الرياضي - Local sports club (football based) with swimming pool adjacent

Typical hours - 08:00-22:00

Rough GPS - 25.266 , 51.483 Street - off Al Nadi St - Fereej Al Soudan / فريج السودان Public Transport - Bus 31, 32 , 301 Contacts - +974 4444 8080 alsadd@mcs.gov.qa www.al-saddclub.com

Ali Bin Hamad Al Attiyah Arena / ملعب علي بن حمد العطية - A multi-purpose indoor arena for Handball, Badminton, Boxing, Wrestling

Typical hours - 08:00-23:30 Entry charge – per some events

Rough GPS - 25.270 , 51.490 Street - Al Nadi St - Fereej Al Soudan / فريج السودان Public Transport - Bus, 31,33a,34,136,136a,137,137a Metro Al Sudan Contacts - +974 4032 5529 www.abha-arena.com

Al Rayyan Racing & Equestrian Club / مضمار السباق والفروسية - An impressive Horse Race Track and Show Jumping Arena with world class facilities and viewing options. The schedule is weekend oriented however major events spread over the several months from Oct-May.

Typical hours - As per racing and event schedule - check media - events are usually on Wednesday Thursday (Thursday is the most regular) afternoon - from 15:30. Entry charge - usually no charge -

Rough GPS - 25.280 , 51.427 Street - Furousiya St - Muaither / معيذر Public Transport - Bus 40 or 43, 57

+ 974 4482 5708 info@QARec.gov.qa www.QARec.gov.qa

Racing & Equestrian Club / نادي السباق والفروسية - Events are held from November - April, especially on Wednesday & Thursday from 16:00. The grandstand can accommodate 3,000 spectators, which is good as it's a free-to-enter track. The parade ring and winners enclosure are beautifully laid out. The ideal day to visit is of course for the Amir's Sword race - held on the last Saturday in February. There is a riding school within the overall complex and Qatar Equestrian Federation www.qefed.com

Typical hours - as per event Entry charge - usually no charge -

Rough GPS - 25.278 , 51.428 Street - Furousiya St - Muaither / معيذر Public Transport - Bus 43, 67 Contacts - +974 44825708 info@QARec.gov.qa www.QARec.gov.qa

Souq Al Ali / سوق العلي - This is a low cost traditional, as in before the glitzy shopping malls, shopping area. A mix of shops with grocery, pet shops, clothing and fast food.

Typical hours - Independent shops

Rough GPS - 25.319 , 51.470 Street - Junction Khalifa St and Doha Expressway - Al Luqta / اللقطة Public Transport - Bus 45

Al Wajbah Fort / قلعة الوجبة - Built by the start of the 19th c this small fort is to the west of Doha's centre. The fort is a courtyard type with a range of rooms opening directly onto the courtyard. It has been substantially restored. Currently not open it is set between two very high security buildings, do ensure you adhere to non-photography of these and any prohibited notifications.

Rough GPS - 25.302 , 51.393 Street - south of Dukhan Rd. - Al Wajbah / الوجبة Public Transport - Bus 40,41,42,57 (2km walk)

Mall of Qatar - A vast shopping mall, far from other attractions, the Mall of Qatar is on the road to the Camel Race Tracks and west coast. Its full of franchise shops with a few local brands – however is it different enough to make the drive worthwhile.

Typical hours - 10:00-23:00

Rough GPS - 25.324 , 51.350 Street - off Dukhan Highway / National Day Ceremonial Rd - Al Rayyan / الريان Public Transport - Bus 104, 104a from Al Ghanim Bus Station Contacts - +974 4034 6000 www.mallofqatar.com.qa

Al Rayyan Stadium (Ahmed bin Ali Stadium) - West of Doha on the Dukhan Highway. One of the World Cup 2022 stadiums

Rough GPS - 25.330 , 51.341 Street - Dukhan Highway - Al Rayyan / الريان Public Transport - Al Riffa Green Line & Bus 104, 104a

Mathaf: Arab Museum Of Modern Art / متحف: المتحف العربي للفن الحديث - Mathaf: Arab Museum of Modern Art occupies a re-purposed school building and was opened in 2010. Part of the Qatar Foundation. It is based around the collection of Sheikh Hassan bin Mohamed bin Ali Al Thani, who created the sculpture Motherland in the National

Museum. The museum organises frequent exhibitions, principally of local artists. The museum offers a broad range of learning opportunities and resources and periodically holds show from students. A substantial area of outdoor sculptures adds interest to a visit as does a selection from its permanent collection. A small gift shop and cafe adds to the experience.

Typical hours – Sat-Thurs 09:00-19:00 Fri 13:30-19:00 Entry charge - QAR50 (non residents of Qatar) on-line booking https://qm.org.qa/tickets/select-tickets/ -

Rough GPS - 25.310 , 51.419 Street - Al Luqta St, just before start of Dukhan Highway via Gate 1 entrance (or from Al Rayyan Al Jadeed St) - Education City / المدينة التعليمية Public Transport - No public transport - however Mathaf has operated a shuttle service Mathaf>Qatar National Library> Fire Station>Museum of Islamic Art>Qatar National Museum (make enquiries specifically about this) Contacts - +974 4402 8855 mathaf_info@qma.org.qa www.mathaf.org.qa

Khalifa International Stadium / استاد خليفة الدولي - In the Aspire zone, with excellent public transport and a couple of hotels, including The Torch.

Rough GPS - 25.264 , 51.447 Street - Al Waab St - Baaya / Aspire / اسباير / بعيا Public Transport - Bus 31, 32, 136, 136a, 137,137a,301 Metro Gold Line Sports

Aspire Ladies Gym Comprehensive fitness centre with swimming pool, gym and exercise classes. Ladies only.

Typical hours - 07:00-20:00 Sat-Thurs Entry charge - from QAR150 monthly -

Rough GPS - 25.261 , 51.447 Street - Junction Al Waab St and Aspire Park Rd - Baaya / Aspire / اسباير / بعيا Public Transport - Bus 31,32,136,136a,137,137a,301 Metro Al Aziziya (Villaggio) Contacts - +974 4413 6430 http://aspire-activeqa.com/ladies-gym-doha/

Villaggio Mall - Perhaps the most interesting mall in Qatar, for visitors. With a boating canal (a short trip QAR15), ice skating & more and a good range of retail outlets including Virgin MegaStore, Carrefour, and high to mid-price brands.

Typical hours - 09:00-22:00 (Friday closed 11:00-12:30 prayer time)

Rough GPS - 25.259 , 51.445 Street - Junction Al Waab St and Aspire Park Rd - Baaya / Aspire / اسباير / بعيا Public Transport - Bus 31,32,136,136a,137,137a,301 Metro Al Aziziya (Villaggio) Contacts - +974 4422 7400 info@villaggioqatar.com www. www.villaggioqatar.com

Villaggio Mal

Cinema Qatar - Within the Villaggio Mall shopping mall there are several screens here, including some with iMax. Though prices are slightly lower than European prices, the downside is that films may be censored to local requirements, having an impact on a story line and audiences behave as if at their home, talking and using phones during screenings.

Typical hours - Check film screenings Entry charge - around QAR75 -

Rough GPS - 25.259 , 51.445 Street - Junction Al Waab St and Aspire Park Rd - Baaya / Aspire / اسباير / بعيا Public Transport - Bus 31,32,136,136a,137,137a,301 Metro Al Aziziya (Villaggio) Contacts - info@cinemaqatar.com support@cinemaqatar.com

Gondolania Ice Rink & Leisure / جوندولينيا للتزلج - Located inside Villaggio Mall possibly Doha's most quirky mall, this is an extensive indoor leisure area, focused on children. Given its name there has to be Gondolas, add in Go Karts from QAR70, Ice Skating QAR35 upwards, Laser Games from QAR40, 10-Pin Bowling, Roller Coaster and so on.

Typical hours - 09:00-23:00 Daily Entry charge - from QAR 30 up to QAR150 -

Rough GPS - 25.259 , 51.445 Street - Junction Al Waab St and Furosiya - Baaya / Aspire / اسباير / بعيا Public Transport - Bus 31,32,136,136a,137,137a,301 Metro Al Aziziya (Villaggio) Contacts - +974 4403 9800 info@gondolania.com www.gondolania.com

The Miraculous Journey - This series of 14 sculptures by Damien Hurst, portrays the development of a baby in the uterus, from conception to birth. These are true to life and unmissable. In any city they would attract controversy, as they have done in Doha. The cost is reported to have been US$20 million

Rough GPS - 25.321 , 51.444 Street - Sidra Medical and Research Centre exterior - Education City / المدينة التعليمية Public Transport - Metro Green Line Qatar National Library and then a 5 minute walk

Education City (Qatar Foundation Stadium) - Sports

stadium in Education City and with good Metro services and a Premier Inn not far away.

Rough GPS - 25.311 , 51.426 Street - Al Rayyan Al Jadeed St - Education City / المدينة التعليمية Public Transport - The closest Metro is Education City, about 600m walk away.

Qatar National Convention Centre / مركز قطر الوطني للمؤتمرات - This is a substantial modern convention centre, home to the spider sculpture Maman by Louise Bourgeois. Exhibition halls, modern auditoriums for conferences as well as entertainment events with smaller halls and rooms offer space for smaller events such as board meetings. Concerts of various types are held in the convention centre, often in the smaller halls. For information and tickets check out https://qatarphilharmonicorchestra.org. Parking availability is substantial with a quoted 2,800 spaces (many of which are used by staff), also there are direct Metro links, good Bus options and of course Taxis offer flexible options.

Typical hours - as per events

Rough GPS - 25.321 , 51.437 Street - Al Luqta St/ Dukhan Highway - Education City / المدينة التعليمية Public Transport - Metro Green Line Qatar National Library Contacts - +974 4470 7000 sales@qncc.qa www.qncc.qa

Maman - Not for people with arachnophobia, Mamam is a giant spider sculpture in the Qatar National Convention Centre. The artist, Louise Bourgeois, must be a fan of the Hobbit & Lord of the Rings with their giant spiders. The sculpture is one of 6 other mothers in locations including the Tate Modern London, National Gallery Canada and Crystal Bridges Museum in Arkansas and they are a reference to her mother in the form of a giant spider.

Rough GPS - 25.321 , 51.438 Street - Qatar National Convention Centre, Al Luqta St - Al Rayyan / الريان Public Transport - No public transport

Qatar National Library / متاحف مشيرب - A massive several story, state of the art modern library; the Qatar National Library functions not only as a normal public library but is a research facility and also the state repository. The building is in a modern deconstructionist style with an extraordinarily bright, rather than a dim style favoured by so many libraries. There is plenty of space to sit and research, it's a vast space. Hidden beneath the floor is a state-of-art book delivery system, where borrowers can deposit a returned book (at ground level) in a receptacle and it is automatically delivered to the correct book shelving using RFID chips.

Typical hours - Saturday – Thursday: 8:00 AM - 8:00 PM Fridays: 4:00 PM - 8:00 PM

Rough GPS - 25.319 , 51.442 Street - Al Luqta St - Education City / المدينة التعليمية Public Transport - Bus 42,57 Metro Green Line Al Shaqab Contacts - +974 4454 6039 qnl@qnl.qa www.qnl.qa

VCU Gallery (Virginia Commonwealth University School Of The Arts In Qatar) / جامعة فرجينيا كومنولث للفنون في قطر - If you are in Education City, drop in here for a changing exhibition of student's art.

Typical hours - 09:00-12:00 Sun-Thurs Entry charge - No Charge -

Rough GPS - 25.314 , 51.434 Street - south of Al Luqta St - Education City / المدينة التعليمية Public Transport - No public transport Contacts - +974 4402 0555 www.qatar.vcu.edu

Education City Golf Club / نادي مدينة التعليمي للجولف - New course 18 hole (+ short course)

Typical hours - 07:00-17:00 Entry charge - membership -

Rough GPS - 25.303 , 51.422 Street - Al Rayyan Al Jadeed St - Education City / المدينة التعليمية Public Transport - Bus 40, 104,104a Contacts - +974 7773 7973 Info@ecgolf.com www.ecgolf.com

Rayyan Castle / قلعة الريان - Rayyan Castle is also known as Sheikh Ali bin Abdullah Fort, Sheikh Ali was the

Emir of Qatar from 1949-1960. The fort is essentially a fortified residence, which then was outside Doha. The substantial wall 180m on each side enclosed a number of other buildings including a mosque. North of the fort is a secondary fortified building. A nice detail is the roofline over the entrance door with detailing in the colour and form of the serrations on the Qatari flag. Currently Rayyan Fort is not open.

Rough GPS - 25.301 , 51.431 Street - Al Rayyan Al Jadeed St - Al Rayyan / الريان Public Transport - Bus 57, 104,104a Metro Green Line Al Shaqab

Mangrove *Avicennia marina*

NORTH-EAST

. . .

Al Bayt Stadium / استاد البيت - This will host matches including semi-finals. Designed to look like an Arab tent with 60,000 seats the stadium is a 60km drive from Doha. With very limited hotels in the area, The Sultan Beach Resort is the best option 7km away.

Rough GPS - 25.652 , 51.484 Street - Al Khor Coastal Rd - Al Khor / الخور Public Transport - Bus 102

Al Uqda, Equestrian Complex / اسطبلات العقدة - Al Uqda Equestrian Complex is a multipurpose facility, with a grass race track, jumping arena and riding school. It periodically holds public events, over a dozen race days (from Nov-Feb), and Arab horse shows and auctions. Winter, as with most sporting events in Qatar, is the best time to see these.

Typical hours - open to suite events

Rough GPS - 25.672 , 51.438 Street - off Dukhan Highway - Al Khor / الخور Public Transport - No public transport Contacts - +974 4482 5708 info@QARec.gov.qa https://QARec.gov.qa/

Al Khor Beach / شاطئ الخور - North-east of Al Khor and east of Al Thakhira after a rough unmarked drive of 4km are a series of small beaches with shallow water - and areas of seaweed and seagrass.

Rough GPS - 25.717 , 51.593 Street - off Al Khor Coastal Rd - Al Khor / الخور Public Transport - No public transport

Al Khor Park / منتزة الخور - Around 9km south-west of Al Khor is a 20 hectare family only (except Sundays), reasonably well maintained park, that is extremely busy at weekends. There are places for children to play at including a Miniature Railway, basketball, skating and as an added bonus a small Zoo with a limited variety of animals that includes Arabian Oryx and a Children's play areas. This offers an alternative to the parks in Doha, the zoo animals would benefit from a better environment.

Typical hours - 08:00-22:00 Entry charge - QAR15/- -

Rough GPS - 25.649 , 51.420 Street - Al Shamal Rd - Al Khor / الخور Public Transport - Bus 102, 727 or 100,101,

Al Thakhira / Al Dakhera / الذخيره - This is the largest area of mangrove in Qatar. Coral reefs, seagrass beds, etc with offshore Hawksbill turtle. The mangroves of Al Thakhira lie opposite Al Thakhira village and near Al Khor town. Flora include *Avicenna marina* (Mangrove), *Anabis setifera, Salsola imbricate, Lycium shawii* etc. The fauna includes over 130 species of birds, and reptiles including Hooded malpolon, Spiny tailed lizard and numerous insects. Kayaking can be done though the mangrove (see operators p235)

Rough GPS - 25.748 , 51.540 Street - Al Thakhira - Al Khor / الخور Public Transport - Bus 102

Al Jassasiya (Al Gasasia) Rock Art / الجساسية - The petroglyphs at Jebel Al Jassasiya are promoted by the Qatari government to illustrated Qatar's history and maritime heritage. Petroglyphs were first noted in Qatar, by non-locals in the 1950s, and these at Jebel Al Jassasiya were noted in the 1960s and recorded in detail in 1974. Quarrying in the area has since reduced the number of these at Jebel Al Jassasiya, but still the site consists of 12 low outcrops of rock with several hundred examples of petroglyphs. They are on either side of the tarmac road, enclosed by a badly damaged fence. Both line art and 'cupules' (small circular round depressions, cups, arranged in clusters) are represented. The cupules are probably a version of mancala, the widespread game play of moving a small object (stone etc) along the cups in a manner to defeat an opponent. The others

Al Jassasiya

are line drawings, typically of various types of dhows. Many of these have been stylistically interpreted to date between the 11th and early 16th century. Other line drawing include wasms (tribal markings) and human figures and animals.

Rough GPS - 25.952 , 51.406 Street - A few kilometres to the east of route 1 - Ash Shamal / الشمال Public Transport - No public transport

Fuwairit Beach / شاطئ فويريت - Fuwairit Beach is public and relatively busy at the weekend. Access is via the Al Shamel Rd and then off road. Attached to the mainland (north of the palaces and abandoned ruins) is a sand-spit which is a key location for Hawksbill Turtle nesting (this beach is closed as a result at peak season 1st April to 31 July). Mangroves line the silted khor (creek).

Rough GPS - 26.059 , 51.354 Street - East of Al Shamel Rd north of Doha - Ash Shamal / الشمال Public Transport - a very long walk of 3 kilometres Bus 101, 201

Al Mafjar Beach / شاطئ المفجر - Opposite the small ruined village of Al Mafjar an isolated beach area and sand spit extend to Qatar's most northerly point. The sand is very loose and a 4x4 is essential no lifeguard, safety equipment of facilities.

Rough GPS - 26.136 , 51.301 Street - off Al Shamal Rd - Ash Shamal / الشمال Public Transport - No public transport

Um Tais Island / جزيرة ام تيس - Um Tais Island (Tais is a male goat – so this is the 'Mother of the Male Goat Island')is substantial sand bar off Qatar's northern coast. It's just separated from the mainland, so is a relatively undisturbed place and so low lying that parts are destroyed and rebuilt during storms. To its northwest is a separate sand bar, Ras Rakan Island, which is more disturbed. Substantial areas of

Mangrove add to Um Tais's attraction. Opposite, on the mainland, is the only hotel in northern Qatar Zulal Wellness Resort.

Rough GPS - 26.156 , 51.276 Street - off Al Shamal Rd - Al Ruwais / الرويس Public Transport - No public transport

Jazirat Ras Rakan (Island) / جزيرة ام تيس - A small sandy offshore island with seagrass off its beaches. Opposite, on the mainland, is the only hotel in northern Qatar Zulal Wellness Resort.

Rough GPS - 26.178 , 51.226 Street - off Al Shamal Rd - Al Ruwais / الرويس Public Transport - No public transport

Al Zubarah

AL RUWAIS, WEST COAST and DUKHAN & CENTRAL QATAR

Ash Shahaniyah Camel Race Track/ الشيحانية ميدان السباق للهجن - If you visit Doha in the winter (Nov - March)

Ash Shahaniyah should be on your list of places to visit. Camel Racing is an important part of Qatari identity as the government promotes it extensively, with not only creating the course but with prizes including the 'Golden Sword'. Camels themselves often have high value and all this does create an entire culture around the sport. Here there are 5 tracks - of varying length, where camels and their robot jockeys careen around an oval track. Each track has a companion car track, where numerous trainers race around in their 4x4 vehicles as if veritable Lewis Hamiltons, screaming encouragement to their jockey & camel via walky-talky! Racing schedules are here https://www.hejen.qa/races or training happens on most days in early mornings or late afternoons. There are plenty of opportunities for photography. The main events have senior members of the ruling family in attendance and substantial prices. The start is to the right of the entrance road & - after completing the vast oval track - the finish and grandstand is to the left - Given the race is several kilometres you can catch both start and finish; there is no charge for grandstand entry. Use the toilets in the petrol station on the Dukhan Highway before the track (or McDonalds is on the south side of the highway going into Doha - just east of the elevated roundabout) - and buy water.

Typical hours - as per race Entry charge -

Rough GPS - 25.402 , 51.205 Street - signed off Dukhan Highway - Al Rayyan / الريان Public Transport - Bus 104, 104a (about 70mins bus and walk 3km or use a taxi)

Sheikh Faisal Bin Qassim Al Thani Museum / متحف الشيخ فيصل بن قاسم آل ثاني - An eclectic private museum collection created by its eponymous founder, the Chairman of City Centre in Doha, amongst other businesses.

Purpose built in 1998, the museum is the wide ranging accumulation of items by Sheikh Faisal Bin Qassim Al Thani. The museum is a single story building, spread over a large area with currently over a dozen halls (the museum is being extended), its over 200m in length fortunately on a single floor. There are exhibits both inside and outside from a wide geographical area, including Japan to the USA and a vast time span, from geology through to the late 20th century.

Though without a particular focus, the exhibits are well laid out, unfortunately without a great deal of information. There are highlights. A vast range of boats from The Gulf region are laid out, mostly indoors; there are so many that it's difficult to take each one in. A weaponry section is set amongst general material about Qatar, including its rulers. There are mannequins with Qatari costumes, though it would be good if the mannequins themselves were more appropriate. The collection of vehicles, motorcycles and other transport, including palanquins is remarkable. The cars are mostly from the USA and include some of the earliest vehicles used in Qatar, all it would appear in road-worthy condition. Part of the interior of a house from Damascus has been relocated into Qatar, and set up as if in use. Enough beautiful carpets to cover a football stadium; the collection goes on and on.

It's a remarkable collection, let down by lack of space (which may be improved soon) and information. Outside and adjacent to the museum it's possible to view Oryx.

Typical hours - Sun-Thurs 09:00-16:00 Fri 14:00-19:00 Sat 10:00-18:00 Entry charge - QAR 75 (100 with tour) -

Rough GPS - 25.351 , 51.262 Street - Al Dukhan Highway - Ash Shahaniyah (near) / الشحانية Public Transport - Bus 104, 104a, 300 Contacts - visitors@fbqmuseum.org www.fbqmuseum.org

Arabian Oryx *Oryx Leucoryx*

Mohamed Al Dosari Zoo / حديقة ومحمية محمد الدوسري - An example of a local private zoo, set up in the manner of a poor mid 20th century animal display, with animals in crowded pens and cages. It will be eclipsed if the Doha Zoo ever reopens. Additionally extra displays and activities with charge including Horse, Camel rides

Typical hours - 07:00-19:00 Sat-Friday Entry charge - QAR10/-

Rough GPS - 25.440 , 51.224 Street - off the Dukhan

Highway taking the exit before Al Shahaniyah Camel Race Track - Ash Shahaniyah / Public Transport - Bus 104a Contacts - +974 44908785 AlDosariZoo@Hotmail.com

Al Wabra Wildlife / منطقة حيوان الوبرة - Set up in the mid 1970s as a private zoo, Al Wabra has more recently developed into a breeding zoo. The animals include Arabian Goitered Gazelle, Arabian Mountain Gazelle and Arabian Oryx. Other species include Sand Cat and Cheetah.

Typical hours - Not open to the general public.

Rough GPS - 25.346 , 51.176 Street - southwest of Ash Shahaniyah Camel track - Ash Shahaniyah / الشحانية Public Transport - No public transport Contacts - office@alwabra.com www.alwabra.com

Al Samriya Stables / اسطبلات السامرية - A well-established livery stable - Al Samriya Stables also offers riding & other lessons. With four arenas and a range of horses, most people who wish to either learn or ride are catered for. There are ride options outside the arenas.

Typical hours - 07:00-11:00-13:00-15:00 daily Entry charge - riding from QAR185 -

Rough GPS - 25.351 , 51.262 Street - Al Dukhan Highway - Ash Shahaniyah (near) / الشحانية Public Transport - Bus 104, 104a, 300 Contacts - +974 4490 2359 info@alsamriyaestate.com www.alsamriyaestate.com

Al Ruwais Beach / شاطئ الرويس - A small beach, not really for swimming (or sunbathing).

Rough GPS - 26.144 , 51.216 Street - off Al Kasooma St - Al Ruwais / الرويس Public Transport - Bus 100, 101, 201

Al Mina Market / سوق الميناء - Here in Al Ruwais Port in northern Qatar is a retail market offering a wide range of products, mainly from Iran. They include inexpensive carpets, handicrafts, cheap manufactured products and dried fruit and nuts. In short, this is a modern Iranian bazar.

Typical hours - 08:00-18:00 / 08:00-20:00 Sun-Weds / Thurs-Sat .

Rough GPS - 26.141 , 51.207 Street - Al Ruwais Port - Al Ruwais / الرويس

Ghost Villages of western Qatar. Over less than 30km along the coast to the south of Al Ruwais are a series of settlements that range from pirate lairs to a UNESCO World Heritage Site. Unspectacular in themselves, certainly compared to the glitz on the other side of the peninsula, they offer up a mournful impression of the hard life in Qatar before oil. As there are no shops in any, bring water to drink and, as they have very dusty or damp ground, come in shoes to protect you that you do not mind getting filthy. As all face west over the sea, sunsets are an atmospheric time to visit. Though buses to run along the tarmac road, a walk from any stop to the sea & a village is several kilometres one-way for many villages, not recommended for most people in Qatar's heat and humidity.

Al Jemail Village / قرية الجميل - The ruined village of Al Jemail has signed east access off the tarmac road south-west of Al Ruwais. This is one of several similar abandoned villages on the west coast road, south from Al Ruwais. Dating from the min 19th c-mid 20th c the houses are mostly dilapidated, with crumbling walls, which are a mix of lime and coral stones. Some buildings still have their ceilings, which show timber beams, matting and mud/gypsum roof. The least derelict building is the mosque, which still has its old minaret standing. The old doorway allows access to the minarets internal stairs for the call to prayer from its top. The village is just above high-tide and at low tide, vast areas of sand are exposed - making for a good walk or jog. From Al Jemail south to Al Zubarah there are innumerable low stone walls in the shallows of the sea. These are inter-tidal fish traps, 'maskar', which trap fish as the tide goes out. Clearly, this opportunity to capture fish must have been a key reason all these small villages grew up along the coast.

Rough GPS - 26.094 , 51.152 Street - about 8km by road south west of Al Ruwais (the last few hundred meters are on a rough track) - / Public Transport - Bus route 100 and a walk on rough ground from the tarmac.

Khadaj village / قريه خداج - Possibly the smallest of these abandoned ruined fishermen's villages of the north west coast. Here there are perhaps the remains of four houses.

Rough GPS - 26.081 , 51.112 Street - Off the tarmac west coastal Rd,; the last 2km is rough track. - / Public Transport - Bus route 100 and a walk on rough ground from the tarmac.

Al Areesh / العريش - Much of the housing, which is late 19th century and early & mid 20th c, is ruined; it was a settlement of the Al Kabesi tribe. A small more modern building, the old school is on the eastern edge. The mosque's minaret is still standing, it has a doorway leading to stairs up to the minaret's upper platform, from where the call to prayer could be made. To the west is the village's cemetery.

Rough GPS - 26.051 , 51.057 Street - Off the tarmac west coastal Rd, near the Coast Guard station; the last 2km is rough track. - / Public Transport - Bus route 100 and a walk on rough ground from the tarmac.

Qalaat Al Thaqab / قلعة الثقب - This small abandoned fort 11km north-east of Zubarah has three towers and a few rooms. It served to protect the water wells next to the fort. The agricultural area clearly suffers from lack of water, which made the fort's purpose obsolete many years ago. It was restored in 2005 and awaits a purpose. The floral shaped structure next to the fort was built in 2015, presumably as a reference to the wells. Stick to the tracks leading east off the tarmac road as the soil is like powder and after rain will trap vehicles. 4x4 is ideal.

Rough GPS - 26.033 , 51.117 Street - About 3km south on a rough track, off of the tarmac west coast coastal road to the south of Al Ruwais. الرويس Public Transport - Bus route 100 and a long walk on rough ground from the tarmac.

Al Khuwair / الخوير - The abandoned 18th century village of Al Khuwair sits on the edge of a desolate area in north-west Qatar. The village was a base for Rahmah ibn Jabir Al Jalahimi known to Britain as a pirate, and a style icon as he may have been the introducer of the key part of a 'pirate's' dress, the eye patch, having lost one eye. He was previously a partner with the Al Khalifa sheikhs of Bahrain, but feeling he lost out on the benefit of the spoils when they occupied Bahrain became their enemy. He co-operated with the Al Saud who periodically raided and occupied the east coast of Arabia in the late 18th c and avoided conflict with Britain, despite attacking shipping in The Gulf, clearly he was an excellent tactician. Rahmah ibn Jabir died in battle in 1826, after deliberately using his own ship as a floating bomb to destroy a Bahraini ship which had one of the Al Khalifa sheikhs on board. The sand banks and coral off the coast, which protected the village from attack, must have been a key reason for settling here.

Much of the housing, which seems to be late 19th or early 20th century, is ruined; the mosque's minaret is the tallest structure. It has a doorway, leading to the stairs up to the minarets upper platform, from where the call to prayer could be made. Al Khuwair village relied on water from the wells at Al Thaqab about 5km south-east. A few modern houses are set to the east of Al Khuwair. Al Ruwais to the north of Al Khuwair has petrol and shops. When driving off the tarmac stick to tracks as the general area is sabkha and soft mud when wet.

Rough GPS - 26.068 , 51.083 Street - Off the tarmac west coastal Rd, marked with a four radio masts; the last 1500m is rough track. Public Transport - Bus route 100 and a walk on rough ground from the tarmac.

Al-Rekayat Fort / قلعة ركيات - Al-Rekayat Fort is a small, square, fort, in the north-west of Qatar. Like most forts in Qatar, this is a single story building. Al-Rekayat Fort has a single round tower on one corner and the other corners are square towers made from rooms that project beyond the main wall. This fort dates to the 19th century, and was renovated about 30 years ago and some work is being done again. Inside a series of rooms abutted onto the exterior walls, and there are a number of collapsed walls within the fort. There is a water-well in the fort & presumably the adjacent farm makes use of other water sources outside.

Typical hours - a free to access open area, though next to a private farm. Entry charge - no charge -

Rough GPS - 26.051 , 51.130 Street - about 13km by road south west of Al Ruwais (the last 1.5km to the south of the tarmac road are on a rough track). Public Transport - Bus route 100

Freiha / فريحة - Freiha is possibly the oldest of the fishing villages in north-west Qatar. It is believed to date from the 16th c judging from ceramic finds by the University of Copenhagen, bringing it to the period when the Portuguese arrived in The Gulf. Carsten Niebuhr, the German explorer, must have visited the settlement in 1765 as it was included in his map of The Gulf. Almost on the beach is a hypostyle mosque, with a courtyard - an ablution well in the southern corner and the minaret in the eastern corner. To its east is a larger building, about 40m on each side that, probably, was a fort. The settlements cemetery is just to the south of the mosque. Courtyard type housing - the classic Arab style - is widespread, of stone and coral with mud plastered walls. The fort and mosque however were of a better quality with a simple lime plaster. To the north of Freiha, just south of the modern house, is a secondary settlement, which had its own cemetery that is walled so presumably has been in use more recently. In between these two sections of Freiha, set back 100+m from the beach area, are waste middens. Another small satellite settlement is to the south of Freiha. Water was obtained from a well in the higher ground to the east of Freiha. East, beyond the tarmac road, is another abandoned settlement from the mid 19th century to 20th c, Ain Mohammed. Freiha show every sign of having an ebb and flow of population and occupancy, presumably this was similar in many of these other neighbouring villages.

Rough GPS - 26.014 , 51.040 Street - About 22km drive south from Al Ruwais on the west coast road - and about 4km north of Al Zubarah Fort. . The final 1km to the west of the road is across open ground - Al Zubarah / الزبارة Public Transport - Bus route 100 and a kilometer walk on rough ground from the tarmac.

Al Zubarah Fort / قلعة الزبارة - This small mid 20th c military fort represents a key period in Qatar's history as it was built in response to Bahrain's building of an outpost on the Hawar Islands to the south-west. The fort is a single story, with three circular towers and a fourth square tower and rooms against the exterior wall, that face into the courtyard. Inside are photo-descriptions of the area, its history and archaeology. Outside, some rather ordinary buildings have a museum about Al Zubarah. Exhibits include explanations about pearling. A rusting ship's canon, an old Land Rover and usually a couple of camels complete the scene. As this fort is used to symbolize Qatar's history there are periodic special events held here. For more information, see the Al Zubarah UNESCO section [p133].

Typical hours - 09:00-17:00 daily Entry charge - No Charge -

Rough GPS - 25.977 , 51.046 Street - on bus route 100 - Al Zubarah / الزبارة Public Transport - Bus route 100 and a 200m walk on rough ground from the tarmac.

Qalat Murair / قلعة مرير - Built in around 1768, the largely invisible remains of Qalat Murair fort is 300m south-west of Al Zubarah Fort. The Qalat Murair fort was around 160m on each of its four sides. The fort, which is contemporaneous to Al Zubarah, protected the numerous shallow water well around it. In the area around Qalat Murair fort were several courtyard houses and a mosque. Qalat

Murair was destroyed in the 1960s, a period when Al Zubarah Fort was improved and a rough track to the peninsula of Ras Ushairiq, to Al Zubarah's west. The material of the fort may have been used for construction of Al Zubarah Fort.

Rough GPS - 25.974 , 51.043 Street - / Public Transport as Al Zubarah Fort

Al Zubarah Town / الآثار الزبارة - The abandoned town of Zubarah sits as a walled 61 hectare site (the UNESCO site's land area is much larger and extends beyond the fort) that extends about 1.5km along a shallow, sheltered bay. A visit offers a partially excavated 200 years old town in an interesting beach setting with white sand, from coral, and rocky outcrops and offshore a few inter-tidal fish-traps, 'al maskar' المسكر. The town has had some excavations by the University of Copenhagen, but has not be developed as a tourist attraction; indeed the excavations have been infilled. Several species of land mammals can be found near Al Zubarah, Dromedaries and very occasionally Sand Gazelle might be seen, along with fox. In the sea Dugongs feeding on sea-grass and, Common Bottlenose Dolphin which hunt for fish. A number of bird can be found throughout the year, including Socotra Cormorant that might be seen on Umm Jatila Island off the north of Al Zubarah. Osprey might be seen hunting for fish in the lagoon. In winter, Greater Flamingo gather on the mud-flats off-shore. *Uromastyx aegyptia*, Yellow Spotted Agama and Sand Vipers are two reptiles found inland. In the sea other reptiles are found including Green Turtle and Hawksbill Turtles.

To reach Al Zubarah, from the fort a walk west, for about 1.6km which will bring you to about halfway along the town's crescent-shaped outer wall.

South of this south is an old canal of some 1.8km, and two screening walls. These are believed to have served Qalat Al Murair, the ruined for south of Al Zubarah Fort, on the southern side of the road. Much of the southern area outside the walls is sabkha which after rain or very high tide with be wet and in places slippy. The entrance into the town is more-or-less at the centre of its length, and lies away from excavated areas. Within the walls a pathway cuts left (south-west) through the inner wall to where the inner wall meets the shore. To provide a flowing route, this description moves from the south towards the north.

Al Zubarah has two town walls. The outer original wall was, presumably higher than its current height, its generally between 0.5 & 1 meter in width and is about 2.5km long with 22 towers. The inner wall, of about 1km in length with 11 towers, dates after the 1811 destruction of the town and is built over earlier buildings, as the later population occupied a smaller footprint.

In the southwest of Al Zubarah are what are described as fortified 'palatial compounds' each square in outline, the larger is set against the outer wall. This large building of over 100m on each side, with a corner tower on each corner, was practically self-contained with date fruit stores and a hammam. Plaster on the walls included common Arabic decorative features, unsurprisingly with a hint of Persian and India. The smaller palatial compound was only 60m along each wall, with square towers on the corner. In between the two palatial compounds is a mosque, which collapsed only in 1965. Photos show it with columns and arches between them. In the north of the town is possibly another mosque. To the east of the larger palatial compound is a square of a similar size; this also lies immediately next to both the mosque and smaller palatial compound.

North of the compound area is a residential section, which unlike older Arab towns has a regular grid-like street layout perpendicular to the outer wall; it was a planned settlement. Most of the housing was of a courtyard type.

In the central beach area was Al Zubarah's souq. Ample evidence from potsherds show trade with Persia. Just north-west of the souq, is what is assumed to be a small fort. This overlooks deeper water to its south-west and may have been an open harbour. It was probably in the area between the fort and the peninsula of Ras Ushairiq to Al Zubarah's west that British warships sank many dhows in 1895, that were believed to be massed for an attack on Bahrain.

In the northern area of Al Zubarah the outer wall extends into the sea for about 50m, this provided a barrier against ships grounding on the shallow offshore reefs in the norther area of Al Zubarah.

Rough GPS - 25.977 , 51.029 Street - On the Al Shamal Rd northwest of Doha - Al Zubarah / الزبارة Public Transport - Bus 100 (a kilometre walk) Entry charge - no charge

Al Reem Biosphere Reserve - Rawdat Al Numan / منطقة الريم المحمية - The overall Al Reem Biosphere Reserve extends from Al Zubarah to the north, east to Al Ghuwaitiya and south west to Zekreet. Limestone cliffs, mesas, wadis, sabkhas and gravel plains make up this terrestrial site. Coastal swampy mudflats, shallow sea waters rich in seagrass beds. It's an open desolate area, with a surprising amount of human development. Probably the most vegetated area is at Al Numan, where there is scattered acacia, along with farms.

Rough GPS - 25.860 , 51.080 Street - Much of the northwest region of Qatar. There are fenced area such as Rawdat Al Numan روضة نعمان that included vegetated areas - the word روضة /Rawdha / Rawdat means meadow which occurs after rain. The area south of film city is also included. - Ash Shamal / الشمال Public Transport - No public transport

Film City / مدينة السينما - In a desolate area, devoid of trees, most other plants and wildlife Film City a 3,000sqm reimagined Qatari village was created for a Qatari TV series in 2000. At only a few thousand sq meters it's not large, so easy to walk around. The style suggests Souq Waqif's re-build may have been inspired by it. There may be a caretaker who usually welcomes visitors. A stone's throw away is a small Oasis with roaming Ostrich, Oryx and Gazelle (these are not tame and therefore care should be taken especially if you have children).

Film City

A 4x4 is needed as with all off road - its best to have a full petrol tank and at least 2 vehicles. Continuing through the wilderness, about a kilometre father north, on the same track, are a number of modern stone 'huts' build on a low escarpment and one created on a 'yardang'. These huts are not far from the sea and a few beaches. The beaches are about 25km from the tarmac, so it's at least a 50km round-trip. Note that the northern area of this peninsula is a couple of hundred meters from Bahrain's territorial waters in which you would be an illegal visitor. Arrests by both Qatar and Bahrain are made for illegal entry into their territorial waters, if an arrest is made few Embassies will be of any assistance.

Typical hours - 24 Hours Entry charge - no charge -

Rough GPS - 25.578 , 50.847 Street - off route 30 /

Dukhan Highway the West Coast Rd taking the track north with your 4x4 from 25.460376, 50.894989 opposite a parking area. The track is about 16kms and do not leave it as the wet areas are Sabkha where you may get bogged down very easily. After about 7.4kms a track west leads to 4 steel 'planks' about 15m high sunk into the ground – the modern art 'East West'. Close to these (1.5km northwest) is a low cliff face used for rock climbing 25.519947, 50.847781. This track west eventually reaches Zekreet. - Zekreet / زكريت Public Transport - No public transport

East West - 'East West' is a sculpture installation in the west of Qatar by artist Richard Serra. Spread over a distance of 850m East West are 4 massive steel boards, in the middle of a stone desert. Kilroy may never have made it here, but plenty of others have made certain people know that they have been

Rough GPS - 25.517 , 50.871 Street - Brouq nature reserve - Zekreet / زكريت Public Transport - No public transport

Zekreet Fort / زكريت - North-west of the modern village at Zekreet are the ruins of Zekreet Fort. The fort was built around the start of the 19th c. It may have been associated with Rahmah ibn Jabir Al Jalahimi (see Al Khuwair). Like Al Zubarah the fort seems to have been abandoned around 1811. The archaeologist Beatrice de Cardi researched the fort in 1974 as part of the Qatar government's initial research into its history. This fort is a simple design of 1,800sqm with three round towers and a square tower, very typical of other Qatari forts. Traces of rooms can be seen against the interior walls.

Typical hours – 24 hours Entry charge – no charge

Rough GPS - 25.490 , 50.844 Street - From the Dukhan Highway take the exit north to Zekreet. Drive through the village (you will be on a dirt-track road) and onto the fort about 500m north of the village. - Zekreet / زكريت Public Transport - No public transport

Zekreet Beach / شاطئ زكريت - About 300m west of the

Zekreet Rd this shallow, sheltered lagoon is relatively quiet. Kitesurfing is done here and the shallow waters are relatively calm. The sand is very loose and a 4x4 is essential no lifeguard, safety equipment of facilities. Also note that the Qatar / Bahrain International Border runs in the sea on the edge of the coastline.

Rough GPS - 25.471 , 50.849 Street - off Zekreet Rd - Zekreet / زكريت Public Transport - No public transport

Ras Abrouq / رأس أبروق - In northwest Qatar a peninsula with not only Film City but a remarkable variety of archaeology. Flint working and scattered tools might be seen on some of the limestone Mesas. Ubaid pottery of a similar period has been found. The beaches here are overlooked by low limestone cliffs. The most northerly point is a small coastguard station, as Bahrain waters are only a few hundred metres off the beaches.

Rough GPS - 25.622 , 50.832 Street - Al Jamiliyah / الجميلية Public Transport - No public transport

Dukhan Beach / شاطئ دخان - Near Dukhan with some shelters next to the beach and Date palm. Easy access from the tarmac road. Other stretches of public beach lie along the next few kilometres north and south. The west of Qatar has an extended coastline at some distance from roads; also note that the Qatar / Bahrain / Saudi International Border runs in the sea on the edge of the coastline.

Rough GPS - 25.414 , 50.759 Street - Corniche Dukhan - Dukhan / دخان Public Transport - Bus 104,104a,137,137a (a walk of 4 kilometres)

Dukhan Water Sports Club / نادي دخان للرياضات المائية - A small well established club, with access to the sea has lots of activities including swimming pool and Jet Skies. This is a membership Club for employees of companies associated with Dukhan, if you are in Qatar from some time check with somebody for an entrance pass.

Typical hours - 08:00-18:00 Entry charge - by invitation only -

Rough GPS - 25.411 , 50.760 Street - off the Dukhan Highway west of Dukhan. - Dukhan / دخان Public Transport - A kilometre walk from the nearest stop at Dukhan Petrol Station Bus 104,104a,137,137a (at least every hour).

Aqua Park / أكوا بارك - A water park, some 45mins drive south-west of Doha. Only 10 years old, yet its showing its age, with below expected maintenance standards and hygiene. At just over 3 hectares with about a dozen activities, most of which are relatively small, the drive out may be as long as is spent enjoying the activities.

Typical hours - 11:00-20:00 Mon-Weds (Tues Ladies 14:00-22:00) / 10:00-22:00 Thurs-Fri (Fri Family Day) / Sat 10:00-20:00 closed Sunday Entry charge - QAR120 entrance / Child QAR100 (plus some rides extra) -

Rough GPS - 25.155 , 51.294 Street - South of Salwa Rd Rawdath Rashid Interchange - Abu Nakhla / ابو نخلة Public Transport - no public transport Contacts - +974 4490 5878 www.aquaparkqatar.com

Heenat Salma Farm / مزرعة هينة سلمة - An organic farm in central Qatar. Here there is an opportunity to participate in farm life; harvest dates (in season) milk livestock, and enjoy natural food. There is a small farm shop. Holistic treatments are also available, and for a lucky few there are comfortable tents to stay overnight.

Typical hours - as per activity Entry charge - from QAR250

Rough GPS - 25.387 , 51.257 Street - Ash Shahaniyah / الشحانية Public Transport - no public transport Contacts - +974 5096 0007 https://heenatsalma.earth

Mudhlem & Musfur Caves / كهف دحل / كهف مظلم المصفر - Mudhlem and Musfur caves (Al Dhal) are small sinkholes with a potentially hazardous scree slope to clamber down to the bottom. The area has a number of small or potential sinkholes that though fenced off many people do gain access into. Musfur cave is at 25.174, 51.211.

Mudhlem's Rough GPS - 25.123 , 51.228 Street - South of Salwa Rd Mekainis Interchange - Mekainis / مكينيس Public Transport - No public transport

Irkaya Farm / مزرعة ارخايا - Here, to Doha's south-west, is a mix of habitants, mostly man-made, that offer good birdwatching opportunities. The natural environment is a scrubby stony desert. However here there are also several dozen pivot fields for fodder, also to the west of the fields is a substantial settling pond for treated sewage water, with rush (Phragmites australis). This vegetation and water attract insects, such as grasshoppers and flies, these attract lizards and birds all year round. Occasionally people may be seen hawking as there is plenty of prey for their falcons. Irkhaya Farm is about an hour's drive from Doha (4x4 is needed as final few kilometres is rough track). The track off the Salwa Rd south of Junction 5, leads past a couple of farms to aggregate plants and heavy equipment yard - you will be in a dusty environment and will need to navigate through dozens of aggregate trucks. The main settling pond is about 4 kilometres west of the truck yard.

Typical hours - 08:00-16:00 (Fridays 08:00-11:00) Entry charge - no charge -

Rough GPS - 25.013 , 51.163 Street - south of Salwa Rd - / Public Transport - No public transport

Umm Al Maa / ام الماء - Umm Al Maa 'The Mother of Water' is an area in west Qatar, close to the beach, with accessible water aquifers and shallow depressions that collect water after rain. About 400 metres from the beach is an area of graves dated variously to the Bronze Age or mid Iron Age. A small late 19th century early 20th c fort is the most obvious marker of the site.

. . .

Rough GPS - 25.818 , 50.991 Street - Al Ghuwariyah / الغويرية Public Transport - No public transport

General Tourist Service Providers

Air tours - Air tours around Doha area great way to see the city, though they do have restrictions regarding the air-space they can fly in. If you have a choice of times - sunset is a magical time - when the lights start coming on over West Bay. Asfary offer a number of flying experiences. Hot Air Balloon, with a small basket, Paragliding or Gyrocopter with a pilot, Helicopter and Small plane. There are some weight restrictions on Paraflying and the Gyrocopter. Qatar Flying Club offer small fixed-wing flights. The extremely well established Gulf Helicopters provide helicopter flights and photo tours. In all cases, booking several days in advance is suggested. Some experiences are only private to you - others are usually made as part of a group of other passengers. Transport to the place of departure is your responsibility - it may be in the centre of Qatar at Ash Shafallahiyah 25.696 51.361 (60km from central Doha)

Typical hours - Entry charge - as per activity -

Contacts - https://asfary.com / www.qatarflyingclub.net / www.gulfhelicopters.com

Blue Pearl - Blue Pearl offers a range of land and sea activities that are great for all ages. KiteSurf, Standup Paddleboarding (SUP), Kayak, Fatbiking in Doha and in the area around the city, and wilderness camping and other eco activities.

Rough GPS - 25.369 , 51.548 Street - off Lusail Expressway - The Pearl / اللولو Public Transport - No public transport Contacts - +974666 02 830 hello@clubbluepearl.com www.bluepearlexperience.com

Doha Bus - Group Bus tours throughout Qatar - a 24 hop-on hop-off type operation - including Souq Waqif (look for Kiosk on Bank St etc). A different bus ventures as a 4x4 vehicle into the sand dunes south of Doha. If you have two or more people in your party its worth comparing the cost compared to private tours by other companies.

Typical hours - as per event Entry charge - from QAR154 -

Rough GPS - 25.268 , 51.495 Street - Doha Expressway/Al Amir St - Al Nasr / النصر Public Transport - Bus, 31,33a,34,136,136a,137,137a Metro Al Sudan Contacts - +97444422444 hello@dohabus.co www.dohabus.com

Falcon Tours - City Tour, Desert Safari, Dhow and Game Fishing, Yacht

Typical hours - as per event Entry charge -

Rough GPS - 25.289 , 51.539 Street - Building No : 38

7th floor Abdullah Bin Jassim St, Doha, Qatar - Souq Waqif / سوق واقف Public Transport - Bus 76, 177 Metro Gold Line Souq Waqif Contacts - +974 3144 0129 info@falcontoursqatar.com www.falcontoursqatar.com

Golden Adventures Qatar - City Tours, Tours to northern & western Qatar, Desert Safari

Typical hours - as per event Entry charge -

Rough GPS - 25.267 , 51.545 Street - Al Khalidiya Street - Najma / نجمة Public Transport - Bus 11, 757 Metro Umm Ghuwailina Contacts - +974 5501 1031 info@goldenadventuresqatar.com www.goldenadventuresqatar.com

Inbound Tours Qatar - Tours throughout Qatar, including Desert Safari, with optional overnight, and Dhow trips.

Typical hours - as per event Entry charge -

Rough GPS - 25.287 , 51.532 Street - South of Souq Waqif - Souq Waqif / سوق واقف Public Transport - Bus Al Ghanim Bus Station. Metro Gold Line Souq Waqif or Red

Line Al Doha Al Jadeda. Contacts - +974 7745 1196 info@inboundtoursqatar.com www.inboundtoursqatar.com

National Cruise - Cruises in a traditional dhow around the bay at Doha. Cruises can include meals, in some dhows a table dining experience is offered. A great option is an evening cruise, that takes in the lights of the skyscrapers on West Bay. The Qatari government hope to install solar-power and LED lighting to makes its fleet of tourist Dhows more environmentally friendly. Other tour companies are available.

Typical hours - Various times including 10:00. from QAR150 for round trip excluding snacks which are + QAR50. Private cruises are also available

Rough GPS - 25.295 , 51.533 Street - Dhow Harbour off Corniche - Dhow Harbour / ميناء الداو قبالة الكورنيش Public Transport - Bus 76, 777 Metro Gold Line Souq Waqif Contacts - +974 77999666 sales@nationalcruise.com www.nationalcruise.com/

Qatar International Adventures - City tours, Desert Safari, Dhow Cruise, Game Fishing, Helicopter,

Typical hours - as per event Entry charge -

Rough GPS - 25.270 , 51.517 Street - 1st Floor, Office # 7, 16 Al Rawabi St - Rawdat Al Khail / روضة الخيل Public Transport - Bus 21,22,94 Contacts - +974 4455 3954 info@qia-qatar.com www.qia-qatar.com

Q-Explorer - A range of programs in Qatar, essentially Q-Explorer offer most of what Qatar can provide, including a variety of City Tours, Desert Safaris, Kayaking, Scuba and Sae Excursions.

Typical hours - as per event Entry charge -

Rough GPS - 25.318 , 51.528 Street - Doha Tower, Corniche - West Bay / الخليج الغربي Public Transport - Bus 76,777 Metro Red Line WestBay Contacts - +974 4472 5146 info@q-explorer.com www.q-explorer.com

Sea excursions - Several companies offer game fishing as a private activity, (not a group program). Game fishing from

Qatar is a good chance to enjoy warm weather and, usually, not too rough seas. Equipment and bait are supplied, you need to bring your passport. You stand a chance of catching sea-bass, tuna, or grouper (hamour). Much of the fishing from Doha is between Banana Island and off Al Wakrah. The start may be from the Dhow Harbour off the Corniche. Dhow cruises are available from Arabian Adventures or Asfary (and other companies), which are typically you will join other people, and private yacht tours. If you travel with a larger group Asfary also offer houseboats, which can cruise up the coast, slowly, and give a unique, very relaxing half or full day out. For sea-tours that are simple for sightseeing or leisure, a great time to do it is to take in dusk, and enjoy the city lights of West Bay.

Typical hours - daylight hours and is best done in the morning. Entry charge - as per request -

Rough GPS - 25.295 , 51.533 Street - Dhow Harbour off Corniche - Dhow Harbour / ميناء الداو قبالة الكورنيش Public Transport - Bus 76, 777 Metro Gold Line Souq Waqif Contacts - https://qittour.com / http://www.arabianadventuresqatar.com/ https://asfary.com

Skydive Qatar - Obviously for the adventurous and those who like heights. Plunge from a plane over central Qatar - with views of course of land, sea and lots of sky. The office is in Al Saad, Jawaan St near the British Council 25.2776519,51.4907862 and it is ideal to speak with them about the location.

Typical hours - as per event Entry charge - QAR1150(upwards) -

Rough GPS - 25.701 , 51.362 Street - Al Khor (13km west of town - final 2 kilometres are on well graded but rough track) / الخور Public Transport - Al Shamal Rd Contacts - +974 40329173 info@skydiveqatar.com www.skydiveqatar.com

Man with hunting Falcon

POSSIBLE EVENTS IN QATAR

These are held annually – however its always best to check if they will be held as normal.

Jan - **Qatar International Book Fair** - DECC - Large retail book fair - compensating for the lack of bookshops in Qatar

Jan - **Marmi Festival** - Katara (base) - Falcon and Saluki hunting festival. Hawking displays and more, in Khor Al Udaid area. - http://algannas.website/

Feb - **Katara International Arabian Horse Festival** - Katara - Festival focused around Arabian Horses - with events and their equipment. https://kiahf.qa/

Feb - **Al Adaid Desert Challenge** - Khor Al Udaid - Off road (up to 60km) cycling & running event - promoted with the Qatar tourism council - www.aladaid.qa/

Feb - **Al Shaqab International Equestrian Competition** - Al Shaqab - A major CHI (Concours

Hippique International) Show jumping and Dressage event - www.alshaqab.com/

March - **Qatar Marine Festival** - off Katara - Marine festival aimed to promote Qatar's maritime heritage.

March - **Aspire International Kite Festival** - Aspire - Professional kite displays and family kite flying events

Sept - **S'hail Hunting & Falconry** - Katara - A major even about hunting and falconry. - https://s-hail.qa

Sept - **Qatar Shopping Festival** - City-wide - A retail event promoting shopping in Qatar

Oct - **Qatar ITF Tennis Tour** - Khalifa Complex - Tennis tournament - one of many throughout the year. - http://www.qatartennis.org/

Nov - **Qatar International Boat Show** - The Pearl - An international boat show aimed at the local market - with some regional overspill - https://qatarboatshow.com.qa/

Dec - **Qatar Balloon Festival** - Several days of multiple hot-air balloon events

Dec - **Qatar National Day** - Nationwide - especially the Corniche - Patriotic events celebrating Qatar as a nation

Dec - **Souq Waqif and Souq Al Wakrah Spring Festival** - Souq Waqif and Souq Al Wakrah - Entertainment and cultural events in Souq Waqif and Souq Al Wakrah

Dec - **Katara Dhow Festival** - Katara - Traditional Dhows, under sail and more. - www.katara.net/

31

RESTAURANTS

Parisia Souq Waqif

CORNICHE, SOUQ WAQIF & CENTRAL DOHA

Afghan Brothers (one of seven branches all are comparable) - Very Good value **Afghani** (& Pakistani) meat and rice based style food with a local Qatari style. Might only have spoons, ask for knife and fork - or use hands. Take away also available as is assorted Afghani sweets.

Typical cost range - * Rough GPS - 25.273 , 51.496

Street - Al Mirqab al Jadeed St Public Transport - Bus 49,94 Metro Joaan Metro 1km over busy rd. Typical hours - 07:00-01:00 Contacts - +974 4488 8556 / Alnasr@afghan-brothers.com / www.afghanbrothers.com

Saravana Bhavan - An extremely well established **vegetarian** restaurant (a major franchise from India). The food is authentically south Indian. There are other branches in Doha.

Typical cost range - * Rough GPS - 25.283 , 51.537

Street - Ras Abu Abboud St Public Transport - Bus, innumerable bus routes & about 500m south of Al Ghanim Bus Station. Metro Gold Line Souq Waqif or Red Line Al Doha Al Jadeda. Typical hours - 07:00-15:00/17:30-23:00 Friday 07:00-11:30 12:30-23:00 Contacts - +974 4443 5557

Al Adhamiyah - Very popular restaurant south of Souq Waqif - serving **Iraqi** style food that is meat & rice based, have one of their great fruit juices. It's possible to dine indoors or outside. The interior is extremely atmospheric especially upstairs - with extensive use of a 'mashrabiya ' style decoration. The service reflects how busy they are, and also its relatively low cost.

Typical cost range - ** Rough GPS - 25.286 , 51.532

Street - Ali Bin Abdullah St, Doha, Qatar Public Transport - Bus Al Ghanim Bus Station Metro Gold Line

Souq Waqif Typical hours - 12:30-midnight (Midnight) Contacts - +974 4432 4326

Bandar Aden - Authentic, in all respects with **Yemeni** food, meat and rice based. The service is very patchy and cleanliness is not ideal; however the food is freshly prepared. Very popular, they must be getting something right. Ask for cutlery or go Yemeni style and choose a sitting on floor option indoors and use your right hand.

Typical cost range - ** Rough GPS - 25.290 , 51.533

Street - Abdullah Bin Jassim St, Public Transport - Bus 76, 177 Metro Gold Line Souq Waqif Typical hours - 06:00-23:00 (Friday 12:30-23:00) Contacts - +974 44375503 / bandaraden@yahoo.com / http://www.bandaraden.com/

Icons Coffee - In the western area of Souq Waqif, in between the mosque and the camel pens. This fresh looking coffee shop has everything needed to give you a boost when sight-seeing, **coffee, delicious cakes** and more.

Typical cost range - ** Rough GPS - 25.289 , 51.532

Street - Inside Souq Waqif Public Transport - Bus 76, 177 Metro Gold Line Souq Waqif Typical hours - 10:00-midnight Contacts - 974 4408 7777

Pak Pakwan Restaurant - This is a busy ,small local restaurant, with good **Pakistani** food. Good value grilled meats and curries are supported by rice dishes with food and, usually, quick service.

Typical cost range - ** Rough GPS - 25.286 , 51.523

Street - Al Diwan St Public Transport - Bus 40, 41,42,43,45,55,56, 100, 101,101,102x, 104 Metro Msheireb (Hub) Typical hours - 11:30-23:30 (Friday 12:30-23:30) Contacts - +974 3382 2399

Shujaa Restaurant - Small, always busy and inexpensive, share your table with others and enjoy this restaurant's golden anniversary in 2022. The food is loosely **Lebanese** in style. Meat based dishes are available in the evening. This is a stone's throw away from the opulence of

Parisa or just south of the more expensive Al Shurfa. Expect a rushed service and you will not be disappointed.

Typical cost range - ** Rough GPS - 25.289 , 51.533

Street - near Corniche in Souq Waqif Public Transport - Bus 76, 177 Metro Gold Line Souq Waqif Typical hours - 14:00-midnight Contacts - +974 5586 7895

Turkey Central Restaurant - A large, simple restaurant where you probably will be sharing a table with other diners. This is a well established **Turkish** restaurant, geared to high turnover business especially with take-aways. It offers good value food.

Typical cost range - ** Rough GPS - 25.274 , 51.496

Street - Al Mirqab Al Jadeed St Public Transport - Bus 41, 94, Metro Gold Line Joaan Typical hours - 09:30-01:30 Contacts - +974 4443 2927

Al Shurfa Arabic Restaurant - One of the more interesting views in Doha from this restaurants upper floor balcony - it overlooks the Corniche and is great following sunset. The **Middle Eastern** food is coupled with Arabic games and water-pipes and makes a good dinner choice. One of two restaurants within the small Al Jumrok Hotel.

Typical cost range - *** Rough GPS - 25.289 , 51.533

Street - off Corniche Public Transport - Bus 76, 177 Metro Gold Line Souq Waqif Typical hours - 12:00-23:00 Contacts - +974 4433 6666 / res.vswq@tivolihotels.com / https://www.-tivolihotels.com/en/souq-waqif-al-jomrok-boutique-hotel?

Lamazani Grill - Busy, excellent value **Persian** style kebab restaurant. The location and decoration may not have the appeal of some other options - but a 30 minute walk from Souq Waqif does have its rewards.

Typical cost range - *** Rough GPS - 25.280 , 51.537

Street - Ras Abu Abboud St Public Transport - Bus, innumerable bus routes & about 500m south of Al Ghanim Bus Station. Metro Gold Line Souq Waqif or Red Line Al Doha Al Jadeda. Typical hours - 12:00-01:00 (Friday 14:30

-01:00) Contacts - +974 55526345 (Mobile) / info@lamazani.com / www.lamazani.com

SMAT Restaurant - A contemporary version of Qatari & **Gulf food**, with lightly spiced meat and rice, though it offers much more than that. The restaurant's location is good, overlooking a small park and beyond that the sea. Well worth a visit from the National Museum or Museum of Islamic Art.

Typical cost range - **** Rough GPS - 25.290 , 25.290

Street - East Corniche Public Transport - Typical hours - 08:00-01:00 Contacts - +974 4410 6600

Zaman Al Khair Restaurant - A well-established **Lebanese** / Syrian restaurant, with excellent mezze, mains and fruit juice. This is on route to Inland Sea – with a choice of dine-in or takeaway.

Typical cost range - **** Rough GPS - 25.186 , 51.600

Street - Al Wakrah Main St Public Transport - Bus109,119,129 Typical hours - 08:00-midnight Contacts - +974 4498 6111 / info@zamanalkhairrest.com / www.zamanalkhairrest.com

Azraq At Banana Island - With various cuisines and an **International buffet** offering the wide selection of a typical Gulf style main dining restaurant, though slightly skewed towards seafood. Choice of indoor or outdoor dining.

Typical cost range - ***** Rough GPS - 25.295 , 51.646

Street - from Corniche 25.292010, 51.534803 Public Transport - Bus 76,777 (Airport), Metro Gold Line Souq Waqif & Ferry from Dhow Harbour 25.292135, 51.534429 Typical hours - 06.30 -23.00 Contacts - +974 4040 5050 / fbreservations.adoh@anantara.com / https://www.anantara.com/en/banana-island-doha/restaurants/azraq

The Village - Stylish dining in one of three dining options here. Choose from **Arabic, Iranian or Turkish** cuisines. It's just to the south, outside the main Souq Waqif. The other branch on the Salwa Rd (25.265308, 51.498197) is comparable - but not quite as beautifully decorated.

Typical cost range - ***** Rough GPS - 25.287 , 51.533

Street - Al Souq St Public Transport - Bus Al Ghanim Bus Station Metro Gold Line Souq Waqif Typical hours - 08:00-23:30 Contacts - +974 4411 1243 / www.thevillageqatar.com

Al Nahham Restaurant At Banana Island Resort - Offering **Lebanese** / Gulf style Arabic food with indoor or outdoor dining overlooking the sea. Premium prices, you should expect a premium experience and overall you receive it.

Typical cost range - ****** Rough GPS - 25.295 , 51.646

Street - Banana Island Public Transport - Bus 76,777 (Airport), Metro Gold Line Souq Waqif & Ferry from Dhow Harbour 25.292135, 51.534429 Typical hours - 13:00-17:00 / 19:00 - 17:00 Contacts - +974 4040 5116 / fbreservation-s.adoh@anantara.com / https://www.anantara.-com/en/banana-island-doha/restaurants/al-nahham

Argan - This opulent restaurant in a modern Moroccan style offers an update on **Moroccan** cuisine - with a few International dishes thrown in. Its inside the Al Jasra Hotel - the Tivoli group do have a remarkably good dining choice in Souq Waqif.

Typical cost range - ****** Rough GPS - 25.289 , 51.531

Street - Al Jasra St, Doha, Qatar Public Transport - Bus 76, 177 Metro Gold Line Souq Waqif Typical hours - 13:00-23:00 Contacts - +974 4433 6872 / https://www.-tivolihotels.com/en/souq-waqif-al-jasra-boutique-hotel/restaurants

Mercato Antico (Also Branch In Tawar Mall) - A rustic style restaurant, with an extremely simply looking set-up. Overlooking beach a sepia toned interior looks out over blue sea and sky. Premium priced **Pasta and Pizza** are largely worth the visit.

Typical cost range - ****** Rough GPS - 25.172 , 51.611

Street - off Al Wakrah Main St Public Transport - Bus 129 Typical hours - 16:00-midnight (Friday & Saturday 13:00-

midnight) Contacts - +974 4441 0020 / info@mercato-antico.com / www.mercato-antico.com/en/

Parisa Souq Waqif (Also At Sharq Village) - A destination in itself with décor a fusion of style from the Golestan Palace. The **Persian** food is good, with matching service and, usually, light live music in the background. This is dining as a total sensory experience.

Typical cost range - ****** Rough GPS - 25.288 , 51.533

Street - Inside Souq Waqif Public Transport - Bus 76, 177 Metro Gold Line Souq Waqif Typical hours - 12:00-midnight Contacts - +974 4441 1494 / dining.sharq@ritzcarlton.com / http://www.ritzcarlton.com/en/hotels/qatar/sharq-village/dining/parisa-souq-waqif

Q Lounge & Restaurant At Banana Island - Overlooking a pool, beach, sea and in the distance Qatar Airways taking off and landing at Hamad International Airport, the **Asian / Indian** style food is also good.

Typical cost range - ****** Rough GPS - 25.295 , 51.646

Street - Banana Island Public Transport - Bus 76,777 (Airport), Metro Gold Line Souq Waqif & Ferry from Dhow Harbour 25.292135, 51.534429 Typical hours - 06.30-10:30 / 12.00-23.30 Contacts - +974 4040 5116 / fbreservations.adoh@anantara.com / https://www.anantara.com/en/banana-island-doha/restaurants/q-lounge-and-restaurant

Riva At Banana Island - A **Mediterranean** themed restaurant with a remarkably good mix of taste and service.

Typical cost range - ****** Rough GPS - 25.295 , 51.646

Street - Banana Island Public Transport - Bus 76,777 (Airport), Metro Gold Line Souq Waqif & Ferry from Dhow Harbour 25.292135, 51.534429 Typical hours - 13:00-22:00 (Closed Sunday) Contacts - +974 4040 5116 / fbreservations.adoh@anantara.com / https://www.anantara.com/en/banana-island-doha/restaurants/riva

. . .

West Bay

Royal Istanbul Restaurant (Behind Westbay Petrol Station) - The name aside is a simple **Turkish** restaurant, which is popular due to its convenient location, with a takeaway service.

Typical cost range - * Rough GPS - 25.326 , 51.517

Street - Al Istiqal St / Al Intisar Public Transport - Bus 78 Typical hours - 11:00-midnight Contacts - +974 4498 1268 / RoyalIstanbul@BakeMartDoha.com /

Spice Market (W Hotel) - Set in the W Hotel, general **Asian** themed menu offered in a room with very subdued lighting. A very popular option, with co-operative staff.

Typical cost range - *** Rough GPS - 25.328 , 51.530

Street - Diplomatic St Public Transport - Bus 57,74,76,777 Metro Doha Exhibition and Convention Center (DECC Consider the , paid, shuttle coach services the general West Bay area every 15mins for all West Bay Hotels Typical hours - 07:00-midnight (Friday from 08:00) Contacts - +974 4453 5135 / bnfreservations.wdoha@whotels.com / https://www.spicemarketdoha.com/

W Café (W Hotel) - Set in the W Hotel, this is a good alternative **coffee-shop** to Starbucks, at not much more cost.

Typical cost range - *** Rough GPS - 25.328 , 51.530

Street - Diplomatic St Public Transport - Bus 57,74,76,777 Metro Doha Exhibition and Convention Center (DECC Consider the , paid, shuttle coach services the general West Bay area every 15mins for all West Bay Hotels Typical hours - 07:00-midnight (Friday from 08:00) Contacts - +974 4453 5135 / bnfreservations.wdoha@whotels.com / www.wcafedoha.com

Applebee's (Chain) - Part of the APPLEBEE Franchise,

one of several branches in Doha. American style **Ribs and fast food** options. Predictable, food quality and efficient service.

Typical cost range - **** Rough GPS - 25.326 , 51.530

Street - Conference Centre Public Transport - Bus 78,Metro Doha Exhibition and Convention Center (DECC) Typical hours - 10:00-23:00 Contacts - +974 4493 4880 / contact form / www.applebeesme.com/qatar/

Olive Oil Rotana City Centre (all day dining breakfast/lunch/dinner) - A good buffet in the Ritan that is very convenient for the Conference Centre and City Centre Mall. The food is a typical Gulf **International style**.

Typical cost range - **** Rough GPS - 25.324 , 51.533

Street - Diplomatic St / Conference Centre St Public Transport - Bus 74,777 Metro Red Line Doha Exhibition & Conference Centre (DECC) Typical hours - 06:30-23:30 Contacts - +974 4445 8727 / Contact Form / https://www.rotana.com/rotanahote-landresorts/qatar/doha/citycentrerotanado-ha/diningout/oliveoil/booknow

Al Sultan Brahim - **Seafood** near, but not on the sea in West Bay. Though the gardens are attractive to dine in, the interior decor is almost bland. Choose your own fish bar.

Typical cost range - ***** Rough GPS - 25.349 , 51.531

Street - off Lusail Highway Public Transport - Metro Red Line Al Qassar Typical hours - 12:00–16:30pm

18:30–23:30pm Contacts - +97444460000 / dining.reservations@stregis.com / www.alsultan-brahimdoha.com

Boston's - Popular American themed bar style restaurant, with live sports.

Typical cost range - ***** Rough GPS - 25.326 , 51.531

Street - Omar Al Mukhtar / Conference Centre Public Transport - Bus 78,Metro Doha Exhibition and Convention Center (DECC) Typical hours - 17:00-02:00 Contacts - +974

4445 8888 / fb.citycentre@Rotana.com / www.rotanatimes.-com/citycentrerotanadoha/dining/1368

La Spiga By Paper Moon (W Doha) - A small **Italian** Restaurant with appropriate wine bar in the W Hotel. The décor is more anonymous than Italian, while outside the overlooking skyscrapers may not be to everyone's taste.

Typical cost range - ***** Rough GPS - 25.328 , 51.530

Street - Diplomatic St Public Transport - Bus 57,74,76,777 Metro Doha Exhibition and Convention Center (DECC Consider the , paid, shuttle coach services the general West Bay area every 15mins for all West Bay Hotels Typical hours - 12:00 - 16:00 / 17:00-midnight Contacts - +974 4453 5135 / bnfreservations.wdoha@whotels.com / www.laspigadoha.com

Sridan - A very comfortable restaurant offering an **Arabian** style menu in a convenient location for NECC and City Centre Mall.

Typical cost range - ***** Rough GPS - 25.325 , 51.533

Street - Conference Centre/Diplomatic St Public Transport - Bus 74 , 777 Metro Doha Exhibition and Convention Center (DECC). Typical hours - 6.00am – 10.30am / 12.00noon – 3.00pm / 6.00pm – 10.00pm Contacts - +974 4429 5000 / Contact Form / https://www.-marriott.com/hotels/hotel-information/restaurant/dohjb-jw-marriott-marquis-city-center-doha/

Teatro - Another winning option when in NECC or City Centre. Good option for a **fusion meal** from Japanese through to Italian, designed to appeal to everyone; it also has a good range of alcohol.

Typical cost range - ***** Rough GPS - 25.324 , 51.533

Street - Conference Centre Public Transport - Bus 74,777 Metro Red Line Doha Exhibition & Conference Centre (DECC) Typical hours - 12:30-02:00 am (Friday and Saturday from 17:00) Contacts - +974 4445 8888 / contact form / https://www.rotana.com/rotanahote-landresorts/qatar/doha/citycentrerotanado-ha/diningout/teatro/booknow

Trader Vic's (Hilton) - Part of the established chain of **Polynesian**-themed restaurants - it's been in the region for almost 40 years. Frequent theme nights add to the appeal. They have a dress code to gain entry.

Typical cost range - ***** Rough GPS - 25.327 , 51.541

Street - Diplomatic St Public Transport - Bus 74 , 777 Metro Doha Exhibition and Convention Center (DECC Consider the , paid, shuttle coach services the general West Bay area every 15mins for all West Bay Hotels Typical hours - midday-midnight Contacts - +974 4423 3118 / www.tradervicsdoha.com/

Wahm (W Hotel) - Live music and a fashionable **bar** in the W Hotel in Doha.

Typical cost range - ***** Rough GPS - 25.328 , 51.530

Street - Diplomatic St Public Transport - Bus 57,74,76,777 Metro Doha Exhibition and Convention Center (DECC Consider the , paid, shuttle coach services the general West Bay area every 15mins for all West Bay Hotels Typical hours - 17:00-02:00 Contacts - +974 4453 5135 / bnfreservations.wdoha@whotels.com / www.wahmdoha.com

Al Hubara Restaurant - Well established venue in the slightly dated public lobby of the Sheraton. The good is generally good, though an unadventurous **International** style.

Typical cost range - ****** Rough GPS - 25.318 , 51.536

Street - Corniche Sheraton Public Transport - Bus 777 Metro Red Line Doha Exhibition & Conference Centre (DECC) Typical hours - Breakfast Buffet: 06:00 AM - 11:00 AM

Lunch Buffet: 12:00 PM - 15:30 PM

Dinner Buffet: 19:00 PM - 23:30 PM

Friday Brunch: 12:30 PM -16:00 PM Contacts -

+97444853000 / F&Breservations.doha@sheraton.com / www.alhubararestaurant.com

Ipanema (Marriot Marquis Hotel) - Remarkable **Brazilian** restaurant (with a few dishes that have immigrated from elsewhere) with good food, range of alcohol and often live music. It's well worth dining in.

Typical cost range - ****** Rough GPS - 25.325 , 51.528

Street - Omar Al Mukhtar Public Transport - Bus 57, Metro Red Line Doha Exhibition & Conference Centre (DECC) Typical hours - 18:30-23:00 (plus Friday 12:30-17:00) Contacts - +974 4419 5000 / http://www.marriottmarquisdohadining.com/restaurant/hotels/hotel-information/travel/dohmq/restaurant.aspx?id=010

Market By Jean-Georges - A very simple European design for the restaurant, with a similar approach to the quality food. It's a **general offering** - from the British Isles, through Lebanon - to Japan.

Typical cost range - ****** Rough GPS - 25.328 , 51.530

Street - Diplomatic St Public Transport - Bus 57,74,76,777 Metro Doha Exhibition and Convention Center (DECC Consider the , paid, shuttle coach services the general West Bay area every 15mins for all West Bay Hotels Typical hours - 06:00-11:00/12:00-16:00/17:00-23:30 (Friday 12:00-16:00/17:00-23:30) Contacts - +97444535135 / bnfreservations.wdoha@whotels.com / www.marketdoha.com

Nobu - Worth visiting for the views, as its just off the beach - with amazing views over West Bay. Although a beachfront location, there is a dress code. This is a decidedly premium, mainly **seafood** offering, the service and food struggle to match the price.

Typical cost range - ****** Rough GPS - 25.323 , 51.541

Street - Diplomatic St (Four Seasons Marina) Public Transport - Bus 74,777 Metro Red Line Doha Exhibition & Conference Centre (DECC) Typical hours - 18:00-01:00 (Friday 12:30-16:00) Contacts - +974 4494 8600 / contact form / www.fourseasons.com/doha/dining/restaurants/nobu_doha/

Shanghai Club - A modern take on **Asian** cuisine with a good alcohol selection. In the evening there is a smart dress code. The views of Doha Bay and occasional live music add to the experience.

Typical cost range - ****** Rough GPS - 25.325 , 51.533

Street - Diplomatic St/ Conference Centre Public Transport - 57,74,76, 78,777 Metro Doha Exhibition and Convention Center (DECC). Typical hours - 12.30-16.00/ 18.30-23.30 Contacts - + 974 4429 5050 / shanghaiclub.sldh@shangri-la.com / https://www.marriott.-com/hotels/hotel-information/restaurant/dohjb-jw-marriott-marquis-city-center-doha/

Zengo (Kempinski Residences) - **Asian** menu with good alcohol selection. Ask for window table to enjoy an airplane view from 61st floor across Doha Bay to The Pearl.

Typical cost range - ****** Rough GPS - 25.328 , 51.531

Street - off Diplomatic St Public Transport - Bus 74 , 777 Metro Doha Exhibition and Convention Center (DECC Consider the , paid, shuttle coach services the general West Bay area every 15mins for all West Bay Hotels Typical hours - 12:30-midnight (Closed Saturday) Contacts - +974 4453 5135 / Zengo@zengodoha.com / www.zengodoha.com

The Pearl & Katara

Layali In Lagoona Mall - A reasonable **Lebanese** restaurant in a building that looks like an afterthought in an expensive area. The interior is more on-point as is the food.

Typical cost range - *** Rough GPS - 25.377 , 51.526

Street - off Pearl Boulivard Public Transport - No public transport Typical hours - 09:00-23:30 Contacts - +974

44310005 / layali@adaragroup.co / www.layalirestaurantqatar.com/

Shakespeare and Co Chain - Part of a Gulf-wide chain decorated surprisingly an Edwardian meets Louis XVI fusion theme decor & not Jacobean, but its ideal for Instagram. An **International** style range of light meals are offered.

Typical cost range - *** Rough GPS - 25.373 , 51.543

Street - Port Arabia Drive Public Transport - No public transport Typical hours - 08:00-23:30 Contacts - +974 6629 3821 / corporate@shakespeareandco.ae / www.shakespeare-and-co.com

L'wzaar Seafood - Seafront sea food restaurant, what's not to like? From **Sushi to Fish & Chips** a complete range of sea-food overlooking the sea in Katara. In cooler weather choose outdoor, especially in the afternoon when the sun drops behind the building; otherwise ask for window seats.

Typical cost range - **** Rough GPS - 25.358 , 51.526

Street - off Al Moasses St/Lusail Highway Public Transport - Metro Red Line Al Qassar Typical hours - 12:00 16:00 - 19:00-23:30 (Friday 13:00 16:00 - 19:00-23:30) Contacts - +974 4408 0710 / info@lwzaar.com / www.lwzaar.com/

Sukar Pasha - **Turkish** restaurant set directly on an extension on the Katara beach. Indoor dining or in less humid weather choose outdoor. The location is difficult to beat, however the service and quality of food is patchy, which is unexpected at its premium price.

Typical cost range - **** Rough GPS - 25.357 , 51.527

Street - off Lusail Expressway Public Transport - Metro Red Line Al Qassar Typical hours - Fri 08:00-11:00/12:30-01:00 Contacts - +974 4408 2000 / info@sukarpasha.qa. / http://sukarpasha.qa

Al Sufra - Uniformly excellent **Lebanese** food and wine. The service and attractive, subdued Arabic inspired ambiance does make for a relaxing meal.

Typical cost range - ***** Rough GPS - 25.376 , 51.549

Street - Marsa Malaz Kempinski, Pearl Boulivard Public Transport - No public transport Typical hours - 12:30-midnight Contacts - +974 4035 5011 / restaurants.-marsamalaz@kempinski.com / https://www.kempinski.-com/en/doha/marsa-malaz-kempinski-the-pearl-doha/dining/restaurants/al-sufra/

Saffron Lounge - Elegant surroundings and good **north Indian** food. With Ghandi's Three Monkeys sculptures outside, its an easy place to find.

Typical cost range - ***** Rough GPS - 25.359 , 51.526

Street - off Lusail Express (adjacdent to Katara Hall) Public Transport - Metro Red Line Al Qassar or Katara Typical hours - 12:00-22:00 (Friday 13:00-23:00) Contacts - +974 4408 0808

Yasmine Palace - An opulent complex with four dining locations (one is a café style). The overall concept is Arabian Nights - with **Levant style** food. The location isn't the easiest to get to - but the food, ambiance and service make it a worthwhile journey.

Typical cost range - ***** Rough GPS - 25.365 , 51.543

Street - Porto Arabia Drive Public Transport - No public transport Typical hours - 07:00-midnight Contacts - +974 7711 1504 https://yasminepalace.com/

Gordon Ramsay At The St. Regis - Simple décor and a modern take on **Mediterranean** along with alcohol appropriate to the cuisine.

Typical cost range - ****** Rough GPS - 25.350 , 51.529

Street - off Lusail Express Public Transport - No public transport Typical hours - 18:00-23:00 (Closed Sunday) Contacts - +974 4446 0105 / dining.reservations@stregis.com / www.gordonramsaydoha.com

Hakkasan (St. Regis Doha) - Probably the most expensive in Doha, it's reasonable to expect it to be the best and it may well be. Being well established does mean that the restaurant has had more than enough time to find what works and what doesn't. The stylish decor and ambiance set the theme for excellent **Chinese** cuisine, with a style that reflects the restaurant's interior. The restaurant does operate a restrictive door policy including on children below 11 - booking for tables advised.

Typical cost range - ****** Rough GPS - 25.350 , 51.529

Street - east of Lusail Highway Public Transport - No public transport Typical hours - 19:00-23:30 (also weekends 13:00-16:00) wine bar (18:00-01:00) Contacts - +974 4446 0170 / reservation.hakkasan@stregis.com / www.hakkasan.-com/locations/hakkasan-doha/

Morimoto (Mondrian Doha) - Stylish **Japanese** restaurant in the Mondrian hotel (part of Accor) with food and service commensurate with cost.

Typical cost range - ****** Rough GPS - 25.377 , 51.523

Street - Pearl Boulivard/ Lusail Expressway Public Transport - No public transport Typical hours - 18:00-23:30 (Closed Sunday) Contacts - +974 4045 5999 / Wineanddine-mondriandoha@sbe.com / www.morganshotelgroup.-com/mondrian/mondrian-doha/

Nozomi (Marsa Malaz Kempinski) - With a view over the man-made lagoon around Marsa Malaz Kempinski, Nozomi is a premium **Japanese** restaurant in a premium hotel - the food and service are excellent, the interior and exterior don't live up to them.

Typical cost range - ****** Rough GPS - 25.377 , 51.549

Street - Pearl Boulivard/ Lusail Expressway Public Transport - No public transport Typical hours - 19:00-23:00 (Thurs & Friday also 12:00-15:30) Contacts - +974 4035 5089 / info@nozomidoha.com / http://www.nozomi-doha.com/

Toro Toro (Marsa Malaz Kempinski) - Overlooking the lagoon of Marsa Malaz Kempinski, this is a taste of **Latin**

America in Doha, complete with occasional Havana cigar smoke.

Typical cost range - ****** Rough GPS - 25.377 , 51.549

Street - The Pearl Boulivard Public Transport - No public transport Typical hours - 19:00-01:00 (Friday 19:00-02:00) Contacts - +974 4035 5101 / contact form / www.torotorodoha.com

Vine (St Regis) - An elegant restaurant with spacious interior and options to dine outside. This is one of the better all day dining options in Doha serving an **International** range of foods, though they do have theme evenings throughout the week.

Typical cost range - ****** Rough GPS - 25.350 , 51.529

Street - off Lusail Highway Public Transport - No public transport Typical hours - 06:00-11:00/18:00-23:00 and Friday (12:30-16:00) Contacts - +974 4446 0105 / dining.reservations@stregis.com / www.vinedoha.com/

Doha South & East

The Cellar - This is now a Hyatt managed property. With a good range of drinks this **Spanish** themed restaurant is a welcome change from the plethora of Middle Eastern and Indian -sub-continent cuisines throughout Doha.

Typical cost range - *** Rough GPS - 25.268 , 51.554

Street - Al Nahda School St / C Ring Rd. Public Transport - Bus 94, 119, 129, 747, 757 Metro Red Line Umm Ghuwailina Typical hours - 12:00-02:00 Contacts - +974 4402 3454 / Contact Form / https://www.hyattrestaurants.com/en/dining/qatar/doha/spanish-restaurant-in-hamad-International-airport-the-cellar

Al Nafourah Garden - A change from a Rotana to Hyatt management, but still a nice courtyard dining experience. Not the widest choice of food in this **Lebanese** restaurant but what there is offers a good option. The water-pipes add to the experience.

Typical cost range - **** Rough GPS - 25.268 , 51.554

Street - Al Matar St Public Transport - 49,747, 11901,12901 Typical hours - 12:00-02:00 Contacts - +974 4402 3333 / https://www.hyattrestaurants.com/en/dining/qatar/doha/lebanese-restaurant-in-doha-s-business-district-al-nafourah-garden

Stock Burger Co - A mix of good **Burgers**, alcohol and the main attraction, live sport coverage.

Typical cost range - **** Rough GPS - 25.273 , 51.543

Street - Al Matar St Public Transport - Bus 11.747, 11901, 12901 Metro Al Doha Al Jadeda Typical hours - 12:00-02:00 Contacts - +974 4031 3333 / www.ihg.com/holidayinn/hotels/gb/en/doha/dohbp/hoteldetail/dining#

Paper Moon (1st Floor Jaidah Square Complex) - A comfortable modern style restaurant with option of indoor or outdoor tables. This may well be the nicest overall experience in an **Italian** restaurant in Doha.

Typical cost range - ***** Rough GPS - 25.273 , 51.545

Street - Umm Ghuwailina St / Al Matar St Public Transport - Bus 747, 11901, 12901 Metro Red Line Umm Ghuwailina Typical hours - 11:30 - 22:45 Contacts - +974 4016 6000 / info@papermoondoha.com / www.papermoondoha.com/

Jazz Club (Oryx Rotana) - A very good choice for a night out. There is usually live music, occasionally televised sports - supported by a good selection of drinks and **sliders & burgers**.

Typical cost range - ****** Rough GPS - 25.268 , 51.554

Street - off Al Matar St/ C Ring Rd Public Transport - Bus 94, 119, 129, 747, 757 Metro Red Line Umm Ghuwailina Typical hours - 17:00-02:00 (Closed Saturday) Contacts - +974 4402 3444 / https://www.hyattrestaurants.com/en/dining/qatar/doha/International-restaurant-in-al-matar-street-jazz-club

Education City & Doha West

Saj Boutique - Fast-food **Arabic style** with the staple Shawarma (flat pitta type bread with meat or falafil filling) type takeaway nicely cooked and presented. Though popular as a take-away - the restaurant is nicely laid out - one of 2 branches.

Typical cost range - * Rough GPS - 25.270 , 51.477

Street - Al Wab St / Al Bustan St Public Transport - Bus 32,41,304 Metro Gold Line Gold Line Al Sudan Typical hours - 07:00-01:00 Contacts - +974 6607 8444

Al Sultan Restaurant - Al Saad - Good value, though with a tired decor, **Lebanese** restaurant (one of two in a chain) with selection of Fruit Juices

Typical cost range - ** Rough GPS - 25.274 , 51.505

Street - Al Mirqab Al Jadeed Public Transport - Bus 49, Metro Gold Line Al Saad Typical hours - 08:00-23:00 Contacts - +974 4441 1865 / info@al-sultanrestaurant.com / www.al-sultanrestaurant.com/

Beirut Restaurant (With Branches) - Simple well established, low-cost, popular **Lebanese** restaurant.

Typical cost range - ** Rough GPS - 25.285 , 51.509

Street - Al Jazeera St Public Transport - Bus 78, Metro Gold Line Al Saad Typical hours - 03:00- 13:00 yes - closed over lunchtime - these opening times give an insight into the strange working or non-working hours of people in Qatar or possibly the service attitude of this company. 15:00–23:30pm. Contacts - +974 4435 5258 / info@beirutrest.com / www.beirutrest.com/

Summer Land (Qatar Petroleum Service Station) -

Turkish & Syrian style restaurant offering low priced food. This is one of the larger restaurants in this petrol station forecourt. It offers dine-in and take away. There must be a dozen other choices in the same petrol station forecourt that are ideal for a late night takeaway or a picnic when driving north.

Typical cost range - ** Rough GPS - 25.350 , 51.457

Street - Doha Expressway (Al Shamal Road) /Al Khafji St Public Transport - Bus 102, 170 Typical hours - 08:00-02:00 Contacts - +974 4444 2056

Miz Bar And Terrace (The Westin Doha) - Popular bar with indoor and terrace seating - serving **light meals**, supported by a good range of alcohol, and providing good service.

Typical cost range - *** Rough GPS - 25.275 , 51.514

Street - Salwa Rd Public Transport - Bus 49,304 Metro Gold Line Bin Mahmoud Typical hours - 17:00-02:00 (Sunday closes at midnight) Contacts - +974 4492 1555 / www.mixbardoha.com

Atrium Lounge - With live piano music and light **International** food in a spacious atrium - this is a good choice for a quick meal if in the area .

Typical cost range - **** Rough GPS - 25.284 , 51.496

Street - Al Manara St, Jawaan St, Public Transport - Bus 32,41,49, 78,94,304, Metro Gold Line Joaan Typical hours - 07:00-23:30 Contacts - +974 4 424 7777 / info.mdoh@millenniumhotels.com / https://www.millenniumhotels.com/en/doha/millennium-hotel-doha/atrium/

C.Taste (Centro Capital Hotel) In Al Jazeera St - A limited but well produced **International** menu from this modern well run all-day restaurant in the Centro Hotel.

Typical cost range - **** Rough GPS - 25.284 , 51.512

Street - Al Jazeera St Public Transport - Bus 78, Metro Gold Line Al Sadd - 1km away Typical hours - 06:00-22:30 Contacts - T: +974 4455 5000 / centro.capitaldoha@rotana.com / https://www.rotana.com/centrohotels/qatar/doha/centrocapitaldoha/dining

Di Capri Ristorante (La Cigale Hotel) - Vivid ambiance with a hint of the late 1950s modern **Italy**. The food lives up to the promise.

Typical cost range - **** Rough GPS - 25.280 , 51.508

Street - , C Ring Rd /Suhaim Bin Hamad Street Public Transport - Bus 32,42,78 Metro Gold Line Al Sadd Typical hours - 11:30-15:00 / 07:00 - 23:00 Contacts - +97144288840 / info@lacigalehotel.com / http://www.lacigalehotel.com/sub_category.php?intCategoryId=4

Ocean Basket (Mall Of Qatar) - **Seafood** as fast-food. A reasonable option if visiting Mall of Qatar or Villaggio Mall

Typical cost range - **** Rough GPS - 25.324 , 51.350

Street - Dukhan Highway / National Day Ceremonial Road (a complicated junction) Public Transport - Bus 104, 104A from Al Ghanim Bus Station Typical hours - 11:00-23:00 (Friday 01:00-23:00) Contacts - +974 4490 2944 / www.qatar.oceanbasket.com/

Shebestan Palace Restaurant - Extremely well established **Persian** restaurant, with a subdued, classic and spacious interior. The food and service is also less overwhelming than in other Persian restaurants in Doha, though at an appreciably lower price.

Typical cost range - **** Rough GPS - 25.281 , 51.504

Street - Al Saad St Public Transport - Bus 31,32, 301 Metro Gold Line Al Saad Typical hours - 12:00-midnight Contacts - +974 4432 1555

Sabi Thai (Westin Hotel) - This is an authentic **Thai** restaurant, though alcohol offering could be improved.

Typical cost range - ***** Rough GPS - 25.275 , 51.514

Street - Salwa Rd Public Transport - Bus 49,304 Metro Gold Line Bin Mahmoud Typical hours - 12:00 -15:00/18:30-23:00 Contacts - +974 4492 1555 / dining.doha@westin.com / www.sabaithaidoha.com

Hunters Room & Grill (The Westin Doha) - Potentially a good **steak house**, supported by a range of light-meals - though surprisingly let down by inconsistent service.

Typical cost range - ****** Rough GPS - 25.275 , 51.514

Street - off Salwa Rd Public Transport - Bus 49,304 Typical hours - 12:00 - 16:00

19:00-23:00 Contacts - +974 3359 8514 / dining.doha@westin.com / www.huntersdoha.com/

Seasonal Tastes (Westin Hotel) - An **International** restaurant with nightly themed food nights

Typical cost range - ****** Rough GPS - 25.275 , 51.514

Street - Salwa Rd Public Transport - Bus 49,304 Metro Gold Line Bin Mahmoud Typical hours - 18:30-23:00 Contacts - +974 4492 1555 / dining.doha@westin.com / www.seasonaltastesdoha.com/

Three Sixty (360) Torch Doha - **Mediterranean & Seafood** restaurant (no alcohol) set on the 47th floor of The Torch. The food is good but what make this outstanding is the revolving view - best enjoyed from just before sunset (arrive early to catch the skyscraper lights coming on in West Bay). Very Smart Casual, or suit & dress (appropriate national dress) . The other restaurants in The Torch are also good, but the revolving restaurant does make it especially worth the journey.

Typical cost range - ****** Rough GPS - 25.262 , 51.445

Street - off Al Waab Street, Al Buwairda St Public Transport - 31,32,40, 136,137,301,306. Metro Gold Line Sport City Typical hours - 12:00-15:00 / 19:00-23:00 Contacts - +974 4446 5600 / reservation@thetorchdoha.com / www.thetorchdoha.com.qa

North-East

. . .

Al Mandarin Restaurant (one of several branches) - Good Value restaurant, offering fresh juices and Falooda (fresh juice and ice cream) and **light meals**. Other branches (not listed here) for example in Souq Waqif have Fresh Juice only. They operate a semi-permanent 'pop-up' style so may appear in most stadiums for the World Cup.

Typical cost range - * Rough GPS - 25.647 , 51.489

Street - Al Bayt Stadium Public Transport - no public transport Typical hours - 24 Hours Contacts - +974 4442 0808

Maha Al Khaleeg (it was Miknas Cafeteria) - A low cost restaurant, opposite the harbour in Al Khor, with Indian food - especially with a **south Indian** flavour. Outside seating available.

Typical cost range - * Rough GPS - 25.686 , 51.514

Street - Al Khor Coastal Rd / Al Khor Town Rd Public Transport - Bus 102, 102X Typical hours - 05:00-midnight Contacts - +974 500 60179

Pearl Of Beirut Restaurant - Very simple restaurant overlooking sea and Dhow harbour with limited outdoor seating also available. As the name says it's a **Lebanese** style restaurant - the food is good value and the service is better than the price and decor would suggest.

Typical cost range - * Rough GPS - 25.686 , 51.515

Street - Corniche Al Khor (opposite fish harbour) Public Transport - Bus 102, 102X Typical hours - 06:30-23:00 Contacts - +974 4472 0123

Turkiye Kebab - Good for take-away and **Turkish** meals in the north of Qatar - main restaurant upstairs.

Typical cost range - * Rough GPS - 25.679 , 51.497

Street - Al Khor Coastal Rd / Al Khor Town Rd Public Transport - Bus 102, 102X Typical hours - 10:00-23:00 Contacts - +974 4411 4150

. . .

Al Ruwais, West Coast and Dukhan & Central Qatar

Iskender Pasha - About as far north as you can get in Qatar. This is an inexpensive restaurant, basically furnished with simple **Turkish, and Mediterranean** food. There are several other restaurants (including Tea Time) on the same street, compare these if you wish.

Typical cost range - * Rough GPS - 26.126 , 51.204

Street - Madinat Al Shamal Rd / Al Ghayra Rd Public Transport - Bus 101, 201 Typical hours - 09:00-23:00 Contacts - +974 3357 4304

VARIOUS LOCATIONS

Tea Time - A Qatari Gulf-wide franchise. Spiced tea, with a wide range of options, and more is the theme. The **snack food** isn't quite as good as the tea, but all-in-all this is a great alternative to a burger.

Typical cost range - * - various locations (13+) in Qatar including Souq Waqif 25.287, 51.533

Typical hours - 24 Hours Contacts - https://teatime.qa/

Wrap It - In Food Court Of Several Shopping Malls (Gulf Mall, Landmark Etc) - The Gulfs most popular snack, the **Shawarma**, branded here as Wrap-it. Here you can individually select the filling, a Subway style of getting exactly what you want.

Typical cost range - * - various locations

Typical hours - 09:00-23:30 (or as in specific food court opening hours)

32

HOTELS

W Hotel

Corniche, Souq Waqif & Central Doha

Century Hotel - Spacious rooms and good facilities in a convenient location. The hotels is new - unfortunately the staff may also be as their service is inexperienced. A choice of 3 dining options. Well located for National and Islamic Art museums & with good access to National Museum Metro (Gold Line) Number of rooms - 215

Typical cost range - * Rough GPS - 25.286 , 51.547

Street - Sheraouh St Public Transport - National Museum Metro Location in Qatar - Al Hitmi الهتمي Contacts - +974 4445 5111 / info@centuryhoteldoha.com / www.centuryhoteldoha.com

Grand Qatar Palace Hotel - Simple style, locally operated and slightly dated, especially the bathrooms with their simple shower & bath, but acceptable decor and good value. Established hotel, with a selection of restaurants, small pool and gym. About 1 kilometre to Souq Waqif and Msheireb Museums. There are several similar hotels adjacent to this. Number of rooms - 92

Typical cost range - * Rough GPS - 25.281 , 51.530

Street - Al Areeq St. Public Transport - Large number (27+) of bus routes stop on Al Diwan St (50metres away), Metro Musherib (Hub) Location in Qatar - Msheireb مشيرب Contacts - +974 4441 4140 / info@grandqatarpalacehotel.com / www.grandqatarpalacehotel.com

Kingsgate Hotel - Modern functional and colourful - part of the Millennium Hotels chain. A small pool and gym with reasonable facilities for price. The key bonus is the proximity to the bus station and Souq Waqif (600metres) , Gold Souq, Al Ghanim Bus Station and a kilometre away the Islamic Museum or National Museum Number of rooms - 140

Typical cost range - * Rough GPS - 25.286 , 51.538

Street - Ali bin Abdullah (Al Mirqab Roundabout) Public Transport - Bus Al Ghanim Bus Station Metro Gold Line Souq Waqif Location in Qatar - Old Al Ghanim الغانم Contacts - +974 4408 5555 / reservations.kgdoh@millennium hotels.com / www.millenniumhotels.com/en/doha/kingsgate-hotel-doha/

Ramada Encore by Wyndham - Simple, bright decor giving a sense of space in relatively compact rooms. Small pool, gym restaurant About 1 kilometre to Souq Waqif and Msheireb Museums. There are several similar hotels adjacent. Number of rooms - 111

Typical cost range - * Rough GPS - 25.280 , 51.530

Street - Al Areeq St Public Transport - Large number (27+) of bus routes stop on Al Diwan St (50metres away), Metro Musherib (Hub) Location in Qatar - Msheireb مشيرب Contacts - +974 4444 3444 / info@ramadaencoredoha.com / www.ramadaencoredoha.com

The Town Hotel Doha - New hotel with generally attractive and simple muted colour decor. Single restaurant, small pool on roof (often closed). About 1 kilometre to Souq Waqif and Msheireb Museums. There are several similar hotels adjacent. Number of rooms - 120

Typical cost range - * Rough GPS - 25.280 , 51.530

Street - Al Areeq Public Transport - Large number (27+) of bus routes stop on Al Diwan St (50metres away), Metro Musherib (Hub) Location in Qatar - Msheireb مشيرب Contacts - +974 4410 7100 / reservations@thetownhotelqatar.com / www.thetownhotelqatar.com

Tourist Hotel - A budget hotel with inexpensive middle-east style decor. small gym and simple restaurant. Extremely convenient for National Museum and close to Museum of Islamic Art and less than 2km from Souq Waqif, I Number of rooms - 120

Typical cost range - * Rough GPS - 25.287 , 51.547

Street - Al Aaliya St Public Transport - Bus 76, 109 Metro

Gold Line National Museum Location in Qatar - Al Hitmi الهتمي Contacts - +974 4432 1321 / contact form / www.touristhoteldoha.site

Jouri Hotel - With a warm welcoming theme and good service, this hotel is part of Katara Hospitality, the Qatari government group. Other hotels within the group include The Avenue. With 3 restaurants and a small gym and spa - the facilities are good for a short stay. Well location for National and Islamic Art museums & with reasonable access to National Museum Metro (Gold Line) Number of rooms - 136

Typical cost range - ** Rough GPS - 25.287 , 51.545

Street - Muthaf St Public Transport - National Museum Metro Location in Qatar - Al Hitmi الهتمي Contacts - +974 4004 1000 / info@jouridoha.com / www.jourihotel.com/

Saray Mshereb Deluxe Hotel Residence - Comfortable, though using domestic fittings for kitchens. Rooms in muted earth tones encourage sleep. Small pool, gym, sauna, Number of rooms - 216

Typical cost range - ** Rough GPS - 25.283 , 51.522

Street - Al Meyyah

Street/Al Adhwaa St Public Transport - Bus, 31,32,33,33a,34,49,136,136a,137,137aSalwa Rd (100metres) Location in Qatar - Msheireb مشيرب Contacts - +974 4015 0555 / contact form / www.saraymsherebhotel.online/

Fraser Suites Doha - Warm rooms with a range of sizes, many have (ask for these) sea view. Choice of dining, gym, spa and roof-top pool with great views. Museum of Islamic Art, National Museum, Corniche and just over a kilometre away to Souq Al Waqif. Number of rooms - 138 apartments

Typical cost range - *** Rough GPS - 25.290 , 51.544

Street - Al Meena St near Corniche Public Transport - Bus 109,777 Metro Gold Line National Museum Location in Qatar - Al Mirqab المرقاب Contacts - +974 442 43443 / sales.doha@frasershospitality.com / www.doha.frasershospitality.com

Al Najada Doha Hotel By Tivoli - A fresh spacious property with focus on service and ambiance. well appointed hotel with range of facilities (some shared with adjacent Al Najada Hotel by Tivoli) short walk from Souq Waqif, museums and Corniche. Very easy access to transport. Number of rooms - 151

Typical cost range - **** Rough GPS - 25.285 , 51.534

Street - Barahat Al Jufairi

Street, Grand Hamed St Public Transport - Bus Al Ghanim Bus Station Metro Gold Line Souq Waqif Location in Qatar - Msheireb مشيرب Contacts - (+974) 4470 4444 / alnajada@tivolihotels.com / www.tivolihotels.com/en/al-najada-tivoli

Alwadi Hotel - Looking rather utilitarian, this is not a hotel for an Instagram experience. What it excels in is the excellent location for both leisure and business and the service and attention to detail. 3 restaurants and lots more in nearby areas. South-west of Souq Waqif Number of rooms - 213

Typical cost range - **** Rough GPS - 25.286 , 51.531

Street - Wadi Msheireb St. Public Transport - Souq Waqif Metro with bus M138, Msheireb Tram Location in Qatar - Msheireb مشيرب Contacts - +974 4009 9999 / Reservations.alwadihotel@accor.com / https://all.accor.-com/hotel/8395/index.en.shtml

Sharq Village & Spa, Ritz-Carlton - Established hotel. Opulent Arabesque style with a series of low rise buildings set like pleasure pavilions in a manicured environment. Selection of restaurants, including extremely scenic outdoor option, pools, gym, 250metre beach. Near National Museum & Museum of Islamic Art , Dhow yard and along the Corniche to Souq Waqif and more of Doha's sights. Number of rooms - 174

Typical cost range - ***** Rough GPS - 25.284 , 51.557

Street - Corniche Public Transport - Bus 109,777 Metro Gold Line National Museum Location in Qatar - Corniche

الكورنيش Contacts - +974 4425 6666 / sharq.leads@ritzcarlton.com / www.ritzcarlton.com/en/hotels/qatar/sharq-village

Souq Waqif Boutique Hotels - Tivoli A Collection Of 9 Individual Small Properties See List - Very authentic option in central Doha. The style is restrained but opulent Most of these hotels are small and might share some facilities, after a short walk) Surrounded by Souq Waqif and close to Qatar's main museums. Number of rooms - Small individual boutique properties

Typical cost range - ***** Rough GPS - 25.289 , 51.532

Street - Al Souq St Public Transport - Bus 76, 177 Metro Gold Line Souq Waqif Location in Qatar - Souq Waqif سوق واقف Contacts - +974 4433 6666 / / www.tivolihotels.com/en/qatar/souq-waqif-doha

Banana Island Resort Doha By Anantara - A stylish resort, with good access to Doha's attractions but with a sense of getting away. A small 25 hectares island about 1/2 hour boat ride from Doha's Dhow Harbour. A private 600metre beach with a choice of 9 dining options (some included under suggested restaurants). A Surf Pool and main Pool along with Bowling Alley gives a range of activities. Open views to Doha and across to Airport, with surprising lack of noise. Number of rooms - 141 Rooms

Typical cost range - ****** Rough GPS - 25.295 , 51.646

Street - In Doha Bay Public Transport - Bus 76,777 (Airport), Metro Gold Line Souq Waqif & Ferry from Dhow Harbour 25.292135, 51.534429 Location in Qatar - Banana Island Doha Bay جزيرة بنانا Contacts - +974 4040 5050 / doha@anantara.com / www.anantara.com/en/banana-island-doha

West Bay

. . .

Marriott Executive Apartments - A 24 story tower with comfortable furnishings and decor. Offers good value for money. Pool, Gym and well-appointed rooms and suites. Modern easy to use kitchens and bathrooms. Just off the Corniche in West Bay, close to DECC and City Centre Mall Number of rooms - 254

Typical cost range - *** Rough GPS - 25.328 ,51.530

Street - 'Diplomatic Area Doha, Qatar Diplomatic St' Public Transport - Bus 74 , 777 Metro Doha Exhibition and Convention Center (DECC Consider the , paid, shuttle coach services the general West Bay area every 15mins for all West Bay Hotels Location in Qatar - West Bay الخليج الغربي Contacts - +974 4497 1111 / contact form / www.marriott.-com/hotels/fact-sheet/travel/dohec-marriott-executive-apartments-city-center-doha/

The Curve Hotel - Good value for the location though the large number of rooms would benefit from more restaurants and facilities. Roof Top pool, gym, a few dining options, The DECC and City Centre Mall along with the modern sights in West Bay. Number of rooms - 600

Typical cost range - *** Rough GPS - 25.326 ,51.538

Street - Doplomatic St Public Transport - Bus 75, 777 Metro Doha Exhibition and Convention Center (DECC) Location in Qatar - West Bay الخليج الغربي Contacts - +974 400 78888 / reservation@ezdancurve.qa / www.ezdancurve.qa/

Fraser Suites West Bay Doha - The rooms, as you would expect, offer clean relaxed surroundings and excellent options for a business traveller. A rooftop pool, gym, 3 restaurants. A modern hotel with good range of facilities. The Fraser Suites near the National Museum does offer a better option for tourists. Close to the DECC and City Centre Mall along with the modern sights in West Bay. Number of rooms - 396 rooms (one of Doha's largest hotels) on 46 floors.

Typical cost range - **** Rough GPS - 25.325 , 51.522

Street - Al Intisar St Public Transport - Bus 74 , 777 Metro Doha Exhibition and Convention Center (DECC Consider the , paid, shuttle coach services the general West Bay area every 15mins for all West Bay Hotels Location in Qatar - West Bay الخليج الغربي Contacts - +974 4495 5000 / sales.westbay-doha@frasershospitality.com / www.westbay-doha.frasershospitality.com/en

Intercontinental Doha Hotel - This is an attractive relatively low rise hotel, with a beach protected by Al Safliya Island . The let-down is patchy service. A mix of hotel and adjacent apartments on a 400metre beach front. With 10 dining outlets , several pools and very stylish interior. a modern mix of buildings and close to Katara - a 3km walk is possible along the coast with a small detour around Magical Festival Village Number of rooms - 375

Typical cost range - **** Rough GPS - 25.348 , 51.528

Street - East of the Lusail Expressway, on Onaiza St Public Transport - No public transport Location in Qatar - West Bay الخليج الغربي Contacts - +974 4484 4444 / / www.ihg.com/intercontinental/hotels/us/en/doha/dohha/hoteldetail

W Doha - Modern, fresh with almost an oriental touch. Selection of dining options, pools and gym. The DECC and City Centre Mall along with the modern sights in West Bay. Number of rooms - 442

Typical cost range - **** Rough GPS - 25.328 , 51.530

Street - Diplomatic St Public Transport - Bus 57,74,76,777 Metro Doha Exhibition and Convention Center (DECC Consider the , paid, shuttle coach services the general West Bay area every 15mins for all West Bay Hotels Location in Qatar - West Bay الخليج الغربي Contacts - +974 4453 5000 / wdoha.reservations@whotels.com / www.marriott.com/hotels/travel/dohwh-w-doha/

Four Seasons Hotel Doha - Restrained and opulent - the style is welcoming and does hint at the Arab world A private beach and views are intangible facilities to this hotel.

The height of the hotel gives sea views from many rooms. A small marina and Nobu restaurant completes the marine theme. A choice of 9 dining venues The DECC and City Centre Mall along with the modern sights in West Bay. Number of rooms - 232

Typical cost range - ***** Rough GPS - 25.325 , 51.539

Street - Diplomatic St Public Transport - Bus 74 , 777 Metro Doha Exhibition and Convention Center (DECC). Location in Qatar - West Bay الخليج الغربي Contacts - +974 4494 8888 / contact form / www.fourseasons.com/doha/

Kempinski Residences & Suites - The tallest hotel in Doha (till the next one) this offers a luxurious stay with most suites having sea views. The style is modern and simple. All you could expect from an upmarket hotel; plus unexpected facilities such as a boardroom - for the company on the move! Just off the Corniche in West Bay, close to DECC and City Centre Mall Number of rooms - 368 on 60 floors

Typical cost range - ***** Rough GPS - 25.328 , 51.531

Street - Diplomatic Area Public Transport - Bus 74 , 777 Metro Doha Exhibition and Convention Center (DECC Consider the , paid, shuttle coach services the general West Bay area every 15mins for all West Bay Hotels Location in Qatar - West Bay الخليج الغربي Contacts - '

+974 4405 3333' / reservations.doha@kempinski.com / www.kempinski.com/en/doha/residences/

Sheraton Grand Doha Resort & Convention - Very well established extremely well located hotel (its possibly overall the best located property in Doha), focused probably more on the business traveller - it is still an excellent choice for leisure. Beach, pools, gym, racquet courts and more - probably the best pub in town. The DECC and City Centre Mall along with the modern sights in West Bay. Number of rooms - 371

Typical cost range - ***** Rough GPS - 25.318 , 51.536

Street - Corniche Public Transport - Bus 777 Metro Red Line Doha Exhibition & Conference Centre (DECC)

Location in Qatar - West Bay Corniche / الخليج الغربي الكورنيش Contacts - +974 4485 4444 / sheraton.doha@Sheraton.com / www.marriott.com/hotels/travel/dohsi-sheraton-grand-doha-resort-and-convention-hotel/

The St. Regis Doha - Clean, fresh, slightly Arabic in feel. The grounds though are smaller than the number of rooms would suggest. Over 10 dining choices, small beach, pool, gym and all the little touches you would hope for at the cost. a modern mix of buildings and close to Katara - less than 3km walk is possible along the coast with a small detour around Magical Festival Village Number of rooms - 336

Typical cost range - ****** Rough GPS - 25.350 , 51.529

Street - East of the Lusail Expressway, on Onaiza St Public Transport - No public transport Location in Qatar - West Bay/The Pearl الخليج الغربي Contacts - +974 4446 0000 / The hotel avoids disclosing emails. / www.marriott.com/hotels/travel/dohxr-the-st-regis-doha

The Pearl & Katara

Marsa Malaz Kempinski - One of the better hotels in Doha, set on a man-made island in a man-made lagoon. The hotel aims to provide a true 5* service to its guests. With 11 dining option, small private beach, tennis courts and Butler service. A short drive from Katara and the other modern developments of The Pearl and West Bay Number of rooms - 281

Typical cost range - ***** Rough GPS - 25.376 , 51.547

Street - Pearl Boulivad Public Transport - No public transport Location in Qatar - The Pearl اللولو Contacts - +974 4035 5555 / reservations.marsamalaz@kempinski.com /

www.kempinski.com/en/doha/marsa-malaz-kempinski-the-pearl-doha/

The Ritz-Carlton - Well established hotel, with very comfortable luxury rooms. It lacks the opulent style of Ritz-Carlton's Sharq Village Hotel. Overlooking the sea with grounds, pools and access to man-made beach and marina. Convenient for Katara cultural and the business area of West Bay. Number of rooms - 374

Typical cost range - ***** Rough GPS - 25.380 , 51.532

Street - off Lusail Expressway Public Transport - No public transport Location in Qatar - The Pearl اللؤلؤ Contacts - +974 4484 8000 / doha.reservations@ritzcarlton.com / www.ritzcarlton.com/en/hotels/qatar/doha

Doha South & East

Al Liwan Suites - An older style accommodation with spacious slightly dated rooms. As an established hotel (10 years old) it offers a non-pretentious place to stay that gives good value. Options of 3 locations for meals, the best is the roof-top with Frangipani and a take on an old Qatari house. Small pool, gym, airport transfer, this is an older area in Doha (relatively speaking) that offers interest and reasonably easy access to tourist areas and airport. Number of rooms - 84 rooms/suites

Typical cost range - * Rough GPS - 25.275 , 51.547

Street - Umm Ghuwailina St Public Transport - Bus 49 Metro Red Line Al Jadeda Location in Qatar - Umm Ghuwailina ام غويلينا Contacts - +974 44242888 / mohsen.khattab@alliwansuites.com.qa / www.alliwansuites.com.qa/

Chairman Hotel - With comfortable furnishings and spacious rooms - the hotel offers very good value. A single dining option. In one of the older areas of Doha. Number of rooms - 68

Typical cost range - * Rough GPS - 25.269 , 51.538

Street - Najma St Public Transport - Al Mansoura Metro , Buses 10, 11, 12 Location in Qatar - Najma نجمة Contacts - +974 4426 0444 / reservations@chairmenhotel.com / www.chairmenhotel.com/

Holiday Inn Doha - The Business Park - Relatively new, modern, with range of facilities expected in a Holiday Inn Pool, Gym with three dining options Convenient to the Airport and transport to other areas. Major construction work is being done close to the hotel, request quiet rooms. Number of rooms - 307

Typical cost range - * Rough GPS - 25.273 , 51.543

Street - Al Matar St Public Transport - Bus 11.747, 11901, 12901 Metro Al Doha Al Jadeda Location in Qatar - Najma نجمة Contacts - +974 4031 3333 / holidayinndoha@ihg.com / www.ihg.com/holidayinn/hotels/us/en/doha/dohbp/hoteldetail?

La Villa Suites - Very old-fashioned rooms, that offer reasonably good value with a small kitchenette. Rooms are differently furnished - check yours before checking-in. A single dining choice. Close to the Najma souq area - with a wide variety of low cost goods. Number of rooms -

Typical cost range - * Rough GPS - 25.271 , 51.539

Street - Ibn Firnas St Public Transport - Al Mansoura Metro and MetroLink M115, Buses 10, 12, 757 Location in Qatar - Najma نجمة Contacts - / info@lavillahospitality.com / https://lavillahospitality.com/

Strato Hotel By Warwick - Comfortably furnished though with patchy service. Consider for early morning or late night flights and short stay. Rooftop pool, gym, Sauna and a couple of dining options. Convenient for Airport, National Museum and Museum of Islamic Art Number of rooms - 97

Typical cost range - * Rough GPS - 25.269 , 51.552

Street - C Ring Rd / Al Matar St Public Transport - Bus 49, 747, 11901, 12901 Metro RedLine Umm Ghuwailina Location in Qatar - Umm Ghuwailina ام غويلينا Contacts - +974 4041 4444 / info.stratohotel@warwickhotels.com / https://warwickhotels.com/strato-hotel/

Al Madina Suites - Slightly older look that is offset by spacious rooms and comfortable facilities. Buffet style restaurant and gym. An older area (around 30 years old) of Doha - less than 2km from Souq Al Waqif and Corniche. Number of rooms - 40 small suites with small kitchenette

Typical cost range - ** Rough GPS - 25.276 , 51.534

Street - Al Nada Street Public Transport - Buses 10,11,12,94,747,11901,12901 and Red Line Metro Al Jadeda Station Location in Qatar - Al Mansoura المنصوره Contacts - +974 4431 8800 / info@almadinasuites.com / www.almadinasuites.com/

Holiday Villa Hotel & Residence - A very distinctive hotel architecture with large open courtyard overlooked by 10 stories. Though an Asian chain the service standards are generally lower than many of other international chains. This is offset by the good value for money otherwise. Five restaurants, pool and gym. There is a wide range of room options each with different decor, ask to see before booking. Close to local car rentals though quite far from Corniche and other tourist areas. A large park is opposite the entrance. Number of rooms - 356 rooms in a large complex

Typical cost range - ** Rough GPS - 25.265 , 51.525

Street - Rawdat Al Khail St / C Ring Road Public Transport - Bus 94 Location in Qatar - Al Mansoura المنصوره Contacts - +974 4408 4888 / info@holidayvilladoha.com / www.holidayvilladoha.com

Hyatt Regency Oryx - A former Rotana Hotel – it is still a modern functional hotel Gym, Pool Spa & several restaurants very easy access to Airport and Transport Number of rooms - 400

Typical cost range - *** Rough GPS - 25.268 , 51.554

Street - off Al Matar St Public Transport - Bus 94, 119, 129, 747, 757 Metro Red Line Umm Ghuwailina Location in Qatar - Umm Ghuwailina ام غويلينا Contacts - +974 4402 3333 / contact form / www.hyatt.com/en-US/hotel/qatar/hyatt-regency-oryx-doha/dohrd?

Al Wakrah, Mesaieed & South Qatar

Souq Wakra Tivoli - South of Doha on a public beach in a leisure area. A charming hotel, in a modern reimagined village setting. The hotel is one or two floors set around a series of courtyards. In general the hotel lives up to its government high classification. The low density and courtyard style means that you are unlikely to feel you are in anything other than a private home. A choice of 5 restaurants including Mahaadeg with views of The Gulf. Number of rooms - 101

Typical cost range - **** Rough GPS - 25.174 , 51.610

Street - Al Loulou St Public Transport - Bus 109 & 129 - Al Wakrah Metro & MetroLink bus M128 Location in Qatar - Al Wakrah الوكرة Contacts - +974 4428 7888 / souqalwakra@tivolihotels.com / www.tivolihotels.-com/en/souq-al-wakra-tivoli

Sealine Beach, A Murwab Resort - Low rise property, with only 35 rooms in the main building- this is a chalet & villa property. Owned by a Qatar government organisation, though not run by a brand name chain, unlike several others in Doha. This is one of the more established hotels in Qatar. Pool, Gym, Spa and 1.3km beach. not far from the sand dunes and inland sea. Number of rooms - 95 Units

Typical cost range - ***** Rough GPS - 24.862 , 51.514

Street - Sealine Beach Rd Public Transport - No public transport Location in Qatar - Khor Al Udaid / Mesaied مسيعيد

خور العديد / Contacts - +974 4021 4000 / info@sealinebeachqatar.com / www.sealinebeachqatar.com/

Education City & Doha West

Asherij Hotel - Newly built hotel with decorations on an Arabic style Limited options, a small gym and coffee shop. Larger suites have small kitchenette. Rooms have different decoration - ask to see what's available. A mix of residential and business this is just inside the C Ring Rd and about 2.5km walk to the Corniche. Number of rooms - 100

Typical cost range - * Rough GPS - 25.282 , 51.508

Street - Al Quds St /Majda St Public Transport - Bus route 78 / Gold Line Metro Al Saad Location in Qatar - Fereej Bin Mahmoud فريج بن محمود Contacts - +974 440 828 28 / info@asherijhotel.com / www.asherijhotel.com/

Premier Inn Doha Education City - Simply furnished, though comfortable. The hotel offers very good value low cost (meals extra) modern accommodation that could be a good choice for a business person. A pool, gym and restaurant. The hotel does offer a complimentary shuttle into town. This area is principally the educational focus of Doha, about 10km west of the corniche. In the general area is the new Qatar National Convention Centre, National Library, Mataf Arab Museum of Modern Art and Shaqab Equestrian Stables Number of rooms - 219

Typical cost range - * Rough GPS - 25.322 , 51.430

Street - east of Garafat Al Rayyan Rd Public Transport - Bus 56 Garafat Al Rayyan Rd (1km after crossing main road), Metro GreenLine Education City - 800metre walk Location in Qatar - Education City المدينة التعليمية Contacts - +974 4007 8333 / reservations.dec@mena.premierinn.com / https://global.premierinn.com/en/hotel/doha-education-city

Qatar Youth Hostels Association - A relatively simple offering of accommodation, though far from basic its focus is students or similar at the nearby Education City. Do check the rooms before you confirm. A basic coffee shop and do-it-yourself laundry. Number of rooms - 40

Typical cost range - * Rough GPS - 25.317 , 51.464

Street - Al Rayhan St Public Transport - Bus 45 Location in Qatar - Al Luqta اللقطة Contacts - +974 4421 7157 / / as with so many lower cost hotels there is only the option to book through on-line agencies.

Centro Capital Doha - Simple clean rooms creates a modern look. All day dining, with bar, A small rooftop pool & gym along with 2 good restaurants (below) A newer area of Doha - about 2km walk from Corniche Number of rooms - 229

Typical cost range - ** Rough GPS - 25.284 , 51.512

Street - Al Jazeera St Public Transport - Bus 78, Metro Gold Line Al Sadd - 1km away Location in Qatar - Fereej Bin Mahmoud فريج بن محمود Contacts - +97444555000 / Contact Form / www.rotana.com/centrohotels/qatar/doha/centrocapitaldoha

Zubarah Boutique Hotel Doha - A small well run hotel, with warm comfortable facilities Limited facilities include a small Spa and thee small dining options. Mainly a mix of residential and small business area. Number of rooms - 45

Typical cost range - ** Rough GPS - 25.270 , 51.518

Street - Al Rawabi St Public Transport - Bus 21,22 Location in Qatar - Rawdat Al Khail روضة الخيل Contacts - +974 4447 0000 / info@zubarah.com / www.zubarahhotels.com/

The Torch Doha - The most distinctive hotel in Doha, opened for Asian Games, Rooms are simple in appearance alongside modern opulent design. The restaurants are distinctive and all worth a visit esp 360. There are no grounds. Eight dining options, gym and remarkable small swimming pool. near sports stadiums and Villaggio Mall. Its well out of the city centre. Number of rooms - 163 rooms on 51 floors.

Typical cost range - **** Rough GPS - 25.262 , 51.445

Street - off Al Waab

Street, Al Buwairda St Public Transport - 31,32,40, 136,137,301,306. Metro Gold Line Sport City Location in Qatar - Baaya / Aspire اسباير / بعيا Contacts - +974 4446 5600 / reservation@thetorchdoha.com / www.thetorchdoha.com.qa

The Westin Doha Hotel & Spa - Modern exterior is matched with the interior. Spa, gym and fitness, along with sheltered gardens. Several good restaurants - southwest of town centre Number of rooms - 364

Typical cost range - **** Rough GPS - 25.275 , 51.514

Street - Salwa Rd Public Transport - Bus 31, 32, 33.34, 137, 136, 301 Location in Qatar - Fereej Bin Mahmoud فريج بن محمود Contacts - +974 4492 1555 / No email / www.marriott.com/hotels/travel/dohwi-the-westin-doha-hotel-and-spa/

North-East

Al Sultan Beach Resort - Quirky hotel, on beach with pool. A premium price compared to 5* hotels in Doha for a more modest offering. Helpful staff. Beach and Pool with simple restaurant Sea, Beaches & mangrove swamp; Dhow harbour Number of rooms - 187

Typical cost range - **** Rough GPS - 25.685 , 51.522

Street - Corniche Al Khor Public Transport - Bus 102, 102X Location in Qatar - Al Khor الخور Contacts - +974 4472 2555' / / www.alsultanbeachresort.com

Simaisma Al Murwab Resort - A property of villas set overlooking the sea. Owned by a company of the Qatari government. Pool, gym, Tennis and beach Opportunities for scuba diving Number of rooms - 52 all villa

Typical cost range - ****** Rough GPS - 25.584 , 51.488

Street - off Al Khor Coastal Rd Public Transport - No public transport Location in Qatar - Sumaysimah سميسمة Contacts - +974 4479 9555 / info@simaisma.com / www.simaisma.com/

Al Ruwais, West Coast and Dukhan & Central Qatar

Zulal Wellness Resort - A new upmarket hotel, with all the pluses and minuses of brand new properties. On Qatar's northern tip it's a wellness spar and resort. Opposite the hotel, on Qatar's northern tip, are two islands and a few kilometres away is Al Ruwais town. Number of rooms - 120

Typical cost range - ***** Rough GPS - 26.155 , 51.242

Street - Public Transport - Location in Qatar - Al Ruwais الرويس Contacts - +974 4008 4999 / info@msheireb.com / www.msheireb.com/zulal-wellness-resort/

33

INDEX

INDEX

Made in the USA
Monee, IL
12 October 2021